VEDANTA FOR THE WEST

RELIGION IN NORTH AMERICA

Catherine L. Albanese and Stephen J. Stein, *editors*

VEDANTA FOR THE WEST

The Ramakrishna Movement in the United States

Carl T. Jackson

Indiana University Press

Bloomington & Indianapolis

The paper used in this publication meets the minimum require-
ments of American National Standard for Information Sciences—
Permanence of Paper for Printed Library Materials, ANSI
Z39.48-1984.

⊗™

Manufactured in the United States of America

Library of Congress Cataloging-in-Publication Data

Jackson, Carl T., date
    Vedanta for the West : the Ramakrishna movement in the
United States / Carl T. Jackson.
        p.   cm.—(Religion in North America.)
    Includes bibliographical references and index.
    ISBN 0-253-33098-X (cloth)
        1. Ramakrishna Math—Missions—United States—History.
2. Ramakrishna, 1836–1886.   3. Vivekananda, Swami,
1863–1902.   4. Hinduism—Missions—United States—
History.   I. Title.   II. Series.
    BL1280.35.U6J3   1994
    294.5'55'0973—dc20   93-24702

1 2 3 4 5 98 97 96 95 94

For Margaret

Contents

Illustrations follow page 36

Foreword

To INVOKE THE name of Vedanta, for students of South Asia, is to point toward a religious past that is centuries old. Vedanta means, literally, what comes at the end of the Vedas, the ancient sacred scriptures of India. Still more, as a philosophical term Vedanta is shorthand for the monism that forms one of the two major metaphysical systems that have shaped South Asian culture.

For students of the United States, however, to invoke the name of Vedanta is to point toward a past that is very recent. Vedanta appeared in America close to the nineteenth century's end and near the dawn of a new religious era in the twentieth century. At a time when the spiritual anxieties of the Gilded Age were already hinting that the golden day of mainstream Protestantism had passed its high-noon mark, Vedanta came to America in the form of Vedanta societies. Decisively initiated by Swami Vivekananda, who arrived in Chicago as participant in the World's Parliament of Religions at the Columbian Exposition of 1893, the societies were from the first small and distinctly elitist. Vedantists discussed religious philosophy and pondered speculative cosmologies. Their favored religious mode was the lecture, and their preferred form of ritual was serious conversation.

But behind the first impressions that Vedanta societies created lay a heritage of intense devotionalism and, more, religious ecstasy. Vedanta societies comprised the American arm of the Indian Ramakrishna movement, and Ramakrishna—the guru who had profoundly moved and molded Swami Vivekananda—was one of India's celebrated modern saints and seers, a mystic who was hailed by devotees as a God-realized man, an avatar. So the Vedanta societies in the United States had their other side, their devotionalism and even mysticism that moved suggestively beneath the formal structure of lecture and discussion. Quietly and without much ado, the societies took hold in the land, a tiny, almost symbolic presence of religious South Asia exported to American shores.

Until the decades following 1965 and the decisive changes in the American immigration law that brought the large-scale presence of South Asians—and among them South Asian religious teachers—Vedanta societies formed one of the few small and privileged enclaves for Indian export religion. Here alternative religious ways could be modeled for non-Asian Americans. Then, after 1965, Vedanta societies, like some other forms of export Hinduism already here, became at least a temporary religious home for numbers of South Asian immigrants to America. Indeed, some observers who watched the faces of those who exited from Vedanta weekly services on the East Coast in the late eighties and early nineties thought that Vedanta societies were made up almost exclusively of Asian Indian peoples. The societies appeared at casual acquaintance to be ethnic religious structures to accommodate the needs of a generation of new immigrants.

To say this much is to suggest the paradigmatic nature of Vedanta societies as classic religious vehicles for the introduction of South Asian religious belief and practice to Americans. To say more would be to intrude on Carl Jackson's story. And it is an important story indeed. This is especially the case because surprisingly little work has been done on the Ramakrishna movement in the United States, and much of what exists is comprised of in-house accounts with all the localist's perspectives and problems. Not to say that these local and more general participant accounts do not possess their valued stores of information and their insights. But a comprehensive and critical account of the movement is decisively needed, and Jackson's study here promises to go far to address the need. Based on thoroughgoing archival research, the Jackson study also profits from the careful interview work that its author has carried out among contemporary participants in Vedanta societies.

The results are contained in a crisp and pithy no-nonsense account that, with admirable economy, surveys and summarizes a century's Vedantan presence in the nation. Jackson reads the Ramakrishna movement as a kind of "middle way" between meditation forms of Hinduism in America like Transcendental Meditation and devotional ones like the International Society for Krishna Consciousness (the Hare Krishna movement). As the oldest forms of organized Hinduism among us, he tells us, Vedanta societies are worthy of notice. As classical forms, they are even more so.

As editors for the Religion in North America series, we can add that, as an exercise in mapping one distinctive piece of the pluralism that shapes religious America in the late twentieth century, Jackson's is a valuable study. His examination of Vedanta gives us a view of South Asian religion that shows it to be at home and comfortable in the land. If the swamis ruled peaceable kingdoms here, as they seem to have done, they signaled a Hinduism not strange and "exotic" but flexible and adaptable to mainstream American religious attitudes and requirements. We need to learn more about this new and acculturated Hinduism, and Jackson invites us to let him, with his own facility and ease in the Ramakrishna world, become our tutor. We invite readers to accept the invitation and to experience its rewards.

Catherine L. Albanese
Stephen J. Stein
Series Editors

Preface

Few AMERICANS TODAY can be completely unaware of the presence of Asian religious teachers and groups in our midst. Primarily offshoots of Hinduism and Buddhism, these include such movements as the International Society for Krishna Consciousness, better known as the Hare Krishnas; Maharishi Mahesh Yogi's Transcendental Meditation; the Divine Life Society, founded by Swami Sivananda; Guru Maharaj Ji's Divine Light Mission; the San Francisco Zen Center, directed by Roshi Shunryun Suzuki; the Tibetan Nyingma Meditation Center, founded by Tarthang Tulku; and the late Chogyam Trungpa's Naropa Institute—to name only a few of the best-known groups. Though Asian spiritual movements have appeared in America quite recently—in most cases only since 1965 when the passage of the Immigration and Nationality Act opened the way for significant immigration from South and East Asia—Eastern teachers have clearly succeeded in transplanting several strains of the Asian religions to the fertile soil of the New World. The event represents an important turning point: for centuries Western missionaries have carried Christianity throughout Asia; now, in a historic reversal, Asian teachers are bringing Hinduism and Buddhism to the West. Though a few Western intellectuals sensed the importance of such a meeting of East and West at least as far back as the eighteenth century, it is only since the 1960s that most Westerners have begun to appreciate the significance of the present East-West encounter.

In the United States the body which pioneered the way, representing the first Asian movement to present its teachings on American shores, was the Ramakrishna movement. Inspired by the life and teachings of a remarkable nineteenth-century visionary named Ramakrishna, the movement was originally brought to the United States in the 1890s by Ramakrishna's disciple, Swami Vivekananda, who spoke at the 1893 Chicago World's Parliament of Religions. Today the movement launched by the two men carries on as the Ramakrishna Math and Mission, which simultaneously promotes the reform and revival of Hinduism in India while spreading Hinduism in the United States and Europe. Headquartered at the Belur Math, near Calcutta, the Ramakrishna movement remains very much alive a century later, with more than ninety centers scattered across India and twelve Vedanta societies based in the United States. The movement also has branches in Bangladesh, Sri Lanka, Singapore, Fiji, Mauritius,

Japan, Great Britain, France, Switzerland, Canada, and Argentina. To celebrate the centennial of its appearance in the United States, the movement played a leading role in organizing a 1993 Parliament of World Religions, which, like the 1893 congress, convened in Chicago. Though changes have occurred, the Ramakrishna movement appears likely to remain a force in the United States for many years to come.

In view of its significant role in the history of modern India, it seems astonishing that, to date, no comprehensive scholarly study of the Ramakrishna movement has appeared. As my bibliographical essay indicates, a growing body of literature on the movement now exists, but much remains to be done. Let me hasten to add that the intention of the present work is not a comprehensive history, but a more modest examination of the movement's American activities. I have discovered that this is ambition enough. More specifically, the pages that follow will trace the history of the Ramakrishna movement in the United States, beginning with the body's obscure origins in nineteenth-century Bengal and reaching down to the present. I must confess the hope that my examination will also offer some insight into the general attraction of Asian religion for contemporary Americans. Questions to be considered include the following: Why did followers of Ramakrishna originally initiate work in the West? How authentic is the movement's presentation of Hinduism? (For the moment let us pass over the question posed by recent specialists whether, indeed, there is an entity which we may designate as "Hinduism," or whether what we have called by that name should be viewed as an abstraction created and imposed by eighteenth- and nineteenth-century Western scholars.) To what extent has the Ramakrishna movement modified its message to reach an American audience? What has been the nature of the movement's relations with Christian churches and leaders? What has been the background of the typical American follower? And in what ways have the Ramakrishna movement's work and message in the United States differed from such later Hindu transplants as the International Society for Krishna Consciousness and Transcendental Meditation? The record will show that the movement spawned by Ramakrishna and Vivekananda has been one of the most influential Asian religious movements to appear in the United States thus far.

A word should be added about the distinction between the "Ramakrishna Math" and the "Ramakrishna Mission," the two key organizations that direct the work of the Ramakrishna movement. Also referred to as the "Ramakrishna Order," the Math is the movement's monastic organization. Founded by Ramakrishna in 1886, the Math primarily focuses on spiritual training and the propagation of the movement's teachings. The Ramakrishna Mission, on the other hand, administers the movement's extensive medical, relief, and educational programs. Founded by Swami Vivekananda in 1897, it is primarily a humanitarian organization. In practice, the two bodies are difficult to distinguish, since both are quartered at the Belur headquarters, with the trustees of the Math also serving as the Mission's governing board. Monks from the Math direct much of the Mission's work and occupy many of the Mission's administrative positions. Since the major goal in the United States has always been individual spiritual development rather than social welfare, historically the Mission has played little role in the movement's American efforts.

The research for this study could not have been completed without the assistance of numerous members of the Ramakrishna movement, both in India and the United States. A 1987 visit to the movement's Belur headquarters was particularly useful for an understanding of the Indian side of the movement. The following individuals were especially helpful during my stay at the Belur Math: Swami Hiranmayananda, then the secretary general of the Ramakrishna Math and Mission, who made time in a hectic schedule to speak with me and to provide letters of introduction; Swami Smarananda, who assisted in the selection of the photographs that appear in the center pages of this volume; Swami Lokeswarananda, director of the Ramakrishna Mission Institute of Culture, who painstakingly answered all my questions; and Anil Ganguly, whose constant attention and enthusiastic role as guide made the visit to Belur and the Dakshineswar temple the high points of an extended journey through northern India.

A subsequent tour of the various facilities of the Vedanta Society of Southern California, including visits to the Ramakrishna Monastery at Trabuco and the Sarada Convent in Santa Barbara, provided useful insights concerning the operations and daily activities of the Ramakrishna movement in modern America. At the Hollywood Vedanta Society I owe special thanks to Swami Swahananda, who invited me to participate in all activities at the center, and to his assistant Swami Vedarupananda, who handled the arrangements for the visit. Others who went out of their way to make my stay in southern California both informative and enjoyable were Jnana, Nirvana, Bhaktiprana, Saradeshaprana, Vivekaprana, Bhaveshananda, Prabhavprana, and Anandaprana.

Though unfailingly cooperative in answering my questions, a number of my informants expressed some concern that their comments might be misconstrued. In response, I promised that I would avoid identifying my sources by name, attempting instead to generalize the information provided. With a few exceptions, I have followed such a policy throughout. I only hope that nothing said in the pages that follow will cause any of my informants embarrassment. Acutely aware that Ramakrishna followers will disagree with some of the judgments rendered, I can only ask for their understanding that I have tried at all times to offer a balanced assessment. In any case, none of the individuals named here or elsewhere in the text or notes should be held accountable for the contents of this study; I willingly assume complete responsibility for all statements made.

Finally, I would like to thank the following agencies and individuals for their assistance with a project that has extended over more years than I wish to remember: the University Research Institute of the University of Texas at El Paso, which provided funds needed to carry out much of the research; Ann Schultis, a former head of UTEP's Interlibrary Loan Division, who demonstrated extraordinary talent for locating obscure books in distant places; Flo Dick, who typed an early version of the present study; Verna Lopez and Jesús A. Melendez, who oversaw the final printing of the manuscript; and Sue Cook and Vicki Fisher, who unfailingly met all my requests for assistance. I must also thank the Indiana University Press editors of the "Religion in North America Series," Catherine L. Albanese and Stephen J. Stein, whose meticulous criticisms of the manuscript have eliminated numerous lapses and greatly improved the final product. Finally, Swami Sarveshananda of the Ramakrishna Monastery and Retreat in Fennville, Michigan, and Pravrajika Bhaktiprana at the Sarada Convent in Santa Barbara, California, provided critical assistance in updating my information on recent developments in the movement. Most of all, I am profoundly indebted to Margaret, who has supported all my efforts at every stage through many years. I could never have completed this project without her constant encouragement.

VEDANTA FOR THE WEST

1 | The Nineteenth-Century Background

To UNDERSTAND THE sudden appearance of swamis of the Ramakrishna movement in America in the 1890s requires some awareness of far-reaching changes in India earlier in the century; at the same time, understanding the swamis' success in establishing a foothold in the United States requires some knowledge of changes in the American attitude toward Asian religions in the same years. In a number of ways, the story of the Ramakrishna movement in America is the story of the convergence of the right movement and the right time.

By the early decades of the nineteenth century when the British finally succeeded in establishing their hegemony, India had descended to one of its lowest points in a long and glorious history. "The British found a country in ruins," a recent historian writes.[1] The Indian political system had collapsed, economic life was stagnant, and bandits, the notorious "thugs" who were legendary for their unlikely combination of robbery and ritual murder in honor of the goddess Kali, regularly terrorized the countryside. If anything, the Indian religious outlook appeared even more dismal. Always diverse even in periods of strength, Hinduism presented a confusing spectrum of hundreds of sects, each with its own temples and devotional practices.[2] Seven hundred years of Islamic domination added its impact. Portraying Hinduism as idol-worship, Muslim polemicists contemptuously dismissed India's traditional religion as the degraded faith of a conquered people. Surprisingly, some Hindu spokespersons seemed to agree, echoing the worst charges of Muslim and Christian critics. To cite only one example, Rammohun Roy, now revered as the prophet of modern India, judged his Hindu countrymen as "more superstitious and miserable" in the "performance of their religious rites" than the "rest of the known nations on the earth."[3]

It must be said that the low view taken of Indian religion in the period represented perception as much as reality, a point emphasized by the portrayal of Hinduism by nineteenth-century Christian missionaries. Led by William Carey, a growing number of British, American, and German missionaries filtered into the beleagured country as the century advanced. Though the missionary deserves much credit for his educational, medical, and humanitarian work, at the same time he created a "Black Legend" concerning Hinduism that has distorted the perception of Indian religion in the West ever since. On one side, Hinduism was portrayed as a horrifying religion that emphasized idol worship, gross superstition, and headlong flight from the world. On the other, once they became available, the philosophic profundities of the Upanishads and the Bhagavad Gita, the basic texts of Hinduism, were dismissed. Over and over missionary accounts minutely described such practices as the burning of widows (*sati*), female infanticide, and the worship of lingas (stone pillars venerated by Shivites, erroneously identified with the phallus), claiming that such "perversions" defined Hinduism's true spirit.[4]

At a time of widespread self-doubt among educated Indians, and when Western views were almost automatically accorded respect, it is not surprising that increasing numbers of middle-class Hindus accepted the validity of the denunciations. Indeed, by the latter half of the nineteenth century India's better-educated youths found it almost fashionable to embrace Western values while deriding the ways of their ancestors.

The most important consequence of these developments for our purposes was a widespread awakening among Hindu religious leaders that has come to be known as the "Hindu Renaissance." Both accepting and at the same time rejecting Western criticisms, a diverse group of reformers and movements now emerged to champion the reform and renewal of Hinduism. Through such movements as the Brahmo Samaj, Arya Samaj, and Ramakrishna movement, Rammohun Roy, Debendranath Tagore, Keshub Chandra Sen, Swami Dayananda, Sri Ramakrishna, and Swami Vivekananda helped revive middle-class faith in India's future.[5] Because of the emergence of this "reform Hinduism," countless urban youths who had teetered on the edge of repudiating their religious heritage were drawn back to a renewal of faith in Hinduism and Indian ideals. Western influences certainly sparked the awakening and influenced the direction taken, but the Hindu Renaissance was primarily an Indian movement—or better, a series of movements—directed by Hindu reformers. Recapitulating the response of orthodox Hindus many centuries earlier when Buddhism and Jainism were challenging its dominance, nineteenth-century Hinduism met the threat posed by Christianity and Western science by once again reforming itself.[6] The powerful energies unleashed by this renascence not only altered the history of modern India but radiated out thousands of miles to distant North America.

Often hailed as the "Father of Modern India," Rammohun Roy epitomized the Hindu Renaissance. He was simultaneously the defender of traditional Hindu ideals and an advocate of reform. Roy was born in 1772 into a prominent Brahmin family. He early revealed a scholarly interest in religious questions, which led him to studies of the Vedas and Upanishads.[7] Disturbed by what he regarded as the corruptions of popular Hinduism, he undertook the study of Christianity, attracted by its ethical and monotheistic teachings. The result of his explorations was *The Precepts of Jesus*, a book in which he sympathetically summarized the moral teachings of Jesus; significantly, he systematically expunged the founder of Christianity's reputed miracles and claims to divinity. Though he was strongly drawn to Christianity's ethical teachings, Rammohun Roy remained a defender of Hinduism, pleading with his countrymen to return to the pure teachings contained in the Upanishads. In this spirit he condemned idol-worship, the caste system, and widow-burning as practices inconsistent with true Hinduism. Anxious to spread his message, he founded the Brahmo Sabha (Society of God) in 1828, which subsequently became known as the Brahmo Samaj.

Rammohun Roy's preference for a middle position between those who uncritically accepted Western values and those who dogmatically championed Hindu orthodoxy may be said to define the essential stance of most reformers in the Hindu Renaissance. In his *Sources of Indian Tradition* William Theodore de Bary describes Roy's historic role as follows:

> Some Hindus became Christians, others clung stubbornly to orthodoxy, while a third group tried to combine the best features of both religions. Rammohun Roy carefully distinguished between English virtues and English errors, and defended Hinduism against the criticisms of the missionaries as vigorously as he challenged the orthodox to abandon its excrescences.[8]

De Bary aptly characterizes Rammohun's policy as "war on two fronts." Hindu reformers frequently disagreed concerning the positives and negatives of Western influence, but all agreed on the need for purification and reform of Hinduism.

Turning to the major movements, one may classify nineteenth-century Hindu reformers into three broad groups based upon their reaction to Western influence. Led by Keshub Chandra Sen and the Brahmo Samaj, the liberals called for far-reaching alterations in Hinduism through open adoption of Western practices. Represented by Swami Dayananda Saraswati and the Arya Samaj, the conservatives vigorously rejected Western conceptions and called for a return to the original teachings of Hinduism. The third group, whom we may refer to as the centrists, strongly defended Hinduism against Western attack while selectively borrowing elements from the West. The Ramakrishna movement clearly belongs in this last group.

Rammohun Roy's Brahmo Samaj, founded in 1828, never quite achieved the historic role of maker of modern India that a series of brilliant leaders seemed to promise.[9] Following Roy's death, leadership of the organization passed first to Debendranath Tagore (now mainly remembered as the father of Rabindranath Tagore, India's first Nobel Prize winner), then to Keshub Chandra Sen. Though unquestionably a talented man, Tagore was unable to prevent the Samaj from stagnating, but the movement quickly revived once Sen assumed leadership. For a few years Keshub's powerful oratorical skills and passionate, almost evangelical, style made the Brahmo Samaj the hope of India's educated youths, particularly in Bengal, where it drew its greatest support. Keshub launched campaigns for famine relief, uplift of Indian women, and relief for the poor, attracting international attention when he traveled to Great Britain in 1880. He was one of the earliest Hindu lecturers to address European audiences. Though always small in numbers, the Brahmo Samaj nevertheless played a key intellectual role in awakening Hindu interest in reform.

The Brahmo Samaj openly embraced Western conceptions and practices. In a sharp departure from the traditional Hindu pattern, the organization conducted services much as in the West, featuring congregational worship and a service that included a sermon, hymns, and readings of sacred scriptures. The movement's strong commitment to social and humanitarian uplift, with Brahmo Samajists playing leading roles in most of the day's social reforms, also testified to Western influence. Despite deference to Western opinion, leaders of the Brahmo Samaj defended Hinduism against the attacks of Christian missionaries. One might describe the Brahmo Samaj strategy as immunizing Hinduism against Occidental infection by a selective incorporation of Western conceptions.

In the 1870s the Brahmo Samaj fragmented into three separate bodies, with an anti-Keshub group forming an organization known as the Sadharan Brahmo Samaj. Drifting steadily toward Christianity, Keshub created a new organization known as the New Dispensation Church and proclaimed his acceptance of such Christian dogmas as the divinity of Jesus and the doctrine of sin. He also announced direct revelations from God. As a result, a number of his contemporaries predicted his imminent conversion to Christianity. By the time of his death in 1884 at the age of forty-one, the Brahmo Samaj was falling apart.[10] In retrospect, one can see that the Brahmo Samaj was always too intellectual in approach and in the end too foreign to win the acceptance of India's millions.

The most uncompromising defender of Hinduism in the Hindu reform movement was the Arya Samaj, founded by Swami Dayananda Saraswati in 1875. The swami was born into a pious Brahmin family in northern India. He revealed reformist tendencies as early as the age of fourteen, when he rejected traditional Hindu religious devotionalism as idol-worship. Adopting the life of a wandering sannyasin (a monk who has renounced the world), he spent the next fifteen years as an ascetic, traveling from one pilgrimage site to another. He became convinced by his studies of early sacred texts that the original Hinduism had been corrupted by later additions; as a result, he eventually founded the Arya Samaj to promote a return to the Vedas as the only source of truth. He was a traditionalist in his emphasis on the Vedas, but unorthodox in his claim that originally Hinduism had been monotheistic. Like the Brahmo Samajists, he condemned such contemporary Hindu practices as polytheism, child marriage, caste distinctions, and the ban against widow remarriage. Unlike members of the Brahmo Samaj, he rejected Westernization as a solution for India's ills, instead calling for a return to original Vedic teachings.[11]

The differences between the Arya Samaj and Brahmo Samaj emphasize the wide variations in nineteenth-century Hindu reform. Thus, while Dayananda warned against Western influence, members of the Brahmo Samaj championed acceptance of beneficial outside influence. The Arya Samaj advocated a return to Hindu orthodoxy based on the Vedas, while the Brahmo Samaj fiercely denounced the inflexibility and dogmatism of orthodox Hinduism. Defenders of the Arya Samaj proclaimed Vedic Hinduism as the ultimate religion, while the Brahmo Samajists claimed that all religions shared a common spiritual core and that all expressed the universal religion.

The Ramakrishna movement must be assigned a place somewhere between the Arya Samaj and the Brahmo Samaj. All three movements adopted similar stances in defending Hindu ideals against outside Western attacks, while at the same time assailing what they saw as orthodox Hinduism's corruptions from the inside—the familiar two-front strategy—but the Ramakrishna movement balanced these divergent goals in a quite original fashion. Swami Vivekananda, who assumed leadership after Ramakrishna's death, pioneered the way. In India, the swami hotly defended Hinduism against outside attacks while simultaneously urging internal renewal and a program of humanitarian reforms that frightened orthodox Hindu leaders. In the West, meanwhile, he undertook a separate work, launching the first Vedanta societies in the United States and Europe to disseminate Hinduism to Western people. Ultimately, the Ramakrishna movement would champion Hinduism based on the ancient Vedas and Upanishads in the West, while energetically pushing a humanitarian program in India that clearly revealed inspiration from the contemporary West. In this way the movement may be said to have not only pursued a two-front strategy, but to have actually opened a second front in the West.[12]

Though indisputably Western in origin, one other nineteenth-century movement whose championing of Hindu ideals did much to awaken Indians' pride in their ancestral faith should be noted. I refer to the Theosophical Society, founded in New York City in 1875 by "Madame" Helena Blavatsky and Henry Steel Olcott. In fact, the Theosophical Society was even more vociferous in its defense of Hinduism than were the Hindu reformers.

The woman whose writings and actions dominated the early history of the Theosophical movement has always been a mysterious figure.[13] Helena Blavatsky was born in Russia, immigrating to the United States in 1873. Soon after, she met her future collaborator, Henry Steel Olcott, who at one time had served as agricultural editor of the *New York Tribune*. Discovering that they shared an interest in occultism, the "Theosophical Twins" (as they sometimes referred to themselves) joined together to found the Theosophical Society. The new movement grew rapidly, spreading from the United States to Europe, India, and Sri Lanka. It shifted its headquarters to Adyar, near Madras, in 1882.

Though fraud and frequent schisms nearly destroyed its credibility in later years, for a time in the 1870s and 1880s the Theosophical Society played an active role in the Hindu Renaissance. (As a champion of Buddhism, it played an even more significant role in the Buddhist revival then emerging across South and

Southeast Asia.) At a time when Western nations seemed to be riding the crest of history, educated Asians were electrified to encounter Westerners such as Blavatsky and Olcott who championed the superiority of the religious wisdom of Asia. As reports filtered back to the West, missionary apologists expressed outrage at Theosophy's defense of traditional Hinduism. The Theosophical Society may be grouped with reform movements only in a loose sense, since it stood not so much for the reform of Hinduism as for the defense of Hinduism's high spiritual achievements.

To return to the history of the Ramakrishna movement, Swami Vivekananda's appearance at the Parliament of Religions in Chicago in 1893 was unprecedented but hardly accidental. After centuries of decline, Hinduism was reviving in India, a rebirth that would reestablish its place among the world's great religions. The fact that it did not work alone and that its program paralleled that of other Indian reform groups made the Ramakrishna movement's role more, not less, significant. Because of the new energies unleashed by the Hindu Renaissance, Ramakrishna swamis proved to be only the first in a growing procession of Indian teachers who have carried the message of Hinduism to the West in the twentieth century.

Though profound changes in the religious situation in nineteenth-century India may explain the sudden appearance of Hindu swamis in the West after 1893, Indian conditions do not explain their warm reception. In order to understand why the Ramakrishna movement was the right movement at the right time, focus must now be turned to the United States and to changing American attitudes toward the Asian religions. A rising American interest in and awareness of the Asian religions over the course of the nineteenth century opened the way for Swami Vivekananda and the other Hindu teachers who followed.

In the first decades of the nineteenth century, only a handful of Americans indicated any consciousness of the Eastern religions; by the 1890s, however, awareness had greatly widened. As awareness rose, interest centered mainly on Hinduism and Buddhism, with much greater attention paid to Hinduism in the century's first half and Buddhism in the latter half. Educated Americans also knew something of Confucianism, but most other forms of Asian religions, including Taoism, Shintoism, Sikhism, and Jainism, remained almost unknown. The key influence in determining American attitudes seems to have been the extent of knowledge. Though other factors obviously entered in, almost always the more Americans have known about the Asian religions, the more sympathetic their view of those religions has been. The amount as well as the quality of information concerning the Eastern religions grew rapidly as the century progressed.[14]

The earliest American references to the Asian religions crop up in the late eighteenth and early nineteenth centuries; merchants, missionaries, and magazines provide most of the early reports.

American merchants began to seek out Asian ports as early as the 1780s, pressured to discover new markets after the thirteen colonies broke away from the English empire. The trade in Eastern goods may be dated from 1784, the year in which the *Empress of China* entered port in Canton and in which the *United States* anchored off the coast of India. Except for interruptions during war and economic depression, in subsequent decades a steady flow of American vessels made their way east. While in port, the ship's captains and traders had some limited opportunity to observe Asian life, including religious practices. Simple men of limited education, most shared the reaction of Samuel Shaw, who accompanied the very first voyage to China in 1784 and made three subsequent voyages to that ancient nation. Shaw was amazed and appalled by his visit to a Chinese temple, remarking that the "most seemingly extravagant accounts of their idolatry and superstition" had been fully confirmed.[15] Though most merchant reports are harshly negative, a number contain surprisingly favorable comments concerning the Eastern religions.[16] Such reports would scarcely be worth mentioning, except that they preserve the earliest evidence of American awareness of the Eastern religions.

The first American missionaries dispatched to India went out in 1812, sponsored by the newly formed American Board of Commissioners for Foreign Missions; the earliest Americans to undertake missionary work in China followed in 1830.[17] Despite a frightening death rate and meager success with conversions, the flow steadily grew, making missionaries the most numerous and most visible representatives of the United States in Asia during the nineteenth century. Because the missionaries resided in mission stations for years at a time, they were much better situated to observe Asian religious practices than were merchants. In order to maintain home support as well as to recruit new workers, missionaries in the field regularly reported their activities in the pages of journals such as the *Missionary Herald*, the official journal of the American Board of Commissioners for Foreign Missions.

Eastern religious practices inevitably attracted much attention. Missionary reports concerning the Asian religions were even more critical than the accounts of early merchants. The rationale for their presence in Asia depended on presenting the Asian religions as corrupt and in need of replacement. Thus, for example, almost without exception, Hinduism was portrayed as a totally debased religion, dominated by idol-worship and female infanticide. Hindu reformers were also denouncing these practices, of course, but most Asians were incensed by any form of outside criticism. Indeed, half a century after the first accounts appeared, Indian writers were still bitterly protesting the unfairness of missionary portrayals.[18] Though later missionary accounts embodied a more sympathetic attitude, influenced by the ecumenical view that all world religions contained good points, no group exceeded the missionaries in creating a negative image of Asian religions.

During the nineteenth century, magazines played a much larger role in the intellectual life of the country than they do today. Two were especially vital in introducing American readers to Asian thought in the century's first half—the *Edinburgh Review* and *North American Review*—both high-level journals whose essay-length discussions of Asian social and religious conditions and reviews of new books on Asian life provided readers with well-informed accounts based on the newest scholarship. Though published in Great Britain, the *Edinburgh Review* was widely available in the United States, providing readers regular access to the reports of British travelers and scholars. The *North American Review* published one of the very earliest accounts of Hinduism printed in America, William Tudor's "Theology of the Hindoos," which appeared in 1818. In his assessment, Tudor praised the Vedic concept of God as "just" and likely "to lead the mind to true conceptions" of the deity's character, but he did not conceal his distaste for Hinduism's "barbarous sacrifices and idol worship."[19] Despite such critical judgments, the portrayal of Asian religions in the pages of the *Edinburgh Review* and *North American Review* was much more balanced and sympathetic than in missionary reports. The Transcendentalists, led by Ralph Waldo Emerson, drew heavily on the two journals for information concerning Asian thought.

No movement played a more significant role in bringing the Asian religions to American public attention than Unitarianism. As proponents of greater reliance on reason and less on faith, Unitarians were pioneer advocates of toleration and a universal religious outlook. They were also among the earliest groups to adopt a more favorable attitude toward non-Christian religions. Joseph Priestly, the famous British scientist who resettled in America in the 1790s, led the way with *A Comparison of the Institutions of Moses with Those of the Hindoos*, one of the first works on comparative religions published in the United States. While noting certain parallels between Christianity and the Asian religions, including "some excellent moral maxims," Priestly insisted that the differences between Christianity and other religions were far more important than the similarities.[20]

Unitarian awareness of Asian thought greatly increased after 1820, sparked by interest in the Indian reformer Rammohun Roy, whose controversy with Christian missionaries in India concerning the true nature of God was closely followed in Unitarian journals. Roy's rejection of polytheism and proclamation of a "unitarian" conception of God excited much comment.[21] After Rammohun's death, Unitarians transferred their hope to his successor, Keshub Chandra Sen, with many regarding the Brahmo Samaj as almost Unitarian in its program. Keshub Chandra Sen agreed to undertake an American lecture tour, but events prevented the visit. Keshub's disciple Protap Chandra Majumdar, however, eventually visited both England and the United States in 1874, delivering seventy speeches in just three months in fifty Unitarian chapels. From the 1820s on, Unitarian journals such as the *Christian Register* and *Christian Examiner* published regular articles on all varieties of Asian religion, usually with considerable sympathy. One can hardly exaggerate the importance of Unitarianism in the nineteenth-century American discovery of Asian religion, with Unitarian intellectuals prominent in practically every movement that indicated interest in the Eastern religions.[22]

The Transcendentalists, most of whom were Unitarian in background, increased American awareness of Asian thought. Indeed, it has become almost a truism that Transcendentalists were the earliest Americans to indicate serious interest in the Eastern religions. In fact, they were not first to look East, nor were all Transcendentalists sympathetic to Asian thought; but they may be judged the most illustrious early Americans to view the Asian religions in a positive light. Henry David Thoreau's testimonial concerning his reading of the Bhagavad Gita and Laws of Manu still reverberates 150 years later:

> I cannot read a sentence in the book of the Hindoos without being elevated as upon the table-land of the Ghauts. It has such a rhythm as the winds of the desert, such a tide as the Ganges, and seems as superior to criticism as the Himmaleh Mounts.[23]

The passage provides an excellent example of the romantic conception of the Orient, a view that portrayed the Asian religions in a radically different way than the missionary perspective. Emerson wrote of Eastern thought with equal effusiveness. The Bhagavad Gita was the Transcendentalist's special delight. Though Indian religious thought ranked highest, Transcendentalists also expressed appreciation of Confucius's moral axioms and the writings of Persian poets.

The Transcendentalists read Asian sacred texts not as scholars but as spiritual seekers and writers. Trusting in intuition, relying on the heart rather than the head, they tended to ignore inconvenient differences between the various Eastern traditions and to assume that all somehow represented a single universal religion. As writers, they were less interested in the specifics of Asian religion than in the "lusters" to be found throughout the texts, which they viewed as echoes of the Oversoul or universal spirit.[24] With the exception of scattered references in their published writings, much of the evidence of the impact of Eastern conceptions on Emerson, Thoreau, and other first-generation Transcendentalists remained hidden from public view in their journals. As a result, the significant influence of Asian religious conceptions on their thought was not at first apparent.

The Transcendental exploration of Eastern religion may be said to have climaxed in the 1870s with key publications by James Freeman Clarke, Samuel Johnson, and Moncure Conway, who produced three of the most important American works on Asian religion to appear in the nineteenth century. All three authors earned their livelihoods as Unitarian ministers, and all three revealed close ties to Transcendentalism. Their writings testify how much American awareness of Asia's religious traditions had increased since the first decades of the century.[25]

James Freeman Clarke was active in most of the movements of his time. In addition to working in a long ministry as head of the Church of the Disciples in Boston, he was a close friend of Margaret Fuller's and a regular contributor to *The Dial*, an active reformer, author of numerous books, and lecturer on non-Christian religions at the Harvard Divinity School. He was also the author of *Ten Great Religions*, published in 1871, one of the century's most widely read books on religion, which went through an amazing nineteen editions. For our purposes, the significance of the book is its inclusion of extended chapters on Hinduism and Buddhism among his ten religions. In view of the book's popularity it seems fair to say that *Ten Great Religions* formed the conception many nineteenth-century Americans had of Asian religion. In Clarke's formulation, Hinduism and Buddhism represented dramatically opposed types of religious experience. Hinduism was portrayed as a religion of the spirit, which emphasized the infinite over the finite, spirit over matter, and other-worldliness over this-worldliness; by contrast, Buddhism reversed these priorities, emphasizing the material realm over spirituality and this-worldly morality over other-worldly transcendence. Despite obvious limitations, the most egregious being its gross simplifications and strong Christian bias, in its time *Ten Great Religions* represented a major advance. Its attempt to offer a balanced analysis of the world's religions based on the research of scholars served as a model for future students of comparative religion.[26]

Samuel Johnson resembled Clarke in attending the Harvard Divinity School and in becoming a Unitarian minister, but unlike his contemporary he avoided the limelight, passing his life as an obscure minister of a nonsectarian Free Church in Lynn, Massachusetts. Aside from pastoral duties, he devoted most of his energy to the research and writing of his three-volume magnum opus, *Oriental Religions and Their Relation to Universal Religion*, published between 1872 and 1885, the most ambitious American attempt in the nineteenth century to explain Eastern spirituality. Less sectarian than Clarke, he approached the Asian religions with the assumption that all major religions embodied religious truth and that none, including Christianity, could claim its exclusive possession. "I have written," he explained in the first volume of *Oriental Religions*, "not as an advocate of Christianity or of any other distinctive religion, but as attracted on the one hand by the identity of the religious sentiment under all its great historic forms, and on the other by the movement indicated in their diversities and contrasts towards a higher plane of unity."[27] The controlling assumption behind his portrayal of the Eastern religions was that each Asian civilization had produced a distinctive "mind": the Hindu mind was "cerebral" and contemplative, the Chinese mind "muscular" and pragmatic, while the Persian mind was more "nervous." Arguing that all religions deserved to be judged in their own terms, in *Oriental Religions* he treated even what seemed the most bizarre features of each Asian religion as natural and once-functional adaptations to its particular religious environment. Though his volumes were severely attacked by contemporary scholars, Johnson's sympathetic method and comprehensive approach represented major advances in nineteenth-century American writing on Asian religion.

Barely four years old when Emerson's *Nature* appeared, Moncure Conway may be said to have concluded the long Transcendental affair with the Orient. The son of a Virginia slave owner, Conway subsequently went north to school and became a Unitarian minister. Though he spent much of his adult life abroad as head of the South Place Chapel in London, he always maintained close ties with his homeland. He became attracted to Asian religious thought while a student at Harvard and eventually published the *Sacred Anthology* in 1873, which gave much prominence to Eastern sacred writings. From the time of Emerson, there had been much talk among Transcendentalists of such a work, which would collect the highest expressions of the various world religions in a kind of "universal Bible." Conway finally realized the dream with the *Sacred Anthology*, which gathered key statements from a broad range of Eastern and Western sources and grouped them topically under such headings as "God," "Man," and "Nature." The volume's clear message was a universal religion, which recognized that all religions taught the same truths. A standard work among liberal religionists, the volume was frequently called upon for scriptural readings for Unitarian services.[28]

In the 1880s Conway set off for Sri Lanka and India in order to inspect the Orient firsthand, an experience that he subsequently recounted in *My Pilgrimage to the Wise Men of the East*. Previously, Transcendentalists had always idealized the Orient from a distance; he was unique in confronting the East directly and face to face. Conway found—and the discovery has been frequently repeated among later Western travelers—that the realities of Eastern life often diverged sharply from the romantic image encouraged by Western literary accounts. He would confess that a chance encounter with a group of Hindu ascetics in Calcutta forced the realization that Hinduism was far more appealing in the Hindu sacred writings than when confronted face to face.[29] Chagrined by his experience, he repeatedly complained in the volume of Western distortions of Asian thought. Though he continued to champion Eastern wisdom, his pilgrimage made him much more sensitive concerning what for him were now the Orient's limitations.

Historically, American interest in the Asian religions seems to rise and fall cyclically, with periods of little interest alternating with periods of intense concern. Similarly, interest has periodically shifted from one Asian tradition to another. Early in the century Hinduism and Confucianism had attracted most attention, while Buddhism remained practically unknown. By the century's final two decades, however, the situation was almost reversed. Indeed, for a time the religion of the Buddha became almost fashionable. Consider the remark of Phillips Brooks, the prominent minister of Boston's historic Trinity Church. Traveling in India in 1883, the clergyman confided to his sister-in-law that he had that day visited Buddhagaya, the sacred site where the founder of Buddhism had achieved enlightenment. Brooks explained: "In these days when a large part of Boston prefers to consider itself Buddhist rather than Christian, I consider this pilgrimage to be the duty of a minister who preaches to Bostonians."[30] Though surely spoken in jest, the statement suggests the growing awareness of Buddhism in the United States.

The event that riveted nineteenth-century American attention on Buddhism was the 1879 publication of the English poet Edwin Arnold's *The Light of Asia*. A romantic life of the Buddha rendered into free verse, the volume became an instant sensation, going through sixty English and eighty American editions. More than one million copies were sold in the two nations.[31] Aside from its literary virtues, the special fascination of Arnold's poem was its emphasis on startling parallels between the lives and teachings of Jesus and the founder of Buddhism. Similarities may be cited—for example, the traditional description of Gautama's birth at Lumbini and Jesus' nativity as described in St. Luke; however, Arnold clearly molded Buddhist legends to conform to a Christian pattern. His use of biblical words and references in his telling of Gautama's life further encouraged Western readers to see similarities between the two religions. Whatever its merits, *The Light of Asia*'s publication ignited a stormy debate that continued for the next decade.

Several theories were advanced to explain the strange congruence between Buddhism and Christianity. In 1883 James Freeman Clarke suggested that, logically, the religions' similarities might be accounted for in at least four ways: that Christianity had emerged out of Buddhism, that Buddhism had evolved from Christianity, that both traditions had arisen from a common source, or, as Clarke clearly preferred, that each had evolved independently but developed striking resemblances to one another because human nature was the same everywhere.[32] Several writers went far beyond Clarke, arguing that Jesus had been a Buddhist missionary sent from India to the Middle East. The *reductio ad absurdum* was supplied by a Russian journalist named Nicholas Notovitch in a sensational book entitled *The Unknown Life of Jesus Christ*. During a visit to a Tibetan lamasery Notovitch claimed that he had discovered a document that proved beyond any doubt that Jesus had lived several years in India where he had studied Buddhism at its source.[33] Polemicists kept the controversy alive well into the twentieth century.

The popular debate concerning similarities between Christianity and Buddhism may have contributed little to a better understanding of the two religions, but it certainly underscored the need for more scholarly studies. In fact, Unitarian, Transcendental, and all other early American students of the Asian religions, with occasional exceptions, had shared a common liability: none had either the ability to read the Eastern texts in their originals or the scholarly training essential for their elucidation. This situation changed rapidly in the latter half of the century as a result of the emergence of an American school of Asian scholars, most of whom trained in German universities. The founding of the American Oriental Society in 1842 indicated the rising scholarly interest in the East. Asian religions received much attention in the Oriental Society's journal.

Beginning with Edward Salisbury, America's first professional Orientalist, a succession of able American scholars now appeared, preparing translations and expositions of many of the Asian sacred texts. These included William Dwight Whitney, an expert on the Vedas, who held the Yale professorship in Sanskrit; Charles Rockwell Lanman, editor of the *Harvard Oriental Series*; and Henry Clarke Warren, America's first important Buddhist scholar, whose *Buddhism in Translations* is still consulted by modern students.[34] Breaking away from the romantic Orientalism that had dominated earlier decades, such Oriental scholars sought to approach their subject from a more objective and scientific perspective.

Finally, notice should be taken of the comparative religions movement, which emerged in the United States in the 1880s and 1890s, focusing much attention on the Asian religions. Comparative religionists liked to cite F. Max Müller's observation that "He who knows one language knows none," proceeding to claim that it followed that anyone aware only of one religion was equally unenlightened. The movement's impressive growth in the century's last decades may be traced through the establishment of lectureships and journals devoted to comparative religious studies. Beginning with James Freeman Clarke's 1867 appointment as lecturer on non-Christian religions at Harvard, most leading American universities had established professorships in comparative religions by 1900. For a time journals such as *New World, Open Court,* and *Biblical World* devoted a large portion of their space to articles reflecting the comparative approach. The movement climaxed in the founding of a series of notable Anglo-American lectureships that focused on comparative religious studies, including the Hibbert Lectures (1878) and Gifford Lectures (1888) in Great Britain and the American Lectures on the History of Religions (1891) and Haskell Lectures on Comparative Religion (1894) in the United States.[35]

The significance of the comparative religions movement is that its advocates approached the Asian religions much more sympathetically than most earlier writers. The very act of comparing Hinduism or Buddhism with Christianity tended to legitimize Asian religious conceptions, forcing Westerners to recognize the profundity of much in Eastern religious teaching. The comparative religions movement was particularly important as an influence on seminaries where, reaching across denominational lines, it profoundly influenced the way the next generation of Christian leaders viewed non-Christian religions.

As a result of these developments—the growth of U.S.-Asian trade contacts, a rising flood of American missionaries bound for the East, increased attention paid to Asian religions in nineteenth-century American and British periodicals, discovery of Eastern thought by Unitarians and Transcendentalists, rising interest in Buddhism stimulated by the publication of *The Light of Asia*, and the appearance of Asian scholars and comparative religionists—Americans by the 1890s had become much more aware of and sympathetic toward the Asian religions than at the century's beginning.

One other factor should be mentioned. America's increasing openness to Asian thought in the 1890s may be explained as much as a consequence of a deepening internal crisis within American religion as a result of these developments. Historians such as Paul Carter argue that the final years of the nineteenth century marked a "spiritual crisis" in American religious life. Forced to adjust to a huge internal shift of population from the farm to the city; nearly overwhelmed by the added strain of ministering to the spiritual needs of millions of new immigrants; confronted by the intellectual challenges posed by Darwinists and advocates of the "higher criticism" of the Bible; and more and more divided as the result of a deepening split between liberal and conservative Christians, American Christianity found itself increasingly on the defensive.[36] Recognition of such a crisis suggests the possibility that the growth of sympathy toward the Asian religions in the later nineteenth century represented a vote against contemporary Christian orthodoxy as much as a vote in favor of those ancient faiths. On the rebound, Americans in some cases found themselves willing to contemplate Asian alternatives.

Linkage of rising American interest in the Asian religions to a spiritual crisis has merit, provided the argument is not carried too far. In the first place, any account of a crisis must not be allowed to obscure the intrinsic attractions of Eastern conceptions. Such attraction often began as a romantic interest and deepened into something more substantial. As acquaintance grew, Americans became persuaded of the philosophic profundity and richness offered by the Asian traditions. Westerners who looked East on the rebound from a bad experience with Christianity regularly found more than they anticipated. Here, both a "push" and a "pull" may be deciphered. The eighteenth- and nineteenth-century Hindu and Buddhist revivals in South and Southeast Asia supplied the "push," restoring the dynamism and renewing the self-confidence of those religions, inspiring a series of teachers and movements to carry the message west. Profound changes in the American religious environment and growing acquaintance with Asian thought occasioned the "pull," with the "spiritual crisis" of the Gilded Age undermining older certainties and encouraging a more tolerant, more sympathetic attitude toward non-Christian religions.

One other observation is pertinent. Though it is now clear that nineteenth-century American awareness of the Asian religions was considerably wider than once assumed, such acquaintance was almost entirely confined to the printed page. There were exceptions, of course. A handful of New England merchants and shippers obviously had some opportunity to confront Asian religious life face-to-face; and several hundred Protestant missionaries enjoyed more extended contacts over the course of the century. A limited number of affluent travelers, who made their way east as tourists eager to observe the area's temples and pagodas, joined in later in the century. All other nineteenth-century Americans were forced to rely on the literary record for information concerning Asia and Asian thought.

This brings us back to the Ramakrishna movement. The appearance of Swami Vivekananda and other Asian representatives at the Parliament of Religions in 1893 marked the first time authentic Asian teachers presented their faiths directly to Western audiences. The appearance of Ramakrishna swamis in America in the 1890s inaugurated a new stage in the history of Eastern spirituality in the United States.

2 | The Founders
Ramakrishna and Vivekananda

THE SPIRITUAL FOUNDER of the Ramakrishna movement was an obscure Hindu born in a small Indian village in rural Bengal in the early part of the nineteenth century. He never traveled more than a few hundred miles from his birthplace, he often behaved like a child, and he embraced a great many conceptions that modern Westerners would immediately dismiss as rank superstition. His admirers insist that he was a religious genius in the great tradition of Hindu holy men. Scholars agree that he played a leading role in the modern revival of Hinduism in India and that the movement he inspired has deeply influenced modern Indian history. From a historian's perspective, Ramakrishna's uniqueness was not the originality of his teachings or his ability as a dynamic organizer but the intensity of his spiritual quest and his ability to attract young Hindu disciples of talent and education to carry on his work. In spite of the strange and unsettling events of his life—or perhaps because of them—he has attracted the attention of Western students of religion for more than a century. Max Müller, the nineteenth-century Anglo-German scholar, Romain Rolland, the early twentieth-century French man of letters, and Christopher Isherwood, the Anglo-American writer, are only three of the West's notables who have been fascinated by the founder of the Ramakrishna movement.[1]

Before considering the events of Ramakrishna's life, a preliminary word should be said about *The Gospel of Sri Ramakrishna*, our major source concerning the Bengali's life and teachings. The recorder of the *Gospel* was Mahendranath Gupta, a graduate of the University of Calcutta who at one time had been a follower of Keshub Chandra Sen, the charismatic leader of the Brahmo Samaj. (A significant number of Ramakrishna's major disciples shared Samaj backgrounds.) Gupta was well equipped to take down Ramakrishna's teachings as a result of his vocational background as a teacher. Convinced that anything his master said or did had spiritual significance, Gupta provided an almost stenographic record of Ramakrishna's life and teaching, including the most trivial episodes. The resulting manuscript was eventually published as *The Gospel of Sri Ramakrishna*, with Gupta listed as recorder under the pseudonymn of "M." The volume records Ramakrishna's daily life and teachings only for the last four years of his life (1882–1886). Gupta did not begin publishing the *Gospel* until 1897, more than a decade after his master's death, and he was still editing the manuscript at the time of his own death.[2] Regarded by followers as the sacred scripture of the movement, the volume is the only source for much of our information concerning Ramakrishna.

Gadadhar Chattopadhyaya, as Ramakrishna was known before embracing a religious career, was born in the village of Kamarpukur, in what is now West Bengal, on February 18, 1836.[3] The son of poor Brahmin parents, he grew up in a rural environment almost untouched by the rising Western influence then permeating India—an impact especially strong in nearby Calcutta, the capital of British India. Though the country was rapidly changing, his India remained much the same as in millennia past, an India of peasants, minutely observed caste regulations, and religious orthodoxy.

While much about Ramakrishna's life will always remain unknown, it appears that he early manifested the paranormal religious behavior that was to attract wide attention. Any scholar who considers his life must immediately confront serious difficulty in determining which experiences can be corroborated by contemporary sources and which have been added by subsequent devotees. Legend and history became intertwined at an early point. An example was a remarkable experience said to have occurred when Ramakrishna was only six or seven, when, walking across a field, he chanced to glance up at the sky just as a flight of snow-white geese cut across the darkened thunderclouds above. Instantly falling into a deep ecstatic trance, he dropped to the ground as if he had been shot. The repeated report of such experiences in subsequent years led some, including his parents, to doubt his sanity. Aside from these events, Gadadhar struck most of his contemporaries as a normal, fun-loving village boy. He completed more formal schooling than is commonly believed, attending a village school with some regularity for twelve years. During these years, he read widely in Bengali religious texts, committing long portions of the *Ramayana* and *Mahabharata* to memory. Though hardly well educated by modern standards, he was no illiterate.[4] At the age of sixteen Ramakrishna left his village for Calcutta to assist his elder brother, who had recently opened a Sanskrit academy. Three years later he resettled in the small village of Dakshineswar across the Ganges from Calcutta, where his brother had been recently appointed chief priest of a new temple.

Dakshineswar marked a key turning point in Ramakrishna's life, for it was here that he began worship of the goddess Kali, who would play such a special role in his later life. Known by several names, including Sati, Parvati, and Durga, and viewed by Hindus as the female aspect of God, Kali was believed to personify the divine mother of the universe. The goddess is traditionally portrayed as four-armed, bedecked in a necklace of human skulls, dancing on the chest of Shiva. (For many years Ramakrishna swamis in the United States ignored or downplayed the centrality of Kali in Ramakrishna's life, realizing that most Westerners would have great difficulty accepting such a figure.)

Following his brother's death, Ramakrishna inherited charge of the Dakshineswar temple where he soon began to attract attention by the unusual zeal of his worship of Kali. Bathing, clothing, and offering food to God-images may be commonplace in Hinduism, but Ramakrishna performed these devotions so fervently—tenderly fondling, patiently feeding, and actually speaking to an image of Kali—that acquaintances began to doubt his mental stability. The Bengali visionary became sufficiently concerned that he was, in fact, losing his mind that he began to query visitors for their opinions. The *Gospel of Ramakrishna* relates that a female renunciate who later became his teacher reassured him: "My son, everyone in this world is mad. Some are mad for money, some for creature comforts, some for name and fame; and you are mad for God."[5]

Alarmed by reports of her son's unstable condition, his mother arranged in 1859 for Ramakrishna's return to Kamarpukur. The mother concluded that matrimony might stabilize him, and as a result she quickly arranged marriage to Saradamani Mukhopadhyaya, a five-year-old girl from a neighboring village. (Such child marriages were still widespread in nineteenth-century India, despite vehement condemnations by both English authorities and Hindu reformers. Analogous to the Western betrothal, child marriage committed the partners to one another, with the actual act of living together and assuming family responsibilities delayed until puberty.) Ramakrishna returned to Dakshineswar immediately after the marriage, not to see his child-wife again for many years. By the time his bride joined him, he had already embraced the monastic life of a sannyasin; as a result, the marriage was never consummated, though the two subsequently shared a common living quarter. Meanwhile, Ramakrishna singlemindedly pursued an arduous course of spiritual practices that would ultimately establish his fame throughout India. In the beginning he struggled on his own; sometime in the 1860s, however, he embraced training under a series of teachers.

A woman referred to as the "Bhairavi Brahmani" now introduced Ramakrishna to Tantrism, a significant influence on his early development.[6] Tantrism focuses on the worship of *shakti*, the personification of primal energy; the object of Tantric training is to transcend the barriers between the holy and the unholy as a means of achieving liberation. Traditionally, such training has entailed overcoming aversion to such Hindu taboos as eating meat, drinking wine, and encountering dead flesh. Tantrists believe that violating such taboos will force recognition that, ultimately, all aspects of the natural world are manifestations of the divine *shakti*. Instead of renunciation, the student learns to redirect, transform, and control impulses normally viewed as obstacles to higher consciousness. Tantric rites are considered extremely difficult and only to be taken up under the guidance of a qualified guru.[7]

Apologists for the Ramakrishna movement consistently reveal anxiety that this aspect of Ramakrishna's early spiritual development will be misconstrued. Concern especially centers on the practice of *vamachara*, or the "left-handed" school of Tantra, which prescribes control of semen during sexual intercourse as one means to self-liberation. Biographers insist that the Ramakrishna movement's founder never engaged in these rites. Ramakrishna later warned that Tantric disciplines were dangerous, and he admonished his followers to avoid them. Despite his warnings, modern scholars increasingly agree that Tantrism must be recognized as a major force in Ramakrishna's life and teachings.[8]

Several other teachers played a role in Ramakrishna's spiritual education, but none exceeded the importance of Tota Puri, an itinerant monk Ramakrishna met in 1865 who trained him in Advaita Vedanta. One of six traditional schools of Hindu philosophy, Vedanta was systematized by Shankara in approximately 800 A.D. Emphasizing nondualism, in Vedanta spiritual liberation arises from recognition that the True Self (*atman*) and Ultimate Reality (*Brahman*) are one.[9] Ramakrishna pursued Vedantic disciplines under Tota Puri's direction for nearly a year, culminating in *sannyas*, the final monastic vows normally reserved for unmarried aspirants.

During his spiritual training as well as later, Ramakrishna astonished observers by the ease with which he apparently entered what was known as samadhi and considered as the highest state of transcendental consciousness. Indeed, according to the testimonies of his disciples, he could enter such states of higher consciousness almost at will.[10] Nagendranath Gupta reported one such experience in *Modern Review* in 1927:

> He repeated the word Nirakara two or three times and then quietly passed into Samadhi as the diver slips into the fathomless deep. . . . The whole body relaxed and then became slightly rigid. There was no twitching of the muscles or nerves, no movement of any limb. Both his hands lay in his lap with the fingers tightly interlocked. The sitting posture of the body . . . was easy but absolutely motionless. The face was slightly tilted up and in repose. The eyes were nearly but not wholly closed. The eyeballs were not turned up or otherwise deflected, but they were fixed and conveyed no message of outer objects to the brain. The lips were parted in a beatific and indescribable smile, disclosing the gleam of white teeth.[11]

Most Westerners find themselves troubled by such accounts. Even Romain Rolland, whose sympathetic portrayal of Ramakrishna in *Prophets of New India* helped attract wider Western interest to the Hindu visionary, confessed: "I will not deny the fact that when I had reached this point in my researches, I shut up the book." Other Western investigators have attributed Ramakrishna's transcendental claims to his "nervous excitability" and "mother-fixation," utilizing Western psychological terminology to explain his behavior.[12] Obviously, the explanation preferred will depend upon the view one adopts toward visionary experiences. Familiarity with the accounts of mystics such as Saint Teresa, Meister Eckhart, or Jacob Boehme emphasizes that nearly identical claims have been advanced in the West.[13]

Claims concerning Ramakrishna's visionary experiences are not the only aspect of his life that has struck Westerners. His extreme reaction to what he called *kamini kanchan*, or "women and gold," has also intrigued outside observers. According to Sivanath Sastri, a well-known Sadharan Brahmo Samaj minister, on one occasion he observed Ramakrishna sitting by the Ganges holding dirt in one hand and coins in the other, mumbling the phrase, "dust is money, money is dust, dust is money, money is dust" again and again. When he had convinced himself of the truth of the statement, Ramakrishna hurled both the dirt and coins into the stream. He apparently reacted to physical contact with women in an even more remarkable manner. Indeed, according to Sastri, his "abhorrence of the touch of woman" was so great that he "would not permit" any woman to approach him. If a woman intruded into his space, he would bow and anxiously plead: "Mother! mother! stay there, please come not nearer."[14] Such reactions call up Freudian explanations, though it should be noted that Western monastic practices also emphasize avoidance of money and women through vows of poverty and chastity. Modern defenders explain that when referring to *kamini kanchan*, Ramakrishna spoke symbolically, intending to signify "lust" and "greed" by the words "woman" and "gold."[15]

Following years of spiritual exploration of Hinduism, Ramakrishna apparently also investigated other religious traditions. A chance encounter with a Hindu seeker who had embraced Islam led him to the teachings of the Qu'ran. For a brief period, according to his official biographer, he dressed in Muslim clothing, consumed Muslim food, and attempted to observe all obligations and prayer periods mandated in Islam—meanwhile meticulously avoiding contact with Hindu deities. His biographer reports that, after only three days of such observances, Ramakrishna underwent an experience in which he merged with Muhammad.[16] Sometime later he also considered Christianity. Swami Saradananda recounts the details in *Sri Ramakrishna: The Great Master*, including an unusual visionary encounter with a "marvellous god-man," whom he immediately knew to be Jesus, who proceeded to embrace and merge into him. These experiences apparently convinced Ramakrishna that Jesus was an incarnation of God.[17]

Ramakrishna movement writers make much of these visionary experiences with the founders of Islam and Christianity, claiming that Ramakrishna thereby demonstrated the universality of his teaching for all people. Unlike previous teachers, he had attained higher transcendental consciousness not only in his own tradition but in others as well. However, scholars such as Cyrus Pangborn have objected that such claims may be questioned in view of Ramakrishna's limited contacts with non-Hindu religions—though his expression of interest in Islam and Christianity certainly establishes his broad religious outlook. Pangborn contends that Ramakrishna seems to have experienced Muhammad and Jesus "not on *their* terms but only on his own" and that his "temporary departures from outward Hindu practice" did not thereby make him either a Muslim or Christian. Indeed, one might better say that Ramakrishna had "made Hindus of Muhammad and Jesus by initiating them posthumously into Vedantic Sannyasa!"[18] As we will see, subsequent swamis proceeded to proclaim a Hindu Christ.

Clearly, then, Ramakrishna was not merely a Vedantist, as he has often been presented, but also a devotee of Mother Kali, a Tantrist, and, perhaps at times, a Vaishnavite (worshiper of Vishnu) insofar as he emphasized devotionalism. A close reading of the *Gospel of Ramakrishna* reveals the influence not only of Vedanta but of several other Hindu traditions. Recent Western scholars have traced the misunderstanding back to Swami Vivekananda, who tended to accentuate the movement's Vedantic message so strongly that other formative influences on Ramakrishna were overlooked. Far from being a mere follower of Shankara, Ramakrishna blended elements from Kali worship, Vaishnavism, Tantrism, and Vedanta into his own distinctive teaching.[19]

As word of Ramakrishna's unusual behavior and visionary experiences spread, a procession of curious students, householders, and outsiders made pilgrimages to Dakshineswar to observe the childlike Hindu. Surprisingly, a good number of the visitors were Westernized Indians, who normally should not have found Ramakrishna's traditional Hindu devotionalism and uncontrolled, ecstatic behavior congenial. The Brahmo Samaj leader Protap Chandra Majumdar, who subsequently lectured in America, typified the reaction of such individuals. Reflecting on his encounter with Ramakrishna, Majundar confessed that his mind was "still floating in the luminous atmosphere which that wonderful man diffuses around him." The Brahmo Samajist was apparently astonished by his own reaction, expressing a disquietude that must have been echoed in other Westernized Hindu visitors. "What is there in common between him and me?" Majumdar asked himself. "I, a Europeanized, civilized, self-centered, semi-sceptical, so-called educated reasoner, and he a poor, illiterate, unpolished, half-idolatrous, friendless Hindu devotee? Why should I sit long hours to attend to him?"[20] The impact of such encounters could be far-reaching, as revealed in the later years of Keshub Chandra Sen, the Brahmo Samaj's most charismatic leader. From his first encounter with Ramakrishna in 1875, Sen became a regular visitor at Dakshineswar. Ramakrishna apparently drew Keshub back to a renewed appreciation of traditional Hinduism, while Sen's enthusiastic reports generated wider public interest in Ramakrishna and attracted valuable recruits. (The two men's association altered the subsequent histories of both the Brahmo Samaj and Ramakrishna movements.)

At the height of his powers in the late 1870s, Ramakrishna clearly impressed his contemporaries. Pictorial representations present a small, thin, emaciated man whose bearing suggests an intense, deeply emotional nature. Deep-set eyes, which were never opened very wide, and a dazzling smile that seemed both affectionate and mischievous were dominant facial characteristics. Thanks to the preservation of three nineteenth-century photographs, all taken while he was in an ecstatic state, the Ramakrishna movement may make the novel claim that of all "religious teachers of the highest order," Ramakrishna was the "first to be photographed." Swami Nikhilananda, who taught for many years in New York City, comments: "We know now what an Incarnation looks like."[21]

Anyone who reads the account of Ramakrishna's life as recorded in the *Gospel of Sri Ramakrishna* will find an absorbing portrait. Despite growing fame in

his last years, Ramakrishna never wandered far from the temple precincts at Dakshineswar, where he spent most of his days in worship and conversing with his
devotees. On occasion he joined his followers in a *kirtan*, a Vaishnava ritual in
which the group danced and chanted sacred scriptures. He also spent increasing
time instructing a band of young disciples who would carry on the work after
his death. Throat cancer cut his life short, causing his death in 1886 at the age
of fifty.

If Ramakrishna was the spiritual founder of the Ramakrishna movement, his
young disciple Swami Vivekananda was the movement's chief organizer and publicist. Ramakrishna supplied the teachings and inspiration, but Vivekananda was
largely responsible for the movement's internal form and outward reach. Without
Vivekananda, it seems unlikely that Ramakrishna would ever have attracted significant attention in the West. At the same time their collaboration was an unlikely one, representing a meeting of opposite types. The child of an older India,
Ramakrishna was deeply instilled by the traditional outlook and values of a peas-
ant society; the product of New India, Vivekananda embodied the views and
concerns of an urban society. Ramakrishna may perhaps be best described as a
mystic and traditionalist; by contrast, Vivekananda was an activist and reformer.
Where Ramakrishna looked inward in his search for God, Vivekananda stressed
the need of religion to reach outward. While Ramakrishna passed most of his
life in the circumscribed world of Dakshineswar, where he quietly engaged in the
worship of Kali, Vivekananda circled the world, devoting himself to public lectures, polemics, and humanitarian projects in both Asia and the West. The resulting combination of tradition and modernity, of orthodoxy and reform, of
mysticism and social action, define the Ramakrishna movement's distinctive
message to India and the world.

Narendranath Datta, as Vivekananda was known before becoming a monk,
was born on January 12, 1863, in Calcutta. Raised in a middle-class, professional family, he was originally expected to follow in the footsteps of his father,
who was a successful lawyer. He was educated at Presidency College and a Christian missionary institution known as Scottish Church College; after passing his
examinations in 1884 he undertook the study of law. During these formative
years, he read a good deal of Western philosophy, indicating special enthusiasm
for Herbert Spencer, John Stuart Mill, and Auguste Comte. Along the way, he
also became a Mason, joining the Freemason's Lodge in Calcutta, an affiliation
then considered quite important among India's ambitious younger set.[22] Except
for the influence of a pious mother, these early years reveal little evidence to explain his subsequent choice of a religious career.

Significantly, young Narendra was also a member of the Brahmo Samaj, the
Hindu movement which championed a program of reform Hinduism and humanitarianism that closely resembled and undoubtedly influenced the Ramakrishna movement's subsequent work. At first a follower of Keshub Chandra Sen,

he shifted allegiance to the Sadharan Brahmo Samaj in 1878, following a schism in the movement. Though in later years the swami rarely mentioned the Brahmo connection, it was apparently a significant personal influence. His friend Haromohan Mitra recalled that he had frequently heard Vivekananda declare, "But for Ramakrishna I would have been a Brahmo missionary."[23] For a number of years the future leader of the Ramakrishna movement regularly attended Samaj meetings and actively participated in the group's activities. Though he ultimately followed Ramakrishna, he apparently never officially withdrew from the Brahmo Samaj, a fact corroborated by inclusion of his name on the organization's membership roll as late as 1907.[24] In this he was not unusual, since some prior affiliation with the Brahmo Samaj was almost the norm among many of Ramakrishna's early disciples.

Vivekananda was a youth of eighteen years at the time of his first meeting with Ramakrishna. If the reminiscence of his college classmate Brajendra Nath Seal may be trusted, he hardly seemed the type to renounce the world for a religious career. Seal characterized the future swami as "undeniably a gifted youth," who was "sociable," "unconventional in manners," and a "brilliant conversationalist"; but he also remembered his college friend as "somewhat bitter and caustic" and even something of a "Bohemian."[25] Son of a Calcutta professional family, an enthusiastic reader of Western philosophy, and a member of the reformist Sadharan Brahmo Samaj, the promising youth seemed much better suited to join Calcutta's Anglo-Indian professional class than to adopt the life of a wandering sadhu.

The first fateful meeting that was to change his life occurred in late 1881. Curiously, Vivekananda's original interest in Ramakrishna seems to have been sparked by a Westerner, a teacher at Scottish Church College named William Hastie, who casually mentioned Ramakrishna's name in the course of a lecture on the role of mysticism in Wordsworth.[26] (In view of Keshub Chandra Sen's ripening friendship with Ramakrishna after 1875, Vivekananda must have also heard reports of the Bengali visionary through his Brahmo connections.) In his first encounters, Vivekananda tended to dismiss Ramakrishna as both strange and excessively emotional, but he was unable to ignore the priest of Dakshineswar's intense religiosity. He was struck by the older man's answer to his question of whether he had seen God. Without a moment's hesitation, Ramakrishna had replied: "Yes, I have seen God. I see Him as I see you here, only more clearly."[27]

Over the next several years Narendra was apparently both strongly attracted to and at the same time repelled by Ramakrishna, visiting his future guru with some frequency, but periodically drawing back and refusing to seek the older man out for months at a time, despite his urgent entreaties. Fascinated by Ramakrishna's apparent ability to enter into and to induce altered states of consciousness in others, he was simultaneously repelled by the Dakshineswar priest's worship of Mother Kali, which contradicted his rationalistic Brahmo Samaj convictions. He might have continued to resist Ramakrishna indefinitely but for the unexpected deaths of his father and Keshub Chandra Sen within a single month in 1884, a double blow which seems to have precipitated the profound spiritual crisis that culminated in his decision to pursue a religious life.[28]

Unfortunately, the events between Ramakrishna's death in 1886 and Vivekananda's dramatic American appearance before the World's Parliament of Religions in 1893 are obscure; the seven-year period represents a crucial interim during which Ramakrishna's disciples gradually coalesced into a movement that was to spread their master's teachings across India. There seems to have been little question among the "boys," as the younger devotees were referred to, that Vivekananda should assume leadership, since before his death Ramakrishna had commanded him to keep the disciples together. At the same time, there was no concrete plan of action, and little evidence that Ramakrishna, Vivekananda, or anyone else foresaw the need to create an organized movement to carry Vedanta to the West.

The years immediately following Ramakrishna's death were particularly precarious. In spite of a chronic shortage of funds, suspicion by older followers, and confusion as to what should be done, Vivekananda somehow managed to keep the younger disciples together. Several now took the vows and assumed the names of monastics, thus formally launching the Ramakrishna Order.[29] (Ramakrishna normally should have conducted the ordination ceremony as their guru, but his early death forced them to proceed on their own.) Following the traditional Hindu ideal, in 1887 the youthful monks set off on extended pilgrimages to the sacred sites and religious shrines of Hinduism scattered throughout the Indian subcontinent. Vivekananda joined in, traveling alone much of the time, utilizing a series of names (Sachchitananda, Vividisananda) to mask his identity. (In fact, he did not adopt "Vivekananda" as his monastic name until 1892. Translated as "he who has the bliss of spiritual discrimination," the name was suggested by one of his major supporters, the raja of Khetri.)[30] His extensive travels during these years proved crucial in crystallizing Vivekananda's conception of the Ramakrishna Order's future work. As the full extent of India's debilitating social and religious problems dawned upon him, he formulated his first tentative plans for reform. A nationalist as much as a defender of Hinduism, he now began to refer to his "mission of regenerating the motherland."

During his extended travels in the years following Ramakrishna's death, Vivekananda did not ignore his own mission, regularly seeking out teachers who might assist him in improving his spiritual practice. In the case of an ascetic named Pavhari Baba, he seems to have come very close to abandoning Ramakrishna for a new guru. Though sought out by a steady flow of eager pilgrims, Pavhari rarely left the walled compound where he spent his days in meditation. Vivekananda was deeply impressed by Pavhari's spirituality, spending several months at the compound pursuing raja yoga under the older man's direction.

Many years later, Vivekananda made the surprising confession that he had actually appealed to Pavhari to become his guru, but that the Hindu holy man had refused, explaining that he had committed all his energies to working out his own salvation. By 1890, however, Vivekananda was reaffirming his allegiance to Ramakrishna, and he never again changed his mind.[31]

Why did Swami Vivekananda abruptly decide to go to America in 1893 to attend the World's Parliament of Religions? And what exactly did he hope to accomplish? Though movement histories seem to assume that he had already settled on a fully developed plan for the movement's Western work before departing for the Parliament, close inspection of the swami's actions in the period before and after 1893 suggests that, on the contrary, his conception of the Ramakrishna Order's future work remained fairly hazy until well after the close of the Parliament. At the time he sailed for the United States, the swami's primary concern apparently was not propagation of Vedanta in the West but raising money to finance the humanitarian work he planned in India.

Indeed, Vivekananda's original hope had apparently rested on the rajas of India, for he spent the two years preceding his departure for Chicago searching out wealthy donors who could be persuaded to underwrite his program of uplift for India. Once asked why a monk who had renounced the world spent so much time with princes and rajas, Vivekananda had responded: "Just compare the results one can achieve by instructing thousands of poor people and inducing them to adopt a certain line of action on the one hand, and by converting a prince to that point of view on the other."[32]

Still unsuccessful in locating a raja willing to underwrite his Indian regeneration program when he heard news of the impending Parliament of Religions, Swami Vivekananda immediately sensed that he might find the necessary financial resources in the West and apparently decided to attend. He openly admitted that he had remained in America after the close of the Parliament to raise money. His warm reception at the congress and during lectures in the months afterward persuaded him to launch a separate Western effort in tandem with the Indian work.[33] In short, the idea of establishing Vedanta centers in the United States was an unanticipated result rather than the original intent of his Western trip.

The World's Parliament of Religions, which convened for seventeen days in September 1893 in conjunction with the Chicago Columbian Exposition, was unquestionably one of the unique events of nineteenth-century America. Charles C. Bonney originally proposed the idea for such an event, arguing that in order to present a true representation of American civilization at the Exposition, the nation's spiritual achievements should be on display alongside its material wonders. A series of denominational congresses were also scheduled, but the centerpiece was the Parliament of Religions, in which representatives of all the world religions were invited to present their beliefs. Though the vast majority of participants were Christians, a surprising number of Asian delegates were also present. To mention only a few, these included Protap Chandra Majumdar from India, representing the Brahmo Samaj; Virchand Gandhi, sent by the Jain Association of India; Anagarika Dharmapala of Sri Lanka, representing Buddhism; Pung Kwang Yu, secretary of the Chinese Legation in Washington, D.C., the official spokesman for Confucianism; and a Japanese delegation who represented Shintoism and Japanese Buddhism.[34] From the opening day, the Parliament's sessions were thronged by thousands of Americans, while its deliberations were closely followed in the nation's religious press. For the first time in history, Asian adherents presented the major Eastern religions directly to Americans. As such, the Parliament of Religions was considered a watershed event by contemporary observers.

The 1893 congress also proved to be Vivekananda's great opportunity. Completely unknown when the Parliament doors opened, he quickly became one of the best-known delegates. (All the Asian representatives attracted unusual attention, perhaps as much because of their seemingly exotic dress and cultures as because of their novel message.) Vivekananda's very first words on the Parliament's opening day, "Sisters and Brothers of America," attracted much comment, seeming to capture the spirit of the occasion. Altogether, the swami spoke perhaps a dozen times, addressing both the large general sessions and the more specialized gatherings scheduled during the Parliament. In addresses such as "The Essence of the Hindu Religion" and "Religion Not the Crying Need of India," the swami presented Hinduism's basic teachings and at the same time launched a spirited attack against Western distortions of Indian social conditions.[35]

Though there were dissenting voices, most contemporary accounts suggest that Vivekananda was extremely effective as Hinduism's representative. Harriet Monroe, the founder of *Poetry* and a major figure in early twentieth-century American poetry, was completely won over by the swami's performance. "It was the last of these, Swami Vivekananda the magnificent, who stole the whole show and captured the town. Others of the foreign groups spoke well—the Greek, the Russian, the Armenian, Mazoomdar of Calcutta, Dharmapala of Ceylon—leaning, some of these, upon interpreters. . . . But the handsome monk in the orange robe gave us in perfect English a masterpiece." Unable to say enough, she claimed that his speeches at the Parliament represented "human eloquence at its highest pitch."[36] Even his harshest critics admitted that he was persuasive. His willingness to appear before an American audience to confront and criticize Christian missionary efforts in India excited much comment, triggering a heated series of exchanges with missionary apologists that continued for months afterward. He argued that India's true need was not an alien religion, but food, medicine, and financial assistance to cope with India's massive problems.

Testimonies such as Monroe's have led some later writers to exaggerate Vivekananda's role at the 1893 congress. Ramakrishna movement accounts go so far as to claim that the swami completely dominated the proceedings, overshadowing the large Christian representation at the sessions. The facts suggest a more modest impact. One voice among several hundred, he did not dominate the sessions. Looking back a century later, we can now see that the Parliament of Religions itself was not the watershed event that contemporary enthusiasts proclaimed, nor did it launch a new era in world religious history.

Swami Vivekananda's decision to remain in America after the Parliament's close was not surprising in view of his favorable reception and the continuing need to raise money to launch his work in India. Three years would pass before he finally returned to his homeland. Beginning in late 1893, the swami began a series of lectures that extended through mid-1895.[37] He focused at first on the Middle West, concentrating on Madison, Minneapolis, Des Moines, and Detroit; but he soon expanded his range to include Memphis and the cities of the eastern seaboard. Headlined in reports as the "cyclonic Hindu," the swami usually achieved notice wherever he spoke. His appearance and message continued to excite American audiences. The *Memphis Commercial* described Vivekananda as "in some respects" the "most interesting visitor Memphis has ever had"; the *Appeal-Avalanche* went even further, claiming that the swami was attracting "more marked attention" in Memphis than "almost any lecturer or minister" who had previously visited the city.[38] Extended lecture appearances in Detroit in February and March 1894 were high points of the first year in America.

While generally well received, Swami Vivekananda had to confront rising criticism from missionaries and conservative Christian leaders who deeply resented his continued attacks on missionary work in India. Christian anger seems to have been building since the Parliament of Religions, finally spilling over in Detroit. Upset by a lecture in which the swami advanced a claim to the moral superiority of Hinduism, a Methodist leader shot off an angry letter of protest to all the city's newspapers. A general barrage followed, with the swami returning the fire.[39]

The reverberations of the controversy with American missionaries continued for several years. In late 1894 Frank Field Ellinwood, secretary of the Board of Foreign Missions of the Presbyterian Church, U.S.A., launched a fierce personal assault on Vivekananda in a two-part series entitled "A Hindu Missionary in America." Ellinwood's attack was particularly significant, coming from a missionary spokesperson who, before the Parliament, had been calling for a more tolerant view of the non-Christian religions. Ellinwood confessed that he now felt that Asian delegates had taken unfair advantage of American hospitality to launch an anti-Christian campaign. The *Missionary Review of the World*, perhaps the country's leading missionary journal, was even more hostile, charging that Vivekananda and his countryman Virchand Gandhi had launched an "aggressive movement" to promote their "heathen propaganda."[40] Gandhi's article "Why Christian Missions Have Failed in India," published in the April 1894 issue of *Forum*, fueled the controversy, igniting a furious series of exchanges that extended over the next six months.[41]

Of all American groups, none was more critical of Vivekananda than Christian missionaries. None had more to lose. The swami's questions concerning missionary reports on Indian social conditions and his sturdy defense of the Asian religions threated the very rationale of the whole missionary enterprise. Increasing numbers of missionaries were abandoning the older view of "heathen" Asian religions for a more sympathetic perspective. An ongoing missionary debate that had been rising for decades concerning the appropriate Christian attitude toward non-Christian religions made the swami's observations that much more sensitive. A number of causes undoubtedly contributed to the transformation in missionary views, but the appearance in the United States of Asian lecturers such as Swami Vivekananda certainly played some part.[42]

In April 1894 Vivekananda shifted his campaign to the East Coast, where he launched a second series of lectures that included extended stays in Boston and New York; addresses at Smith, Radcliffe, and Harvard colleges; and classes offered during the Greenacre Conferences in Maine, an annual summer gathering that attracted a diverse collection of liberal Christians and free religionists. The swami gradually gave up his original hope of collecting money ("Now lecturing for a year in this country, I could not succeed at all . . . in my plan for raising some funds for setting up my work"), and instead began to speak of a distinct American work. Indicative of the change, he wrote an Indian disciple in October 1894: "Everybody wants me to come over to India. They think we shall be able to do more if I come over. They are mistaken, my friend." Warning that his Indian supporters should not expect his speedy return, he continued: "Here is a grand field. What have I to do with this 'ism' or that 'ism'? I am the servant of the Lord, and where on earth is there a better field than here for propagating all high ideas?"[43] Apparently, classes in New York City removed all further doubts; the result would be the inauguration of the first Vedanta society in America.

"Organisation has its faults, no doubt, but without that nothing can be done," the swami once confessed.[44] All Asian teachers who have propagated their spiritual teachings in America have faced much the same dilemma: how to create a movement adapted to Western conditions, yet compatible with their Eastern traditions. The problem has been particularly acute for Hindu teachers because Hinduism has not been notable for organization. With few preconceived ideas, the swami felt his way forward hesitantly. At first, he seemed to prefer a skeletal housekeeping structure which would take over all distracting administrative and financial details, leaving religious activities to be carried on by himself and close disciples. Religion, he felt, must not be tainted by a business mentality. If there must be some form of organization, keep it to an absolute minimum, and leave it in the hands of American followers. With such a view in mind, he founded an infant society in November 1894. (The body was so nebulous that it was entirely overlooked by early movement historians.)[45] In time, more substantial arrangements evolved in which administrative and religious functions were combined—making the New York Vedanta Society a board of directors as well as a body of believers. The two types of functions have continued to be distinguished ever since. The result has been a dualistic system in which the swami of each Vedanta society controls all spiritual matters, while financial and administrative concerns are delegated to a local American board.

From the very first, upper-middle and upper-class supporters were active in the swami's American work. Some of the prominent names include the George Hales, whose spacious home served as the swami's base of operations in Chicago; Thomas Palmer, a wealthy Detroit businessman; Walter and Frances Goodyear of Goodyear Rubber Company fame; Sara Bull, the wife of famous Norwegian violinist Ole Bull; well-known soprano Emma Thursby; and Francis Leggett, a wealthy New York businessman—all affluent members of their respective communities. To some extent the pattern has persisted throughout the Ramakrishna movement's history in America, a connection sometimes explained as characteristic of people with excess time and too much money, who have become jaded by more conventional religion and who are forever searching for an alternative. Or perhaps it is that members in the upper levels of society are better educated and more cosmopolitan in their tastes than the working class, circumstances that create greater openness to foreign conceptions.

The special demands of upper-class supporters could pose problems; and, indeed, on several occasions Swami Vivekananda strongly protested efforts to deflect his work toward greater respectability. In one case, a wealthy follower warned the Hindu monk against renting quarters in a less desirable section of New York City. Complaining that the society lady wanted him introduced to the "right kind of people," the swami lamented: "Lord! how hard it is for man to believe in Thee and Thy mercies! Shiva! Shiva!" He observed with satisfaction that he had rejected the advice but that the "right kind" came anyway. On another occasion the swami even crossed swords with Sara Bull, perhaps his most trusted American follower. A heated argument with a Presbyterian polemicist led Bull to admonish the swami concerning the great harm such uncontrolled outbursts could do to his work. Indignantly denying that he had any "work" to perform, Vivekananda erupted: "In one word, I have a message to give, I have no time to be sweet to the world, and every attempt at sweetness makes me a hypocrite." He continued that he preferred to "die a thousand deaths rather than lead a jelly-fish existence and yield to every requirement of this foolish world."[46]

A small group of inner followers has shouldered most of the day-to-day work in the Ramakrishna movement's centers in the United States throughout its history. Aware that the future of Vedanta in the United States would depend on local leaders, Swami Vivekananda broke off his public lectures in 1895 to train a select group of devotees to carry on his work after he returned to India. At his invitation twelve disciples joined him at Thousand Island Park, an isolated retreat on one of the larger islands in the St. Lawrence River.[47] The group included Leon

Landsberg, Marie Louise (no surname has survived), Christine Greenstidel, and Ellen Waldo—all of whom subsequently played critical roles in the movement's American work. Over the next six weeks, the swami gave daily talks and instructed the twelve disciples in deep breathing and meditation. He also spoke openly of Ramakrishna for the first time, apparently hesitant previously to confront Americans with a figure so alien to Western preconceptions.[48] The classes marked a milestone, culminating in the initiation of Landsberg and Marie Louise as sannyasins (monks who have taken the final vows of renunciation), as the first Western-born swamis in American history.

Swami Vivekananda briefly interrupted his American work in 1895 for a trip to England, where he lectured with considerable success. He recruited several outstanding disciples in Great Britain—including Margaret Noble, who became famous in India as Sister Nivedita—but for some reason early Ramakrishna movement efforts in England failed. In retrospect, one of the most important events of the period that followed was the employment of Josiah J. Goodwin to take stenographic notes of Vivekananda's lectures on the swami's return to the United States. Within weeks of taking up his new duties, Goodwin became an ardent disciple. Without Goodwin's conscientious labors, the swami would have left little exposition of his teachings, since he rarely found time for sustained literary activity. Of the numerous volumes included in his *Complete Works*, the only book Vivekananda actually drafted was the *Raja-Yoga*.[49]

In 1896 Vivekananda finally departed America for India, where he discovered that he was a national hero. His prominent role at the Parliament of Religions and his unbending defense of Hindu ideals stirred deep patriotic feelings among the Indian people. From the moment he landed, he was mobbed by adoring crowds, who seemed to look upon him as a national savior. Though warned by doctors that he must conserve his strength in order to cope with the debilitating effects of diabetes, which was already undermining his health, he set off on a strenuous national lecture tour.[50]

The spirit and content of Vivekananda's Indian addresses, published as *Lectures from Colombo to Almora*, differ markedly from earlier Western speeches. The major difference is the much more aggressive, more nationalistic tone of the Indian remarks. The swami obviously had concluded that the tact and caution necessary to communicate effectively in the West could now be abandoned among his own people. Though in the past he had repeatedly warned his followers to avoid sectarianism and name-calling, he now launched fierce attacks against both Theosophical and Bramo Samaj leaders, suggesting that they had frequently resisted his effort to present the true facts concerning Indian society during his sojourn in the West. A strong note of anti-Westernism also cropped up in the addresses. In his very first lecture after his homecoming, "India, the Holy Land," the swami declared that India and Indian ideals had become even more sacred to him since he had seen the West. In a subsequent lecture he abruptly interrupted his remarks to admonish his audience, many of whom were dressed in European-style clothing, against the evils of slavish imitation of the West. While his attack on Western ways became more pronounced, his defense of traditional Hinduism also seemed to harden. Remarking that at one time he had regarded many Hindu institutions as "useless and worthless," he now confided that the older he became, the more hesitant he felt about "cursing any one of them," each representing the "embodiment of the experience of centuries."[51]

Swami Vivekananda's Indian lectures reflected a growing sensitivity to Western influence, perhaps because of his own attraction to Western conceptions. Certainly, the social message he now championed hinted influence from the West. The underlying philosophy was distinctively Hindu, but his emphasis on education, emergency and medical relief, and humanitarianism pointed to the West. He sometimes spoke of his message as "practical Vedanta," an apt description in the sense that he advocated both individual enlightenment and social reform. A rising number of Indians favored social reform and many more proclaimed themselves Vedantists, but few nineteenth-century Indians championed both social reform and Vedantism. As an advocate of "practical Vedanta," Vivekananda insisted that enlightenment could be attained through service to one's fellow human beings as much as through self-renunciation; work for others might be a form of worship. At the very least, his education and years in the West helped clarify and mold his ideas concerning social reform.

In India between 1897 and 1899, Vivekananda concentrated heavily on developing a suitable Indian organization that could carry on the work after his departure. Branch centers were begun at Calcutta, Madras, and other major Indian cities; and a spiritual retreat known as the Advaita Ashrama opened in the Himalayas. He also founded three periodicals to transmit Ramakrishna's teachings more effectively to the public: *Brahmavadin* and *Prabuddha Bharata*, which were published in English, and *Udbodhan*, printed in Bengali. Finally, Vivekananda founded the Ramakrishna Mission Association in 1897, a prototype for the later Ramakrishna Mission, which has coordinated all social and humanitarian work ever since. The Association functioned through two departments: an Indian Work Department, whose responsibilities included overseeing the Indian centers and directing the movement's Indian humanitarian activities; and a Foreign Department, which had the responsibility of managing the movement's Western centers. Ultimately, the Ramakrishna Mission Association and its two departments were superseded by the Ramakrishna Math and Mission, which have directed the movement's work ever since. The movement inaugurated its first famine relief work in 1897 and soon after established the first schools and medical dispensaries.[52]

Apparently, Vivekananda had to overcome strong resistance from other monks as a result of his initiatives, with his associates vehemently claiming that humanitarian activities were wholly inconsistent with Ramakrishna's teachings. Most monks believed that their ultimate mission was self-realization, achieved through meditation and spiritual discipline.[53] It seems clear that the

Ramakrishna movement would almost surely not have embraced a program of humanitarianism and social welfare without Vivekananda's insistent urging. By contrast, the social and humanitarian programs are generally hailed today as among the Ramakrishna movement's greatest contributions and most distinctive trademarks.

In 1899 Swami Vivekananda returned to the West a second time, apparently still hopeful of raising funds for his Indian projects, but primarily to expand his Western beachhead and to ease the huge pressures he faced in India, which were steadily undermining his health. He made brief stops in London and the east coast of the United States, but he primarily concentrated on transplanting Vedanta to the Pacific Coast. Splitting his time between Los Angeles and San Francisco, he eventually established Vedanta societies in both areas. (The Los Angeles group quickly collapsed.) Particularly if compared to his earlier triumphs, the second Western visit was both unsuccessful and anticlimactic. The major result, almost the only result, was the establishment of the San Francisco Vedanta Society, which had to be revived by succeeding swamis. In July 1900 Vivekananda left the United States for the last time, stopping to participate in a conference on the history of religions in Paris before returning to his native land. The swami's health now completely deteriorated, with death occurring on July 4, 1902—an oddly fitting date considering his pioneer labor in the United States.

What, then, was Swami Vivekananda's message in America? If we accept the view of Marie Louise Burke, the movement's most indefatigable scholar, there were actually two distinct messages. According to Burke, there was a "pronounced difference" between the swami's message in the original visit to the United States in 1893–1896 and during his second visit in 1899–1900. While he attempted to outline and explain Vedanta's difficult philosophic teachings during the first visit, he primarily emphasized practical themes on the second tour.[54] Burke goes on to provide the following breakdown of the swami's American talks. Of sixty-six lectures delivered between August 1893 and January 1895, the period from his arrival in America to the close of his first lecture campaign, (1) forty-four focused on India, with heavy emphasis on Indian religion (six of the forty-four were devoted to the condition of Hindu women and two to the Christian missionary effort); (2) seventeen dwelled on the "harmony of religions"; and (3) five dealt with Buddha and Buddhism. Following his return from England in December 1895, he primarily concentrated on expositions of jnana, bhakti, karma, and raja yoga, which his assistant Goodwin carefully recorded for posterity. (A full discussion of the movement's teachings, including an explanation of the four yogas, follows in chapter 4.) On the second Western visit of 1899–1900, Vivekananda delivered some thirty-eight lectures, with six focusing on India's history, customs, and religions; five on religious legends; three on the world's great religious teachers; and as many as thirteen concerned with "practical spirituality."[55]

To summarize, the swami dwelled on three major themes during his lectures in the United States: first, Hinduism, and particularly the essentials of the Vedanta philosophy; second, Indian social conditions, which often boiled down to a defense of traditional Hindu practices against the criticisms of Western detractors; and, finally, the need for East-West understanding, based on acceptance of similarities of the teachings of all world religions. Other recurring topics included the Buddha and Buddhism, which were attracting increased American attention in the century's last decades; the Christian missionary movement; and other world religions. (I speak here only of the swami's public lectures; his emphasis was obviously quite different in classes and private talks, where he concentrated on personal spiritual instructions.)

The Hinduism Swami Vivekananda offered in his public lectures was well suited to appeal to a Western audience, emphasizing the more universal elements in the Hindu tradition. Dismissing a sectarian Hinduism that dwelled on the observance of caste distinctions and ancient taboos—a view he castigated as "don't-touchism"—he spoke in favor of a Hinduism that was reasonable, philosophical, universal, and even scientific.[56] He clearly believed that the essence of higher Hinduism was best expressed in the Vedanta philosophy, an entirely monistic viewpoint derived from the Upanishads as interpreted by Shankara. In one of the most cogent statements of his position and the Ramakrishna movement's message, he once summarized Vedanta's teaching:

> Each soul is potentially divine.
> The goal is to manifest this Divinity within by controlling nature, external and internal.
> Do this either by work, or worship, or psychic control, or philosophy—by one, or more, or all of these—and be free.
> This is the whole of religion. Doctrines, or dogmas, or rituals, or books, or temples, or forms, are but secondary details.[57]

Later Western scholars and polemicists have questioned whether Vivekananda's version of Hinduism and the Vedanta was authentic; what cannot be questioned is the effectiveness of his presentation. More the advocate than the scholar, he presented Hinduism as a viable choice for modern Western people.

The swami almost certainly did not originally intend to concentrate as heavily as he did in his American speeches on Indian social conditions. He quickly discovered, however, that, despite the favorable reports of scholars and literati, popular opinion often reflected an extremely negative conception of Indian life. Articles regularly appeared in the popular press that portrayed Hinduism as synonymous with the horrors of the caste system, child-marriage, and widow-burning. Shocked and inflamed by his discovery, Vivekananda took up defense of Hindu social conditions, while launching an often bitter counterattack against the social evils of the West. As a result, he increasingly became India's apologist.

When he conceded that abuses existed, he argued that (1) they were not central to Hinduism; (2) they had been introduced by foreign conquerors; (3) they represented conceptions and practices that had once served a positive function; or (4) they were badly misinterpreted by Western critics. He liked to remind Western audiences that India's social problems, at least, had originated from an *excess* of spirituality rather than an *absence* of spiritual concern. At times unfair in his indictment of the West, at other times extravagant in his praise of India, in calmer moments he championed the view that all societies and religions deserved understanding and respect. His stout defense of Indian social practices reveals considerable irony. He originally came to the West to seek financial aid to eliminate what he saw as corruptions to be condemned; but, reacting to Western criticisms, he soon found himself hotly defending India's social system, including some of the very things he once assailed.

What about Vivekananda the man? What impression did Hinduism's first teacher make upon Americans? He was clearly a man of complex character who eludes easy classification.[58] Raised in nineteenth-century Bengal, nurtured in a Hindu family, and deeply imbued by his country's cultural and moral values, he was first and always an Indian. But unlike most Indians of his generation, he had also been deeply touched by the Western influences then penetrating India, including an English-style education and wide reading in European philosophy. Americans who got to know him quickly discovered that he was a man of fluctuating moods. Though he could be testy and difficult when angered, normally he impressed Americans as a warmhearted, witty man who made friends easily. Sometimes exuberant, playful, and even boisterous, at other times he seemed quiet, introspective, and withdrawn. Annie Besant, the English Theosophical leader, once described him as a "warrior-monk," adding that the "first impression" was more of the warrior than the monk.[59] However, his letters to Mary and Harriet Hale, the almost-grown daughters of his close supporter George Hale, reveal a tenderness and personal affection that one does not expect in a monk who has renounced the world. (He frequently addressed Hale as "Father Pope" and his wife as "Mother Church," while he teased the unmarried Hale sisters as "old maids.")

In 1962 Harold Isaacs pointed out in his *Images of Asia* that most Americans perceive India and Hinduism through deeply ingrained stereotypes, dominated by images of snake charmers, sacred cows, multiarmed goddesses, and naked fakirs lying upon beds of nails.[60] Many older Americans will conceive the Hindu holy person in the image of Mahatma Gandhi, calling up the image of a partially clothed, emaciated figure whose fasts and championship of nonviolence riveted world attention in the 1920s and 1930s. In Vivekananda's case there is little resemblance either to the naked fakir or to the mild-mannered, emaciated Gandhi image. Physically, the swami appeared to be considerably larger than he actually was, thanks to a barrel chest and broad shoulders—a physique better suited to an athlete than an Indian holy man. Medium in height, Vivekananda's body was topped by a large head dominated by bright, protruding eyes and a jutting "Mongolian jaw"—as he liked to call it. In America he usually dressed in dark trousers, an orange robe, and a yellow turban.

Swami Vivekananda did not look like the stereotypical holy man, and neither did he behave like one. Christopher Isherwood once described him as the "perfect anti-Puritan hero," a man who was the "enemy of Sunday religion" and "outrager of conventions."[61] He obviously enjoyed shocking his Western audiences. On one occasion, he admonished his listeners, "Don't repent. Don't repent," meaning to express his opposition to the doctrine of sin. On another occasion an eyewitness recalled that the swami had sung a well-known missionary hymn, then paused dramatically and, pointing to himself, announced: "I am the heathen they came to save." In the question-and-answer period that followed one of his lectures, a member of the audience had inquired, "Swami[,] have you seen God?" "What!" Vivekananda replied incredulously, his face lighting up with a happy smile, "do I look like it,—a big fat man like me?"[62]

What, finally, may be said of Swami Vivekananda's work and impact in America? Looking back a century later, he clearly deserves credit as the founder of American Hinduism and pioneer Asian teacher who paved the way for all Eastern teachers who have followed. He did not shake the foundations of Christianity, as some of his more zealous followers seem to imagine, but he did succeed in transplanting the seed of Hinduism to the United States and in persuading numbers of Americans that Asian religion offered something that the West needed. Considering the traditional attitude of hostility to non-Christian religions, this was an impressive achievement. The Parliament of Religions provided his opening, generating unprecedented interest in Asian religions; but his talent as a speaker and ability to exploit his opportunity made success possible. The Parliament, after all, opened doors for all the Asian delegates, yet Vivekananda alone succeeded in transplanting a new religion to American shores in the years immediately after 1893.

More directly pertinent to this study, the swami almost singlehandedly created the Ramakrishna movement in America. He brought the movement west and gave it the direction and organizational form it has followed ever since. He founded the first Vedanta societies based on a division of functions between Indian authorities and local followers, with the swami and Ramakrishna Math in India exercising spiritual control and American devotees responsible for financial and administrative matters. He also pioneered the method of presenting Vedanta to Americans, which combined Western-style public lectures with a traditional Hindu emphasis on individualized instruction by a guru. He initiated the first American swamis and conducted the first spiritual retreat (*ashrama*) at Thousand Island Park. He also molded the message to be presented in the United States. His decision not to emphasize Ramakrishna but to dwell on philosophic

Hinduism as embodied in the Vedanta has largely dominated down to the present. (Devotionalism and the "cult" of Ramakrishna have become prominent in American centers only in recent decades.) The very fact that he placed such high priority on the Ramakrishna movement's American work persuaded his successors in India to commit personnel to the West that would normally have been reserved for Indian needs.

Influences rarely flow in one direction only. If the swami has had some impact on American religious history, the American experience also had considerable influence upon him. When he reached the United States in 1893, he had the roughest outline of his future work in mind, aware only that India needed help and that American generosity might provide the funds needed to underwrite an Indian program of social uplift. By the time he returned to India in early 1897, he had a much surer vision of his mission, including the realization that Hinduism could be transplanted to the West. His Western experience clarified his conception of the specific reforms India needed and the best means to achieve his ends. In a word, if Vivekananda had not come to America, the Ramakrishna movement would not be present in the United States today, nor would the work in India have assumed the shape it has.

Sri Ramakrishna (1836–1886), the spiritual founder of the Ramakrishna movement.
(Unless otherwise specified, photos courtesy of Ramakrishna Math and Mission.)

Swami Vivekananda (1863–1902), the "Saint Paul" of the Ramakrishna movement, who founded the first Vedanta societies in the United States.

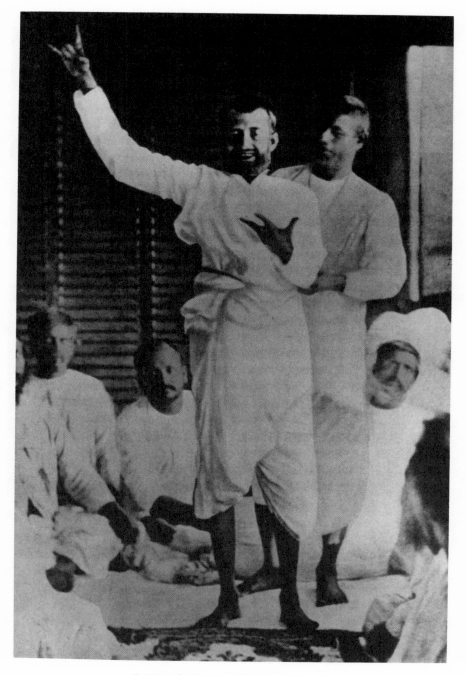

Sri Ramakrishna, standing in ecstasy.

Sarada Devi (1853–1920), wife of Sri Ramakrishna, known as the Holy Mother.

Swami Vivekananda at the Parliament of Religions in Chicago, 1893.

Vivekananda with Western disciples, Kashmir, 1898. From left to right: Josephine MacLeod, Sara Bull (Mrs. Ole Bull), the swami, and Sister Nivedita (Margaret Noble).

Swami Vivekananda in California, 1900, dressed in Western garb.

Swami Abhedananda (1866–1939), early head of Vedanta Society of New York and third Ramakrishna monk to come to the United States.

Hindu temple at Vedanta Society of San Francisco, originally constructed in 1906 and now a city landmark.

Jesus as a Yogi. (Courtesy of the Vedanta Society of Southern California.)

Sri Ramakrishna Temple on Belur Math grounds, near Calcutta, dedicated in 1938. The temple incorporates elements from a Christian church, Moslem mosque, and Buddhist temple, as well as Hindu motifs.

3 Trials of Survival
The Organization of an American Movement

BETWEEN THE 1890s and the present a steady flow of Hindu teachers and lecturers have made their way to the United States to propagate their teachings.[1] In some cases such individuals remained for extended periods, conducting classes, delivering lectures, and founding centers to spread their message. Most eventually developed some following and attracted a certain amount of media attention. In almost every instance, however, nothing came of these stirrings. There are undoubtedly various explanations for lack of success, depending upon the particular teacher, but the most important surely has been the failure to create an effective organization to sustain the work. Though charisma might attract followers, a permanent structure has been absolutely essential to the survival of any movement beyond the passing of its founder.

Creation of an effective organization has not been easy for Hindu leaders. Historically, the message of Hinduism has been passed from generation to generation, not through promulgation of officially sanctioned creeds or the creation of hierarchies to defend the faith, but by individual transmission of the tradition from teacher to disciple. Such an arrangement has worked well in India for thousands of years; however, Hindu teachers who have come to the West have been repeatedly forced to confront the need for greater structure. The creation of an effective organization is one of the major reasons why the Ramakrishna movement has survived in the United States, while other Hindu movements quietly passed away.

The challenge organization posed for the Ramakrishna movement is evident early on. When Swami Vivekananda returned to India from his first trip to the West in 1897, he experienced major difficulty in persuading other monks of the need to come together and to incorporate their work. And, indeed, Vivekananda himself apparently felt deeply ambivalent about such activity. When his disciple Marie Louise wrote to complain that the members of the New York Vedanta Society were not supporting her efforts, threatening to shift her allegiance to Theosophy if a more effective organization was not created, Vivekananda responded: "Perhaps you forget that we have no organization nor want to build any. Each one is quite independent to teach, quite free to preach whatever he or she likes." He argued that Theosophy's method could never be adopted, since it was an "organized sect": "Individuality is my motto. I have no ambition beyond training individuals up."[2] At every stage of his teaching in America he seemed to fear resort to organization, preferring a more fluid, open work. According to a recent study, his policy was to "let things grow," which meant "laying down no rules, giving no preaching directions to his ordained disciples, enlisting no followers, introducing no rituals, and establishing no society except that which was essential to handle the secular, or external, side of his work."[3] Paradoxically, Vivekananda resisted organization and, yet, did more than any other person to establish the institutions and procedures that formed the Ramakrishna movement as we know it today.

Swamis of the Ramakrishna movement were forced to confront several perplexing issues in establishing Vedanta societies in the United States. Stated concisely, the four most important were authority, methods, money, and message. In the case of authority, the question was: Were decisions to be made by the local swami in charge, by American followers in the Vedanta society, or by officials at the Belur Math headquarters? Put differently, the question was, To what extent were decisions to be made locally and to what extent were they to be made in India? Though a division of responsibilities was eventually established, the possibility of conflict constantly existed, and on several occasions tensions over local control led to disruption and schism.

Second, what were the appropriate methods for carrying on Vedanta work in the United States? Traditionally, Hinduism has emphasized personalized instruction under the guidance of a guru, pilgrimages to sacred shrines, and devotional activities. Swamis who came to the United States had to decide to what extent to adhere to traditional practices, which would appear alien to most Americans, and to what extent to embrace Western methods, such as advertising in newspapers, holding organized services featuring lectures and music, and sale of books and magazines. All swamis who taught in the United States found it necessary to accommodate to Western practices, but some acculturated much more completely than others. (For example, Swami Turiyananda, who resided in the United States from 1899 to 1906, made almost no concessions to American ways; on the other hand, Swami Paramananda, who founded the Boston Vedanta Society, eagerly embraced Western procedures.)

Third, there was the troublesome matter of money. As monks, each swami had taken vows of renunciation, which included avoidance of material possessions of all types. To what extent must the swamis concern themselves with financial considerations? In the West, one could hardly avoid frequent contacts with money or, in the case of Vedanta societies, financial transactions. Since all Vedanta society costs had to be met with funds gathered from local sources, financial pressures often weighed heavily. The first years after the founding of a new center were particularly difficult.

Finally, what was the appropriate Ramakrishna message for America? All swamis were committed both to the Vedanta philosophy and to Ramakrishna's teachings, but to what extent should each be emphasized? Should the movement primarily restrict its message to the philosophy, which would be more acceptable to Westerners? How far should they encourage the "cult of Ramakrishna"—the worship of Ramakrishna's image and the introduction of traditional Hindu devotional practices? As will be seen, these four issues refused to die, with frequent differences among the swamis concerning their resolution.

Though the unprecedented events of the Parliament of Religions encouraged belief by Vedantists that America was wide open to Hinduism, the decades between 1890 and 1930 proved that the newly established Vedanta societies would have to struggle heroically for bare survival. Claiming to speak for the oldest world religion at the Parliament, the Ramakrishna movement in succeeding decades was forced to face the attacks and contemptuous dismissal reserved for the new religions—what the general public often designates as "cults." Three Ramakrishna swamis stand out during this period: Swami Abhedananda, who succeeded Vivekananda in New York; Swami Trigunatita, who broke new ground in San Francisco; and Swami Paramananda, who achieved a degree of success in Boston and Los Angeles unequaled by any previous swami. Other Ramakrishna swamis appeared in the United States in the period, but most soon returned to India, with little impact on the American movement. The trio expanded the beachhead established by Swami Vivekananda, with each making a distinctive contribution toward a permanent Western movement.

Swami Abhedananda, who followed Vivekananda in New York, was easily the best-known Asian religious teacher in the United States in the century's first two decades. He was the third monk of the Ramakrishna movement to come to the United States, remaining in the country almost continuously from 1897 to 1921. (Swami Saradananda preceded him in 1896, but remained less than two years.)[4] In addition to directing the New York Vedanta Society, Abhedananda was instrumental in establishing short-lived branch centers in Brooklyn, Washington, D.C., Pittsburgh, San Francisco, Los Angeles, Paris, and London. He also delivered literally hundreds of lectures before social clubs, church groups, and general audiences across the country and authored an impressive shelf of books explaining the Ramakrishna movement's teachings. Most unexpectedly, he ended his career by abandoning the American work and breaking away from the Ramakrishna Order to found his own organization.

As we will see, most of the Ramakrishna monks who came to America had similar backgrounds, though there were also distinctive variations. Abhedananda was born in Calcutta in 1866, the son of an instructor in English at an institution known as the Oriental Seminary. Like Vivekananda, he had undergone an English-style education and was well read in both Indian and Western philosophy (particularly John Stuart Mill, Herbert Spencer, and G. W. F. Hegel). He was a gifted lecturer who ranks as one of the most intellectual monks to teach in America. Despite such obvious assets, the swami apparently had difficulty achieving close relations with his American followers. One of his disciples observed that no one, not even his closest followers, could completely break through his reserve.[5] Contemporary photographs reveal a handsome man, distinguished by a well-proportioned face, high forehead, and slim build.

Abhedananda arrived in the United States in August 1897, after nearly a year in England, and almost immediately plunged into a course of three lectures a week in Mott Memorial Hall in New York City, delivering eighty-six lectures in all from September 29, 1897, to April 30, 1898. In addition to the lectures, the swami's round of daily activities included teaching classes in deep breathing and meditation, private interviews with students, extensive writing, frequent speaking engagements, and a good deal of travel.[6] (Swamis who remained in the United States for any period quickly learned that the vocation of religion required a high energy level and a combination of the skills of teacher, writer, organizer, and confessor. The unaccustomed strain took its toll, particularly in the movement's first years. A surprising number of the swamis suffered physical breakdowns and had to return to India.)

Like Vivekananda, Abhedananda showed special talent in reaching a wider audience, repeatedly speaking before large gatherings. For the most part, invitations came from groups on the perimeter of American religion. Thus, he spoke a number of times to enthusiastic gatherings of Spiritualists at camp meetings in New York and Indiana (even though the Ramakrishna movement has generally downplayed emphasis on psychic phenomena, which are believed to deflect the seeker from true spirituality). One audience numbered 7,000 persons.[7] During 1899–1900 he regularly reached audiences of 500 and more, including addresses to 1,000 persons at a session of the Free Religious Association and 800 people at a local congress of religions convened in Boston. He also spoke frequently at meetings sponsored by mental scientists, divine healers, and New Thought practitioners, connections that proved especially important in the movement's early work, as suggested by the frequency with which Vedanta followers revealed New Thought and Mental Science backgrounds.[8]

Unlike Vivekananda, Abhedananda never seemed to have any doubts concerning the need for organization. Indeed, of all the early swamis, he paid most attention to creating an efficient organization to advance the Ramakrishna movement's work in America. He moved quickly to consolidate the New York Vedanta Society, which was still largely a skeletal operation when he assumed command. One of the first steps was to incorporate the society under New York laws. Eager to accommodate the rapidly increasing audiences his lectures were attracting, facilities were repeatedly enlarged. Expansion began with rental of a larger hall for the 1898–1899 season, followed a year later by the addition of space for a central office and library. Then in 1900 an entire house was rented, eliminating the extra expenses formerly incurred for a lecture auditorium and separate living quarters for the swami. The purchase of a permanent home in 1907 marked the final step in the establishment of the New York center.[9]

The role of American followers in running the Vedanta societies was still unclear at the time Abhedananda took over leadership in New York. When forced to confront the matter, Swami Vivekananda had apparently favored local control. "My idea is for autonomic, independent groups in different places," he confided to his close supporter Sara Bull in 1895. Explaining his decision to assemble a group of disciples at Thousand Island Park for special training, he remarked that "I shall make several Sannyasins and then I go to India, leaving the work to them."[10] The Ramakrishna organization in India, on the other hand, largely vested control in the hands of senior monks, whose decisions went unquestioned because of a monastic tradition in which obedience to one's superiors was instilled. Under Abhedananda, membership in the New York Vedanta Society was at first limited to the body's incorporators, with a few handpicked supporters exercising complete control. By 1900, however, participation was greatly widened, with all students and friends of the movement invited to become members; the expanded membership elected a board of trustees to lead the society.[11] The board consisted of six members who served as an executive committee responsible for all day-to-day operations, with Swami Abhedananda left free to concentrate on spiritual matters. Obviously, the American environment, with its emphasis on democracy, exerted influence. Annual elections of new officers and a written constitution marked further steps in the democratization of the New York society.

The management of Vedanta society finances presented special problems for Ramakrishna monks who, in renouncing the world, had vowed to avoid the corrupting influence of money. From the time of Vivekananda, all financial responsibilities were turned over to American followers. Thus, when Swami Abhedananda took over in New York, his American devotees shouldered all financial duties—including raising the money needed to pay the costs of the swami's food, lodging, auditorium rental fees, and general operating expenses. (As monks, the swamis always serve without pay.) Later, arrangements were regularized with the creation of a Ways and Means Committee to handle all financial matters.

The revenues needed to support the New York society's work derived from a number of sources. (Since financial support from India has always been out of the question, Vedanta societies have had to meet all expenses from local American sources.) At first, classes and lectures were free of charge, supported by passing a collection plate around following the lectures and by contributions from the society's more affluent members. However, as the society expanded and moved to larger quarters, new revenue sources became critical. In 1900 dues of $12 per year were instituted, with a life membership costing $250. Nonmembers had to pay 25 cents for admission to Tuesday evening lectures. Reaching further afield, an associate membership was initiated for interested persons residing outside the immediate New York area. For an annual payment of $5, associate members received the society's publication, the *Vedanta Monthly Bulletin*; enjoyed the privilege of consulting the swami about personal spiritual matters; and had the right to use the facilities of the Vedanta society when in New York. Hope was expressed that as the number of outside associates grew, they would form themselves into branch centers, which the swami would visit at intervals. When support became sufficiently strong to justify a full-time swami, a new Vedanta society would be initiated. The financial reports presented at the New York Vedanta Society's annual meetings suggest that these measures were largely successful.[12]

Swami Abhedananda revealed imagination and resourcefulness in delivering his Vedanta message to Americans. In addition to weekly lectures, he inaugurated regular yoga classes, which offered lessons in deep breathing and concentration; he also founded a society library, stocked primarily with books on Indian philosophy and religion, for the more serious student. In an attempt to reach the younger set, he further instituted a Saturday morning children's class, where he read and explained Indian fables. And in 1900, a "Young People's Yoga Association" was launched.[13] (Presumably, the newly formed Young Men's and Young Women's Christian Associations served as the inspiration for the new Hindu organization.) Most far-reaching, he founded a Vedanta press, which made it possible to extend Hinduism's message to every state in the country. By 1906 the total number of books and pamphlets published had reached 50,000. (Vivekananda's and Abhedananda's writings made up a large proportion of the total publications.)[14] The *Vedanta Monthly Bulletin* featured lectures by Abhedananda, articles on Hindu religious subjects, and regular updates on the progress of Vedanta work in the United States.

One would expect that such energetic activity would stimulate significant increases in Vedanta society membership, and, in fact, rapid growth seems to have occurred. As early as 1900, attendance at lectures and classes was reported as greater than in any season since 1896; and at the 1906 business meeting the society's secretary announced both a "greater accession" of new members than in any previous year and a "larger membership than at any time since the organization of the Society."[15]

As we will see, Ramakrishna swamis have varied a great deal in ability and style of work. Abhedananda's special talent was his literary success as an interpreter of Hinduism for Americans. (Swamis Nikhilananda and Prabhavananda achieved even greater success in the following generation.) Today, his books fill a large shelf, offering both general surveys such as *India and Her People* and *Great Saviors of the World* and more specialized discussions such as *Reincarnation*. Revealing a wide acquaintance with Western as well as Eastern thinkers, the swami cited the names of Western philosophers such as Pythagoras, Plato, Immanuel Kant, and Arthur Schopenhauer throughout his writings. Abhedananda's article "Hindu Philosophy of India," included in Sarvepalli Radhakrishnan and J. H. Muirhead's *Contemporary Indian Philosophy*, indicates his recognized stature as a philosopher. Other Asian contributors to the volume include Ananda Coomaraswamy, Rabindranath Tagore, Surendra Nath Dasgupta, and Radhakrishnan himself—the most respected, internationally acclaimed Asian thinkers of the pre-World War II era.[16] The swami revealed a talent for explaining Asian philosophical and religious concepts in a language educated Americans could comprehend.

One of Swami Abhedananda's most unusual claims was the argument that Hinduism offered a perspective consistent with a modern scientific outlook. He supported such a view by tracing the roots of modern scientific conceptions back to ancient Hindu thinkers. To cite an example, he contended that evolution—a theory that most contemporary Westerners surely regarded as quite new—was actually already "well known to the Hindus of the Vedic ages." He similarly argued that the atomic theory, which was usually traced back to the ancient Greeks, had appeared in the *Vaisheshika* philosophy of Kanada (one of the six Hindu orthodox schools) "centuries before the time of Empedocles and Democritus."[17] Indeed, the swami went so far as to claim that Vedanta offered a scientific religion consistent with empirical data. "The religion of Vedanta," he observed at one point, "may be called the 'Science of the Soul.'" Like modern science, which had discovered the laws of nature by avoiding dogma, Vedanta explained the spiritual nature of humankind "through logic and reason."[18] The claim became a stock argument among later Ramakrishna swamis.

Despite an impressive record of almost continuous expansion, the ambitious work which Swami Abhedananda launched began to falter after a decade, culminating in the temporary suspension of the New York Vedanta Society in 1910. The causes of the collapse are difficult to pinpoint but seem to center on deepening tensions between the swami and powerful members of the New York Vedanta Society. Largely ignored in the movement's literature, the period of collapse deserves close attention, providing a rare opportunity to investigate some of the underlying tensions experienced by the Ramakrishna movement in its effort to transplant its message to the United States.[19]

Swami Abhhedananda's extended absences in Europe provided the first warning that all was not well. Though most Ramakrishna swamis seem to travel a good deal, presenting lectures but also engaging in sightseeing and vacationing, Abhedananda easily exceeded all previous records. Thus, he remained in Europe for several months in 1907, for another eight months in 1908, and for still six months more in 1909. The only explanation offered for his prolonged absences was that he was in London and Paris establishing Vedanta centers.[20]

Meanwhile, reports in the *Vedanta Monthly Bulletin* revealed that things were not going well back in New York, despite efforts by several members of the society to carry on during the swami's absence. For the first time, the organization began to show financial strains. A *Bulletin* contributor complained in January 1908 that an "erroneous impression" seemed to exist that the New York Vedanta Society included large numbers of wealthy members who were underwriting the society's expenses. Two months later, the financial situation was again alluded to, accompanied by an urgent request that members contribute what they could or, even, that they donate small articles for sale to sustain the society's work. Then, without warning, the *Vedanta Monthly Bulletin* suddenly suspended publication in 1908 due to lack of funds, though it briefly revived in 1909.[21] By 1910 the New York Vedanta Society had ceased to function, the journal had died, and Abhedananda had severed all connection with his former New York followers.

What caused the collapse of one of the Ramakrishna movement's most dynamic centers? On the surface, at least, the New York Vedanta Society's troubles seemed to stem from Abhedananda's extended absences and the society's increasing financial strains. There was, however, a more fundamental cause, namely, a deep split between the swami and his leading American supporters. Looking back, the warning signals of future trouble were visible as early as 1900, when Abhedananda fell out with Sara Bull and Josephine MacLeod, two of Swami Vivekananda's leading disciples and major sustainers of the New York work. The exact causes of the differences are unclear, but they almost certainly involved both a personality clash and disagreement over the direction of the work. Though urged to intervene, Swami Vivekananda insisted on staying out of the squabble, explaining that his method was "to leave all rows alone!" He urged the society's members to settle the dispute themselves, observing that "in every country we have to follow its own method."[22] Before the matter was resolved, Francis Leggett, who had been serving as the society's president, resigned and withdrew from the New York work.

The swami's differences with leading supporters certainly weakened the New York Vedanta Society, but a more fundamental division over the emphasis in the body's work seems to have been the decisive event in the collapse. According to Cornelius Heyblom, who knew many of the participants and closely observed the events, the New York society's membership consisted of two divergent factions: "old students," who had joined the society during Vivekananda's stewardship and who favored a small, close-knit community in which followers had frequent opportunity for contact with the swami; and a group Heyblom referred to as "new students," who had joined since Abhedananda's arrival and who accepted the more impersonal relationship created by the swami's expansionistic program of reaching out to a wider audience. At first, Swami Abhedananda had spent much time with the inner followers, but as he became more successful he was often unavailable. As a result, the swami soon found himself pitted against the "old students." In Heyblom's words, the students "preferred the quiet simplicity of early days" when they had "experienced the benefit of small, more intimate gatherings," while Abhedananda believed that he had been called "to reach out beyond his little circle," with the success of his work dependent on "meeting with the intellectual and well-to-do people of New York."[23] The question was whether Vedanta's message should be for the few or for the many.

Apparently, in 1906 Abhedananda unwittingly supplied the spark that led to the final blowup when he recruited a young assistant, Swami Paramananda, to join the expanding New York work. More affectionate and personable than Abhedananda, the younger swami was an immediate "hit" with both "old" and "new" members of the New York Vedanta Society. About a year after his arrival, several followers openly expressed a preference for Paramananda over Abhedananda as head of the New York center. In a 1908 showdown Abhedananda offered to resign in favor of Paramananda. Though five or six members voted for the younger swami, Abhedananda managed to retain the support of the majority.[24] Despite his victory, Abhedananda fled the scene, spending many months in Europe over the next three years. During his absence, the New York society disintegrated. Paramananda also abandoned the work, shifting his focus of operations northward to Boston, where he soon established a new society.[25]

In a surprising final act, in 1910 the leaders of the Ramakrishna Order announced Abhedananda's suspension from the movement. When the swami refused a direct order to return to India, his name was dropped from the Order's rolls.[26] Instead of returning to his homeland, Swami Abhedananda remained in the United States another decade, retiring to the rural isolation of an ashrama in West Cornwall, Connecticut, where he was joined by a small group of loyal followers.[27] He closed the Connecticut retreat in December 1919, however, and shifted his base to San Francisco, where he opened a new "Vedanta Ashrama." He taught classes there until his final departure from the United States in 1921. He subsequently created an independent Ramakrishna Vedanta Math in Calcutta, which survives to the present day. Apparently, he reconciled his differences with the Belur Math, for he was reinstated as a trustee of the Order's governing body. He was the last surviving member of Ramakrishna's original band of disciples at his death in 1939.[28]

Obviously, the collapse of Abhedananda's efforts in New York represents one of the Ramakrishna movement's greatest American defeats. Such experiences have rarely been repeated. A strong Indian base of support and a conscious policy of slow expansion have made it possible for the movement to avoid the setbacks many other Asian religious movements have confronted. At the same time, Abhedananda's difficulties indicate that serious tensions existed in the Ramakrishna movement's American work from the first—tensions between swamis and their

American followers, between American followers and the governing body in India, and between one American faction and another. Considering the possibilities for misunderstanding arising from the effort to transplant the seed of Hinduism to American soil, the surprise is not that there have been tensions but that after nearly a century the disagreements have been so few.

The two oldest Vedanta societies in the United States are situated in New York City and San Francisco. Both were launched in the 1890s by Swami Vivekananda and both fell apart soon after the ailing leader returned to India to die. While Swami Abhedananda revived the New York center, Swami Trigunatita did the same for the San Francisco Vedanta Society.[29] The two swamis present a study in contrasts: Abhedananda was a cool intellectual, Trigunatita a passionate activist; Abhedananda was one of the movement's most effective speakers and writers, Trigunatita never fully mastered English; Abhedananda functioned best in a large auditorium, Trigunatita preferred the surroundings of the temple and ashrama. Despite greater public acclaim, Abhedananda ultimately failed in New York, while Trigunatita created a center in San Francisco that never faltered.

Perhaps Swami Trigunatita's only resemblance to Abhedananda was a shared Bengali background. Born in 1865, the son of a wealthy family, Trigunatita attended the Metropolitan Institution where Mahendranath Gupta, who recorded the *Gospel of Sri Ramakrishna*, served as headmaster. Attracted to Ramakrishna, the young man took the monastic name "Trigunatitananda." (Literally translated, "Trigunatitananda" means "he whose bliss is beyond the three gunas." In the Sankhya philosophy, one of the classical systems of Hindu philosophy, a guna is viewed as a mode of activity or strand that binds the universe together.) Teased by Vivekananda—who complimented him on his "world-entrancing, death-defying name"—he later shortened the name to the more familiar "Trigunatita." Before his assignment to America, Trigunatita had been active in famine relief and served as founder and first editor of *Udbodhan*, the Ramakrishna movement's Bengali organ.[30]

Though over time each Vedanta society tended to develop its own character, in most respects all societies resembled one another and worked along similar lines. Certainly, the San Francisco Vedanta Society differed in small ways from the New York Vedanta Society. Officers (president, vice-president, financial secretary, recording secretary, treasurer, auditor, and librarian) were elected annually to oversee the society's day-to-day activities, leaving Trigunatita free to concentrate on spiritual matters. Expenses were met through yearly dues of $18, which entitled a member to attend all lectures and classes, receive deep-breathing instructions, and visit the society's spiritual retreat, which was known as Shanti Ashrama. Private lessons for "unfolding the Inner Self" cost an additional $18 per year and $24 if conducted by correspondence; more advanced students might enroll in lessons for "Esoterics and Adepts." Meanwhile, the establishment of a monthly journal known as *The Voice of Freedom* in 1909 provided a mouthpiece for the society.[31]

Trigunatita introduced two novelties into Vedanta society services: he incorporated vocal and instrumental music and divided congregational seating into male and female sections. A contemporary reporter observed that the decision to segregate the sexes—a practice normal in Ramakrishna temples in India—fell on members "like a bombshell," but eventually won acceptance.[32] The two initiatives establish Trigunatita as both a traditionalist and an innovater, with sexual segregation reflecting his preference for Indian forms, and his introduction of Western music revealing his willingness to embrace Western practice.

Trigunatita considered his greatest achievement the erection of what he grandly proclaimed the "first Hindu Temple in the whole Western world." Personally planned and designed by the swami, it quickly became a San Francisco landmark. The temple was constructed of wood and topped by domes, towers, and pinnacles, supposedly combining motifs from the Taj Mahal, a famous Benares temple, a Shivaite temple, the Dakshineswar temple-garden where Ramakrishna had often strolled, and, incongruously, a European castle. The swami claimed that the building incorporated elements from a Hindu temple, Christian church, Muslim mosque, Hindu monastery, and American residence![33] Just a few months after its completion, the wooden temple barely escaped the 1906 San Francisco earthquake.

One of the most colorful figures in the history of the Ramakrishna movement in America, the swami was a tireless worker who became legendary among his American devotees for his energy and efforts to achieve greater efficiency. On one occasion, he went so far as to install clocks throughout the San Francisco temple, assigning a student the specific duty of regularly checking and synchronizing the clocks with the Lick Observatory. He also placed signs at strategic locations in the society's quarters exhorting members to "Live like a hermit but work like a horse," "Do it now," and, one of his favorites, "Do or die, but you will not die."[34] Quick to recognize that he must rely on native speakers in the society to reach a wider American audience, he launched an ambitious program to train speakers from the membership, drafting a set of guidelines to promote more effective instruction. Though a number of lecturers were apparently trained, there is no evidence that they were ever utilized.[35]

The Ramakrishna movement has always followed a policy of strict neutrality and noninvolvement in political matters, even though this has not prevented it from working closely with the Indian government in recent years on social and educational programs. At the height of Gandhi's campaigns against British rule in the decades before Indian independence, for example, its monks were strongly warned to avoid participation. If anything, the policy has been even more strictly adhered to in the United States, where the movement has consciously emphasized spiritual realization rather than social action. Surprisingly, Swami Trigunatita seems to have flaunted the rule. Though Vedanta remained basic to his message, he frequently devoted attention to political and social issues. Thus, he contributed articles on such sensitive contemporary issues as Hindu immigration, San Francisco politics, and American involvement in World War I; and he lectured on such politically linked themes as "Vedanta and Socialism," "The Future of the American Woman," and "The Future of the United States as Seen by a Vedantist."[36]

Apparently, he believed socialism represented the correct path to political truth as much as Vedanta pointed the way to religious truth. Indeed, he publicly identified himself as both a socialist and a Vedantist. "Yes, I am a socialist," he confessed at one point, "but, I am a great Vedantist, too." Attempting to explain the affinity of the two perspectives, he suggested that both offered "practical philosophies of Self-culture," the difference between them being that socialism worked "from without," while Vedantism worked "from within."[37] In his view, both philosophies might free humanity from false attachments. In a subsequent article entitled "Socialism as a Phase of Vedanta," the swami argued that socialism actually led to Vedantism. Though Ramakrishna authorities in India apparently chose to ignore Trigunatita's unorthodox behavior, the swami's sympathies did not go unnoticed in America. Recognizing a fellow spirit, the Socialist party in San Francisco invited him to address a 1910 meeting, where the swami responded with a passionate speech entitled "Every Man and Woman Is a Born Socialist."[38]

Aside from political radicalism, Swami Trigunatita remained otherwise quite conventional in his religious practice. Each year he sponsored a group of ten to fifteen devotees on a retreat at the Shanti Ashrama for a full month of intensive spiritual training. The schedule of a typical day ran from 3:45 A.M. to 10 P.M., with the waking hours broken up by classes on the Bhagavad Gita and *Gospel of Sri Ramakrishna*, periods of meditation, and work assignments.[39] A solemn, all-night service, held on a hilltop overlooking the camp and including chanting, readings from sacred scriptures, and observance of special purification rites climaxed the annual gathering. Though a Vedantist and a socialist in philosophic outlook, Trigunatita remained an old-fashioned monk when it came to devotional practices.

From an early point, swamis in the United States had to confront urgent requests from serious devotees who wished to undertake full-time monastic life, including *sannyas*, the final renunciation. The question to be settled was how strictly Western students should be expected to meet Belur Math requirements and how far adaptation should be permitted. Vivekananda's experience in this regard was sobering. He had chosen to grant final vows to Leon Landsberg and Marie Louise after only six-week training sessions—and soon after both broke with the movement. Obviously, the rules for American monastics needed to be adapted to Western conditions but still produce a well-trained, disciplined body of monks.

Trigunatita responded to the growing interest in monasticism by establishing a monastery on the third floor of the Hindu temple, which revealed one way in which Ramakrishna swamis adapted to Western conditions. The swami first devised a set of rules, and ten male devotees were inducted as novices. Since all were forced to work in order to meet expenses, the ten devotees spent many hours each day in the outside marketplace, where enforcement of rules was impossible. While inside the temple, however, each was expected to participate in all temple activities, to observe vegetarian diets strictly, and to practice the spiritual exercises prescribed by the swami. Apparently, these arrangements worked fairly well, though there seems to have been a continuous turnover in novices. The monastery closed after Trigunatita's death in 1915.[40]

Soon after the establishment of the monastery, Trigunatita also opened a convent for female monastics, which for its time represented a much more revolutionary action. Generally, the Ramakrishna Order has followed a very conservative policy concerning the role of women, only belatedly establishing a convent for Hindu women in India in the 1950s. Apparently, the female renunciates in San Francisco lived in a separate house near the Hindu temple, and, like their male counterparts, worked at outside jobs to meet their expenses. Unfortunately, little more is known about this important chapter in the early history of Hinduism in America. The convent closed in 1912, three years before the monastery.[41]

In later years Swami Trigunatita moved to demonstrate the compatibility of Vedantism and socialism by founding a Vedanta colony based on cooperative living and self-realization. Perhaps one might characterize Trigunatita's scheme as utopian Vedantism. The original plan called for purchase of a large tract of land, to be broken up and sold to individual members and their families for farming and the development of home industries. Private ownership would prevail, even in a Vedantic collective. A portion of the land was to be set aside for monastics and devotees to farm, with any profits returned to underwrite future extensions of the society's work. Older Vedantists would be encouraged to make the community their place of retirement.

Inaugurated with the purchase of a 200-acre tract of land not far from San Francisco, the colony seemed at first to prosper. Over the course of several years a headquarters building was raised and a number of Vedantists resettled in the colony. As planned, the Vedanta society retained a plot of twenty-five acres for future use, with the balance of land distributed among individual members. Houses were built, wells dug, and crops planted. Swami Trigunatita traveled out to the colony once a week from San Francisco to conduct religious classes and oversee details. Excited by the prospects, he drafted an ambitious plan for a Vedanta temple, library, home for orphan children, hospital, and old-age home, even though welfare activities have never been considered appropriate to the

American work by others. But all work halted with the swami's sudden death in 1915; and within a few years the colony rapidly withered away.[42]

The death of Swami Trigunatita shocked the San Francisco society. On December 27, 1914, a demented, onetime follower had exploded a homemade bomb in the Hindu temple, fatally injuring Trigunatita and badly damaging the building. A subsequent investigation disclosed that the attacker was an immigrant printer named Louis Vavra, who had been the swami's student. He had lived in the Hindu temple monastery but had broken away to join a group known as the Christian Yogis.[43] With Trigunatita approaching fifty-one at the time, his death deprived the movement of one of its most innovative leaders.

The success of the Ramakrishna movement in America has depended heavily on its ability to adapt to Western conditions. That ability in turn has hinged on the ability and temperament of its swamis. In the end, a swami either possessed the qualities and flexibility needed to lead a Vedanta society or did not. The Belur Math's careful monastic training has provided a steady stream of monks well-grounded in Vedanta philosophy and Hinduism, but it has not been able to guarantee that those sent to America would be able to cope with the challenges and culture shock presented by a strange land. Indeed, a good number of those who came—generally men of excellent education, years of careful monastic training, and previous records in India of impressive success—failed to adapt and soon returned home.

No Ramakrishna monk met the American challenge more successfully than Swami Paramananda, who established flourishing Vedanta societies in Boston and Los Angeles and achieved unprecedented acceptance by the American public. Born in 1884, just before Ramakrishna's death, he represented the emergence of the movement's second generation of monks who faced a very different situation from the original disciples. Paramananda was the son of wealthy parents with large landholdings in what is now Bangladesh; he was unusual among monks who came to America in that he never attended college. Because of a cheerful, easygoing, and sunny temperament, he adjusted easily, embracing Western lifestyles with an eagerness that raised eyebrows among his fellow monks.[44]

Swami Paramananda originally came to America in 1907 as Abhedananda's assistant, remaining at the New York Vedanta Society for two years. Following the crisis in New York, he accepted Sara Bull's invitation to establish a new center in Boston. Within a short period Paramananda had to face a problem confronted by swamis from the time of Vivekananda. When he resisted Bull's suggestions for conduct of the work, she exploded: "If you cannot adapt to the Western way of doing things, you might as well go back to India."[45] The nature of his sponsor's proposals is not clear. Instead, he adopted the conservative strategy followed by most Ramakrishna swamis, attempting to build interest through lectures in outlying towns (Brookline, Cambridge, Waltham) and then reserving a hall in Boston, where he inaugurated regular classes and lectures. Despite a warm response, the swami seemed strangely reluctant to make any further commitment. In the end, a group of supporters took the matter into their own hands. While the swami was out of town, several students called an organizational meeting, which approved renting a large hall as a center for his work.[46]

As we have seen, the issue of organization has troubled the Ramakrishna movement throughout its history. If anything, Swami Paramananda indicated even more reservations about a permanent structure than his predecessors. "I came here as a wandering *Sannyasin*," he remarked years later. "I did not expect to settle down and have an established work."[47] Finally, of course, he had accepted the need for some organization, but he strenuously insisted that it be as limited as possible.

In subsequent years, he kept the operations of his centers as informal as he could. There were no bylaws or officers, and there was no fixed membership. One became a member in societies under his direction through attendance at classes and society functions, not through formal application. He also assumed personal responsibility for meeting all expenses incurred in the work—eliminating the usual machinery for insulating swamis from financial concerns. Apparently, he believed that the formation of institutions would occur naturally, without contrivance, as a slow, organic, automatic process.[48] The paradox is that much of the Ramakrishna movement's success and permanence in the United States may be attributed to its sound organization and strong institutional base—unlike most other Asian imports, which have been slow to embrace such institutionalization.

Once settled into his rhythm, Swami Paramananda rapidly emerged as one of America's most dynamic Hindu teachers. The Boston center flourished, while the swami's reach expanded every year. In 1912 the first issue of the society's journal, *The Message of the East*, made its appearance; and in 1914 the purchase of a large house provided a permanent home for the society. Early on, the swami began accepting outside invitations, speaking literally hundreds of times in the succeeding years to a wide collection of bodies—the Boston Metaphysical Club, Buddhist Temple of Pasadena, College Women's Club of Wilkes Barre, New Thought Center in Cincinnati, Unitarian Church of Ayer, Massachusetts, and the Theosophical Center at Krotona, California, to mention only a few.[49]

Despite their diversity, closer inspection of the hundreds of groups Swami Paramananda spoke to reveals a definite pattern. With few exceptions, there are no references to mainstream Christian churches and organizations, while the names of groups on the perimeter of American religion repeatedly recur. Perhaps half of the religious bodies Paramananda addressed were allied with the New Thought movement, with the other half—led by Unitarians, Theosophists, and Rosicrucians—coming from the liberal, outer fringe of American religion. The outside groups addressed by other early swamis reveal much the same distribution. Obviously, in the early decades of the twentieth century groups on the fringes of mainstream religion were much more receptive toward the Ramakrishna movement than mainline bodies. But the pattern changed dramatically after World War II, with Vedanta societies entering into cordial relations with many mainline Christian churches.

After 1915 Swami Paramananda opened a second major theater of operations on the west coast of the United States, centering in southern California. Apparently intended as an auxiliary work, the new commitment soon claimed as much of his time as the Boston center. In addition to Los Angeles, he began to cultivate Vedanta study groups in the neighboring cities of Santa Barbara, Long Beach, and Pasadena. Encouraged by the response, he approved the purchase of 135 acres of mountainous land in the foothills of the Sierra Madre Mountains and, in 1923, founded the Ananda Ashrama as the headquarters of the Western work. Though originally established as a hermitage for meditation and solitude, the Ananda Ashrama almost immediately assumed the functions of a regular Vedanta society as well. Despite its relative isolation, a growing body of devotees came together weekly for lectures and classes. Within a few years numerous buildings, cottages, and a "Temple of the Universal Spirit" dominated the grounds.[50]

An ingenious system instituted to oversee the separated congregations suggests that, whatever his reservations about organization, Swami Paramananda clearly understood the dynamics of directing a transcontinental operation. Moving continuously back and forth between Boston and Los Angeles, he managed to meet the needs of hundreds of followers in both cities. Subsequently, he began to break up his long transcontinental journeys with "roadside centers" in Louisville and Cincinnati. Once these were perfected, the swami followed a systematic rotation, spending approximately six weeks in Boston and six weeks in Los Angeles, broken by highly condensed visits of several days each way at the Cincinnati-Louisville midpoint.[51] He kept all groups informed of his projected arrivals at each center through an intricate system of letters and telegrams. He originally traveled by automobile, but came to prefer the train, which permitted use of the periods between stations for rest and writing. With the inauguration of transcontinental air travel in the 1930s, he began to move by plane. According to one estimate, the swami traveled at least 150,000 miles by train and 100,000 miles by automobile between 1915 and 1921.[52] The exhausting pace undoubtedly helped bring on the heart attack which caused his sudden death in 1940 at the age of fifty-six.

Swami Paramananda managed to cope with the large demands placed on him only because of the critical assistance of a series of women lieutenants who assumed many of his leadership duties. In this regard, he was a major innovator among Asian teachers. During his frequent absences, his four major assistants— Sister Devamata, Katherine Sherwood, Sister Daya, and Gayatri Devi—assumed control at the Boston and Los Angeles centers, conducting services, delivering lectures, instructing classes, and providing spiritual guidance to those who sought it.[53] With the exception of Vivekananda, who also entrusted several of his female devotees with leadership roles, no other Ramakrishna swami gave women so much responsibility. Apparently, some of the other swamis disapproved of his practice, protesting that no monk should spend so much time in the company of the opposite sex. Belur officials never openly opposed Swami Paramananda's policy of assigning women leadership positions, but the Indian headquarters refused to recognize the succession of Gayatri Devi and Sister Daya as leaders of the Boston and Los Angeles centers after Paramananda's death.[54]

Swami Paramananda appealed to Americans because of an attractive personality and open manner, but also because of the practical emphasis of his teachings. In contrast to Swami Abhedananda, who tended to dwell on abstract, philosophical themes, he simplified and personalized Vedanta. Suggesting that religion should deal with "practical life" rather than "theory," he once remarked that emphasis on the practical had been the "dominant thought in every word" he had ever spoken or written. He promised readers that he would present Hinduism's teachings in a "simple, direct way, leaving aside all elements that might seem occult or mystifying."[55] His substitution of English terms for Sanskrit words throughout his writings removed a major barrier for Western students.

Paramananda's emphasis on spiritual healing represented one obvious method of making Vedanta both more practical and appealing to Americans. In principle, most members of the Ramakrishna movement accept the reality of spiritual healing, but the Order has been cautious about emphasizing it. By contrast, Paramananda made it central to his teaching, avoiding condemnation from movement officials by distancing himself from spiritual healing's more radical claims. He emphasized that healing through spiritual means had nothing to do with miracles, magic, or mysticism but entailed the simple transmission of spiritual power. He claimed that anyone willing to "resign himself absolutely and unreservedly" into God's hands could heal others.[56] He not only championed such healing, but frequently resorted to it, with his disciples testifying that he had repeatedly succeeded in removing pain, preventing suicides, and speeding recovery from illnesses.

In a number of respects Swami Paramananda seems to have struck a successful balance between transmitting Hinduism's authentic message and adapting its teachings for American consumption. Though Hindu on the inside, he could be Western on the outside. In matters of worship, he adhered closely to Hindu orthodoxy. Personally more attracted to Hindu devotionalism than Hindu philosophy, he quickly established altars and instituted image-worship at his centers, transmitting the ancient rites of Hinduism to his American followers. Nor did he forget the Indian people. A strong supporter of the Ramakrishna movement's humanitarian projects, for many years he faithfully sent money home to India to support medical dispensaries and schools. At the same time, he tried very hard to eliminate the seeming exoticism of Indian religion by adapting where possible to Western ways. "When I first came to this country," he once remarked, "I imagined that people expected me to talk philosophy, but I found out later that automobiles create a quicker point of contact."[57] Though a swami, he seemed a very Americanized swami. He loved automobiles, wore stylish Western clothing, and played tennis with passion. When radio transmission became possible in the 1920s, he began to present Hinduism over the airwaves; and when commercial air travel dawned in the 1930s, he immediately booked his ticket. More important, he sought to accommodate and domesticate Hinduism's teachings for a Western audience. He frequently alluded in his addresses to Western thinkers, spoke of Jesus with reverence, and presented Vedanta as a practical philosophy relevant to life in the modern world. Observing his behavior, some of his Indian associates dismissed him as the "Hollywood star swami," but his adaptability and openness to the West unquestionably allowed him to successfully reach a wide spectrum of Americans as few Asian teachers have.[58]

Despite the efforts of Swami Paramananda and the others, by 1920, after more than twenty-five years of activity, the Ramakrishna movement in the United States could count no more than four established Vedanta societies, one each in New York, San Francisco, Boston, and Los Angeles. Promising groups existed in several other cities—particularly Swami Paramananda's enthusiastic followers in Cincinnati and Louisville—but none had yet jelled into permanent centers. Measured in sheer numbers, subsequent Hindu movements have done much better. To cite one example, the Self-Realization Fellowship, introduced in the United States in 1920 by Swami Yogananda (known later as Paramahansa Yogananda), grew more in one decade than the Ramakrishna movement did in four. Writing at the end of the 1920s in the first academic study of Hinduism's role in America, Wendell Thomas would conclude that the Ramakrishna movement had become "stagnant." Thomas observed that beyond a tiny membership and scattered pockets of local interest, the movement's influence had to be judged as "scarcely perceptible," while its membership was "generally on the decline."[59]

Growth *was* slow, a fact that may be explained by several factors. To begin with, the Ramakrishna Order had to divide its energies between two fields of operation, spreading its limited staff and financial resources very thinly. India, where the movement was growing like wildfire, demanded most of the Order's energies; as a result, few monks could be spared for the American effort. However, the slow growth may also be explained by the movement's preference for conservative methods. Swami Yogananda's Self-Realization Fellowship once again offers an illuminating comparison. As an example, before lecturing in any American city, Yogananda regularly dispatched staff volunteers ahead to publicize his visit, place advertisements in magazines and on billboards, and book as many appearances as possible.⁶⁰ Such methods obviously paid off, as indicated by the thousands of Americans who turned up at Yogananda's lectures. By contrast, swamis of the Ramakrishna movement rarely employed any form of advertising, relying on word-of-mouth reports to get their message out. In numerous cases, years passed before a Vedanta society achieved a following. Finally, the Ramakrishna movement faced difficulties caused by the loose ties between individual American Vedanta societies and the headquarters in India. More centralization and closer coordination would have promoted a more effective American movement. Located far away in India, Ramakrishna leaders often had a dim understanding of the needs of the American centers. Further, the American Vedanta societies often worked at cross-purposes with one another, compounding the problem. At times, the swamis in America actually seemed to work against one another, competing for the same followers.⁶¹

Despite slow growth and some unanticipated setbacks, the Ramakrishna movement hardly faced extinction in 1920. Indeed, at the very moment that Wendell Thomas announced its stagnation and decline, the Ramakrishna movement was undergoing a rebirth. In a sudden burst of activity extending over the next decade, one Vedanta society after another sprouted in Portland, Hollywood, Providence, Chicago, New York, St. Louis, and Seattle. This impressive expansion in American Hinduism will be the subject of a succeeding chapter.

4 | Vedanta for Americans
The Teachings of the Ramakrishna Movement

THE RAMAKRISHNA MOVEMENT'S essential message in America is the Vedanta philosophy as interpreted by the Advaita or nondualistic school. According to its advocates, Vedanta captures the essence of Hinduism, eliminating extraneous elements while articulating its essential teaching. Tracing its origins back to the Vedas, India's most ancient scriptures, the Vedantic view particularly emphasizes the Upanishads, the latter portions of the Vedas (thus "Vedanta" or "the end of the Vedas"). The late Indian philosopher Sarvepalli Radhakrishnan described the Upanishads as the "foundations on which most of the later philosophies and religions of India rest."[1] In time a number of Vedanta schools arose, of which the most important is the Advaita school, founded by a ninth-century Indian thinker named Shankara. The traditional Ramakrishna story is that beginning in 1893, swamis of the Ramakrishna movement began to transplant the teachings of Advaita Vedanta to the West.

However, the simple explanation of transmission just offered—which defenders of the Ramakrishna movement still proclaim—can no longer be accepted without significant qualification. The Vedantic message that the Ramakrishna movement has brought to America clearly traces back to the Upanishads and the earliest origins of Indian religious life, but it also reveals new emphases and interpretations that arose in the eighteenth and nineteenth centuries. Beginning with Rammohun Roy, leaders of the so-called Hindu Renaissance gradually carried out a far-reaching reinterpretation of Hinduism developed to a considerable degree as a response to Western critiques of Hindu thought and practices.[2] Reacting to criticisms of Hinduism's polytheism, alleged lack of ethical emphasis, and "idol-worship," Hindu apologists insisted that Hinduism was in fact monistic and ethical, and that the worship of images merely served as a way for Hindu seekers to visualize ultimate reality. Insofar as apologists for Hinduism defended their positions in the language and concepts of Western critics, they reconceptualized Hinduism as a religious system comparable to Western philosophical systems. Indeed, Robert Minor has argued that "Hinduism" should always be italicized, in recognition of the Western-influenced reification of a much more amorphous Hindu religious tradition.[3]

More specifically, modern scholars claim that as a result of the influence of such Indian interpreters as Rammohun Roy, Swami Vivekananda, Sarvepalli

Radhakrishnan, and Sri Aurobindo, Hinduism became an ideology that sharply broke with earlier tradition. Agehananda Bharati, one of the leading propounders of the new view, argues that Hindu apologists generally deemphasized Sanskrit terminology, ritual, and traditional practices while emphasizing Hinduism's philosophical profundity and universality. In Bharati's formulation, the leading tenets of the new ideology included the assumption (1) that India "offered a complete solution of all problems" facing the individual and society; (2) that recognition of this truth had been temporarily lost, in part because of the "apathy of her people," in part because of "hostile conquest from outside"; (3) that despite past tribulations, India had remained superior to the West in "matters of the spirit"; and (4) that the essence of Hinduism could be stated as the teaching that "all religions are one" and that "theological differences" and "varying concepts" of God are "unimportant."[4] Though stated in a polemical style, Bharati's arguments seem pertinent to the subject at hand. As we will see, the Hinduism promoted by the Ramakrishna movement clearly represents a merging of ancient tradition and modern thought.

Over the years, swamis of the Ramakrishna Order have routinely prepared summaries of the movement's basic teaching. There is a uniformity in these statements that suggests that in nearly a century there has been almost no deviation from Swami Vivekananda's original formulations. Two samples will be considered. In 1904 the Vedanta Society of San Francisco announced the following ten "doctrines": (1) there is "One Absolutely Everlasting Blissful Intelligence" into which the universe and individual souls will ultimately be merged; (2) all ideas of heaven, hell, and even "God Himself" must be viewed as relative when juxtaposed to the Absolute; (3) human beings are not born-sinners destined for hell; on the contrary, with appropriate spiritual effort, every human being may attain liberation and union with the Absolute; (4) the present human state is the result of "works" in past lives, while subsequent actions will be "additional conditions" for future lives; (5) all religions represent "different paths, leading to one and the same destination"; (6) God "can do anything and everything," including setting aside the laws of nature and appearing "on earth in some human form"; (7) psychic powers exist, but should be avoided as "awful hindrances" to true spiritual development; (8) the method of spiritual development followed should not be based on "blind faith" in any scripture, church, or divinity but "absolutely upon science and reason"; (9) "persons of all sorts," including agnostics and sceptics, "have a place in Hinduism"; and (10) Hinduism is the religion of the Vedas and is "synonymous" with the Vedanta philosophy; "all other sects and religions" may be viewed as "branches" of Hinduism.[5] Though the message is certainly Hindu, the style suggests a Western confession of faith. References to God rather than Brahman and to the necessity of relying on science and reason rather than faith reveal a message aimed at a Western audience.

Almost fifty years later, Swami Satprakashananda, head of the Vedanta Society of St. Louis, reduced the body of teachings to seven principal tenets:

1. The fundamental Reality is Pure Being-Consciousness-Bliss. That alone exists.
2. The phenomenal existence is an appearance; it disappears when knowledge of the Reality is gained.
3. Transcendentally one without a second—formless, feature-less, attribute-less—the Supreme Being-Consciousness-Bliss, immanent in the phenomenal existence as its one all-pervasive Self, is the creator, preserver and absorber of the universe, the God of love, goodness and grace worshipped by the devotees, and the indwelling Spirit in all beings.
4. Man is essentially That.
5. To realize the innate divinity is the supreme end of life.
6. Methods of God-realization vary according to the aspirants' tendencies, capacities and conditions.
7. Different religions are so many ways leading ultimately to Godhead.[6]

In both cases, the very effort to reduce the movement's message to a series of doctrines suggests a process of reconceptualization through Western categories.

In analyzing the Ramakrishna movement's teachings, the beginning point must be the Vedanta philosophy, which serves as the organization's theoretical base. In what follows, I present the Vedantic concepts as the Ramakrishna movement views them. To be precise, one should refer to Ramakrishna/Vedanta concepts, since the movement tends to blur distinctions between the major Vedantic schools. But for brevity's sake I use the term *Vedanta*.

In Vedanta several concepts stand out. Brahman is chief among these. Vedantists traditionally describe Brahman as the first principle out of which all things arise and into which all things disappear; or as the unconditioned ground behind all conditioned experience; or again, as *Sat-chit-ananda*, which may be translated as absolute existence-knowledge-bliss. Ramakrishna swamis often loosely equated the concept with the Western notion of God. In the end, ancient Vedic sages were reduced to denials rather than affirmations in their attempt to describe this ultimate reality. "Neti, neti"—"Not this, not this"—they had proclaimed. Swami Nikhilananda, for many years head of the Ramakrishna-Vivekananda Center in New York, described Brahman in the following words, which echo the words of the ancients: "Though it is spaceless, without it space could not be conceived; though it is timeless, without it time could not be conceived; though it is causeless, without it the universe, bound by the law of cause and effect, could not be conceived to exist."[7] Paradoxically, a very extensive and rapidly expanding literature attempts to explain Vedanta—which has proclaimed that all efforts at explanation must fail.

Maya, a second key Vedantic tenet, must rank as one of the most misunderstood conceptions in all Indian thought. According to a Vedantist, the world of work and play, life and death, and day and night must ultimately be judged as illusory, or maya. However, the individual's inner spiritual state determines the perception. From the perspective of a still-to-be-liberated person, the world (more precisely, the "phenomenal world") is quite real; however, from a transcendental perspective, the liberated person recognizes that it is unreal. In the words of Swami Prabhavananda, former leader of the Vedanta Society of Southern California, the assertion that the "world of thought and matter" is "not real" did not mean that it was also "nonexistent." In fact, he declares, the phenomenal world "is, and is not." In a "stage of ignorance" the outer world is "experienced as is" and exists "as it appears"; but it ceases "to exist as it appears" when one has seen "ultimate reality." Indian philosopher Sarvepalli Radhakrishnan explains the point more tersely: "Unreal the world is, illusory it is not."[8] Maya, then, does not deny the reality of the world from a phenomenal perspective but only transcendentally.

The attitude Vedantists adopt toward other religious and philosophical perspectives depends heavily on the distinction between a phenomenal and transcendental world, or between relative and absolute planes of reality, a perspective that allows them to view dualists, theists, or, for that matter, even atheists with sympathy without in any way compromising their monism. In fact, from a relativistic perspective, all religious and philosophical outlooks deserve respect. Thus, the Christian belief in the divinity of Jesus and the Hindu view of Krishna as an incarnation of Vishnu may be judged as equally valid, representing relativistic conceptions of the godhead. Once liberation has occurred, such beliefs will drop away because of recognition that Ultimate Reality transcends all distinctions.

Writers of the Ramakrishna movement describe atman, another key concept in Vedanta, as the transcendental self or Higher Self. If Brahman may be said to represent the Vedantic idea of God and maya the concept of the world, then atman embodies its view of humanity. In much the same way that one differentiates between a phenomenal and a transcendental world at the macrocosmic level, the Vedantist distinguishes between a phenomenal self and a transcendental self at the microcosmic level. While the phenomenal self, or *jiva*, remains entwined with maya, in a state of enlightenment the transcendental self, or atman, breaks free of all worldly entanglement. For the Vedantist, the central goal of life focuses on successfully completing the journey from the phenomenal world, from a state of *jiva*, to the transcendental realm, to the realization of atman.

Finally, Vedantists affirm that the moment of liberation arrives when the searcher perceives that atman and Brahman are identical. "*Tat tvam asi*"—"That art Thou"—the Upanishads declare; in the words of the Ramakrishna movement, enlightenment dawns with the realization that atman, or the transcendental self, is inseparable from Brahman, or the transcendental ground of all experience. Perhaps its most distinctive contribution to Indian thought, the assertion that atman and Brahman are identical, represents Vedanta's cardinal tenet. Like the concept of maya, the "That art Thou" claim has been frequently misinterpreted. In affirming "That art Thou," that atman and Brahman cannot be distinguished, the Vedantist means, not that every individual is in some sense automatically divine, but only that each has the potentiality for divinity within. Only those who actually achieve self-liberation from the clutches of maya attain transcendental union with Brahman. Such a recognition normally requires many years of strenuous effort.

The concepts just explained pervade the writings of the Ramakrishna movement, but they tend to be assumed rather than explicitly affirmed. Though several swamis who have taught in America have offered systematic expositions of the Vedanta philosophy, most have preferred to focus on more practical problems of religious life. Throughout its history, movement writers have tended to use "Vedanta" and "Hinduism" as practically synonymous and, indeed, as interchangeable terms to describe the essentials of Indian religious belief generally.

If Vedanta has supplied the theoretical foundation for the Ramakrishna movement, yoga may be said to embody its practical teaching. Self-liberation as defined by Vedanta represents the goal, but yoga as explained by Swami Vivekananda has offered the means to that end. As in the case of Vedanta, the movement has simplified and adapted the yogic teachings for a Western audience. Ramakrishna writers have defined "yoga" variously as the "act of yoking or joining," or as "union of the individual soul with the Godhead," or again, as the "method by which such union is achieved."[9] While emphasizing that a variety of different methods exist, Ramakrishna swamis have insistently sought to distinguish the spiritual yoga offered in Vedanta societies from a purely physical yoga, which the movement tended to identify with hatha yoga. Though willing to concede that hatha yoga can be useful in the earliest stages of spiritual discipline, Ramakrishna writers claim that emphasis on physical methods may actually impede spiritual growth.[10]

The four major types of yoga available to a Ramakrishna student are karma, bhakti, jnana, and raja yoga. Swami Vivekananda was one of the earliest Hindu teachers to explain the four types of yoga in a language that Westerners could comprehend. Originally presented as lectures in New York, Vivekananda's exposition has since become authoritative for most followers.[11] According to movement literature, each of the four types has its own distinctive characteristics.

Karma yoga, referred to as the "path of selfless work," is recommended as the yoga best suited for people of active temperaments. In karma yoga work in the world becomes the preferred path to salvation, a conception that squares poorly with the common Western belief that Hinduism emphasizes repudiation of the world. Movement writers claimed that the karma yogi remains *in* the world but not *of* it, seeking to convert every action into a form of worship. The ideals are renunciation and selfless service in God's name; what one renounces is not the action itself, but desire for the fruits of action. Ramakrishna writers insist that no one needs to convert to Hinduism in order to benefit from its disciplines, and, apparently, this is believed to be especially true of karma yoga. According to Swami Nikhilananda, any individual can "practice karma-yoga without believing in a conventional religion or God, or adhering to any creed."[12] Few American followers of the Ramakrishna movement have indicated interest in karma yoga, despite the fact that its emphasis on worldly activity would seem likely to appeal to a typical Western seeker.

According to Ramakrishna swamis, bhakti yoga, or the "path of devotion," offers the best choice for individuals who are strongly emotional in disposition. In this form of yoga the student learns to rechannel his or her emotional energies toward God rather than denying the feelings. Swami Nikhilananda claimed that because it does not require "suppression of normal impulses," bhakti embodies the "easiest and most natural" of the various yogic disciplines.[13] Recommended bhakti yoga practices include image-worship, *japam* (continuous repetition of God's name), and other forms of devotionalism. A critic might question how any proponent of Vedantic nondualism can engage in image-worship and other rituals prescribed by bhakti devotionalism. Movement writers, however, deny any incompatibility. Swami Vivekananda, for example, pointed out that the "Personal God worshipped by the Bhakta is not separate or different from the Brahman"; and that since Brahman was "too much of an abstraction to be loved and worshipped," image-worship and other bhakti forms had arisen.[14] Because of its emphasis on a personal God, Western scholars of comparative religion generally agree that the bhakti tradition represents the Hindu path closest to Christianity.

In sharp juxtaposition to bhakti, jnana yoga is considered by Ramakrishna writers to be the most suitable path for intellectually oriented individuals. The "path of knowledge," it taught the so-called fine discriminations—distinctions between appearance and reality, the One and the Many, and Lower Self and Higher Self. Through close analysis of the transitory world known through the senses, the spiritual seeker could achieve knowledge of ultimate reality. The swamis argued that long practice of intense intellectual exercises would allow the jnani yogi to penetrate the veil of the phenomenal world and to merge with the undifferentiated unity of Brahman. Though regarded as the most difficult of all the yoga disciplines, jnana yoga was apparently the preferred choice of American followers, particularly in the movement's first years. Later swamis have discouraged its practice because of its abstract, philosophical approach; Swami Nikhilananda warned that it presented a "steep and austere" path that was better suited to monks who had renounced the world.[15]

Finally, there is raja yoga, or the "path of formal meditation," which is believed to promote mind-control. Whereas jnana yoga emphasizes knowledge as the path to enlightenment, raja yoga stresses concentration. American students apparently had considerable difficulty distinguishing between jnana and raja yogas. One explanation offered was that raja yoga offers a psychological method for achieving spiritual liberation while jnana yoga emphasizes a philosophic approach. Systematized many centuries earlier by Patanjali, raja yoga emphasized a variety of spiritual exercises, deep rhythmic breathing, and special postures for meditation (*asanas*) believed to still the mind and lead to spiritual realization (samadhi). According to Ramakrishna swamis, a teacher and careful supervision are critical in all forms of yoga, but such safeguards are absolutely essential in the practice of raja yoga. While jnana yoga seemed to attract most attention among American Vedantists in the early years, bhakti and raja yoga have generated greatest devotee interest in recent decades.

The Vedanta philosophy and four yogas embody the Ramakrishna movement's basic message in the United States. Though simplified, codified, and adapted in order to reach a Western audience, the teaching represents a modern restatement of widely held Hindu beliefs that trace back hundreds and even thousands of years. In addition, Ramakrishna added certain distinctive emphases that became an integral part of the movement's teachings. As recorded in the *Gospel of Sri Ramakrishna*, three ideas stand out, which may be said to define Ramakrishna's particular stance toward the nineteenth-century renewal and reinterpretation of Hinduism.[16]

First, direct experience and personal realization provide the only basis of true religion. Despite a commitment to Vedantism, Ramakrishna never had much sympathy for the subtle distinctions of philosophers or theologians. As he liked to say, "The bee buzzes round a flower before it begins to drink the honey. When once it begins to drink, it is perfectly silent." A man of limited education, he deeply believed that reading about, discussing, and theorizing religion were all secondary to direct religious experience and a waste of time without it. Any religion not securely rooted in experience led to theology rather than to God. Apparently, he was also critical of undue emphasis on humanitarianism for the same reason. "You people speak of doing good to the world," he once exploded. "Is the world such a small thing? And who are you, pray, to do good to the world?" As recorded by his disciples, he advised: "First realize God, see Him by means of spiritual discipline. If He imparts power, then you can do good to others; otherwise not."[17]

Second, differences about questions of religious belief represent empty arguments over differences in form. Characteristically, Ramakrishna claimed that the supposed differences among the three classical schools of Vedanta philosophy— nondualism (*Advaita*), qualified nondualism (*Vishishtadvaita*), and dualism (*Dvaita*)—should be viewed, not as absolute divisions, but as complementary stages on the path to realization. He dismissed the distinction between a personal and impersonal god even more casually, suggesting that such a differentiation was analogous to an effort to distinguish fire from the heat it gives off. According to tradition, when asked, "Is God with form or without form?" his reply had been,

"Both with form and without form." He went on to explain that conceived as "Brahman, the Absolute," God was "formless"; but expressed in relative terms God was "my Divine Mother [Kali]. And she has form."[18] Convinced by his own spiritual search that direct experience was fundamental, he found it impossible to believe that any form was crucial.

Finally, all religions are really different paths to the same goal. This statement may be regarded as a logical corollary of the previous point. Ramakrishna's insistence that Christianity, Islam, and Buddhism all offered spiritual paths as valid as Hinduism's emphasizes his break with Hindu orthodoxy. A number of critics attacked Ramakrishna's stance as eclectic, a damaging charge among nineteenth-century religionists. Swami Prabhavananda later claimed that, rather than creating a "new system" of religion by combining the "best in every teaching and teacher"—the accepted definition of eclecticism—Ramakrishna instead had embraced the teachings of other teachers "in toto" and revealed their "essential identity."[19] Apologists insist that Ramakrishna held only that the inner spiritual *experiences* of all religions were the same, not—as Theosophists seemed to believe—that their *creeds* could be reduced to a common core. The only conclusion possible was that individuals everywhere should pursue the path that best suited them: the typical Westerner, presumably Christianity; the Middle Easterner, Islam; and the South Asian, Hinduism or Buddhism. Ramakrishna believed that, pursued faithfully, the end would be the same in every case—namely, the realization of God.

The last point poses a significant question. Assuming that Christianity were judged to be best suited to Westerners and Hinduism most appropriate for Hindus, then the effort of one group to convert another could only be viewed as misguided. Indeed, leaders of the Ramakrishna movement early embraced such a conclusion, which led them to oppose the work of Christian missionaries in India. But if the Western missionary was mistaken in his effort to transplant Christianity to India, would it not follow that the efforts of Indian swamis to transplant Hinduism to the West must also be judged as misguided? Ramakrishna swamis have answered—or perhaps managed to evade—the question by denying that they come as missionaries. They insist that their purpose is not to win converts to Hinduism but to teach the universal oneness of all religions. In fact, thousands of Americans have joined the Vedanta societies since 1893, in the process abandoning Christianity for a modern variety of Hinduism. Despite all protestations, the swamis appear to work as missionaries of Hinduism in the West.

Though the Vedanta message presented in the West by the Ramakrishna movement clearly drew deeply from the well of classical Hinduism, it also diverged sharply from Hindu orthodoxy. The movement's positive view of science offers one of the best indications of its nontraditionalism. The swamis have repeatedly advanced the claim that the teachings of Hinduism and the findings discovered by science represent different but compatible statements of the same truths. Indeed, they go so far as to argue that Hinduism's method approximated the scientific model. "Religion is, in fact, a severely practical and empirical kind of research," Swami Prabhavananda declared at one point, speaking in general terms but clearly referring to Vedanta. "You take nothing on trust. You accept nothing but your own experience."[20] To Swami Abhedananda, yoga particularly exemplified Hinduism's claim to be scientific. He observed that, like any other science, yoga was "based on experience," and that its method of observation and experiment was the "same as that employed by modern science." Swami Vivekananda went a step further, claiming that Vedanta was the *only* religious tradition fully compatible with science. "Of all the scriptures in the world," he remarked, Vedanta offered the "one scripture" whose teaching was in "entire harmony" with the results of modern science.[21]

Such assertions must have seemed startling and even absurd to contemporary Western observers. Western critics demanded to know how a religious perspective as metaphysical as Hinduism's could pretend even superficial resemblance to an empirical science. In fact, the argument usually advanced was not that the conclusions but rather the method adopted in Hinduism resembled the scientific model, with both favoring rigorous, empirical procedures. In the face of objections, the swamis developed several lines of argument. One emphasized the importance of distinguishing between the larger principles and the inconsequential specifics. Conceding that in the Upanishads readers were bound to discover "details" that conflicted with modern science, Swami Vivekananda insisted that, "at the same time," the "principles" were "correct."[22] In another variation, the swamis dismissed apparent incompatibilities by appeal to the familiar Vedantic distinction between relative and absolute planes. Thus, any divergence could be explained away as the result of the difference between relativistic conclusions produced by science and the absolute knowledge possible in Hinduism. In effect, such an argument elevated Hinduism to the perfect science, since its methods could produce unconditioned knowledge.

Whether convincing or not, the effort to establish Hinduism's empirical bent is significant. In claiming that they approached religious questions in the spirit of scientists, the swamis testified a commitment to rational explanation. Swami Vivekananda admonished, "Stick to your reason until you reach something higher; and you will know it to be higher, because it will not jar with reason"; he also warned that "Mystery-mongering weakens the human brain."[23] As rationalists, the swamis generally opposed mystification, repeatedly objecting to the claims advanced by occultists and spiritualists.

A concern with questions of ethics and social responsibility marked a second divergence from traditional Hinduism. Though the claim that Hinduism ignores ethics is surely a gross simplification (what about doctrines such as karma and dharma, for example, which emphasize the moral consequences of one's actions? And what of karma yoga, the spiritual discipline that teaches disinterested action?), at the same time ethical concerns do seem more central in the Judeo-Christian tradition. The writings of Ramakrishna swamis are notable, therefore, for the attention they devote to the subject. Swami Nikhilananda's chapter "Hindu Ethics" in *Hinduism: Its Meaning for the Liberation of the Spirit* provides an excellent example. Presenting a fairly detailed account of the origin and nature of Hindu ethics, the swami emphatically insisted that an ethical outlook provided the "steel-frame foundation of the spiritual life."[24] In explaining the common Western misunderstanding of Hinduism's moral outlook, the swami noted that ethical sensitivity had not so much been absent but had assumed a different form in Hinduism than in the West. While the West stressed social ethics, Hinduism had emphasized the ethics of the individual.

Swami Prabhavananda claimed that, in truth, Hinduism offered a superior foundation for ethical action, thanks to its "doctrine of unity" set forth in the Upanishads, which offered the "only basis" upon which true ethical life could be lived. He contended that Hinduism offered greater justification for moral behavior than other religions. He wrote: " 'Love thy neighbor as thyself,' say the Upanishads, and after them both Buddha and Christ." Why should one love one's neighbor? A Hindu understood: "Simply because he *is* yourself."[25] Only a monist could have made such an assertion. Few other Hindu movements, ancient or modern, have devoted so much attention to ethical questions.

However, the Ramakrishna movement's clearest break with traditional Hindu views was its advocacy of humanitarian aid, an extension of its ethical emphasis and a policy reflected in its heavy involvement in Indian educational, medical, and welfare projects. Once again, Swami Vivekananda seems to have been the decisive influence. Where Ramakrishna tended to show little sensitivity to and, on occasion, outright contempt for humanitarian efforts, Vivekananda proclaimed that Hinduism should be based both on "RENUNCIATION" and "SERVICE."[26] Renunciation has always been a central goal in Hinduism; however, emphasis on service is something new.

Vivekananda's successors have clearly accepted his service ideal, making humanitarianism one of the Ramakrishna movement's identifying characteristics. "There is an impression among some people that the teachings of Vedanta are fit for those only who live like ascetics," Swami Abhedananda remarked in 1905, a view he was at pains to correct. On the contrary, he insisted, Vedanta provided guidance in social as well as individual matters. In some cases, the swamis called not merely for humanitarian aid but for more thoroughgoing social revolution, occasionally sounding almost socialistic in their condemnation of economic exploitation. "The struggle for existence in an increasingly competitive society has become keen, and wealth is not justly distributed," Swami Nikhilananda commented, lamenting that, sadly enough, the Hindu principle of karma was sometimes employed to justify exploitation of the poor. Openly denouncing traditional Hinduism's stress on the "need of secluded life for spiritual aspirants" and the injunction "to work out" their "Liberation by Self-knowledge," Swami Satprakashananda held that followers of the Ramakrishna movement faced a two-fold duty: "Striving after Liberation by solitary practice" and "doing good to the world as a part of spiritual discipline for Self-realization."[27]

In the present context, the very claim that the movement's message was modern seems significant. "Vedanta," Swami Jnaneshwarananda proclaimed at one point, "is the most up-to-date, efficient, practical and universal model of the oldest philosophy in the world."[28] Though transmitters of one of the world's oldest religious traditions, the swamis have again and again insisted that Vedanta provides the answers needed by the modern world. Swami Pavitrananda's *Modern Man in Search of Religion* and Swami Nirvedananda's *Religion and Modern Doubts*, both focusing on modern skepticism and the search for belief, emphasize the desire to deal with contemporary concerns. Swami Akhilananda's *Hindu Psychology: Its Meaning for the West*, which compares Hindu and Freudian psychology, likewise proclaims the importance of Hindu psychological discoveries for an age of anxiety.[29]

At the same time, one must not go too far. However known for their humanitarian work, leaders of the Ramakrishna movement have always argued that such activity must be viewed as secondary to individual self-liberation. In this regard, Swami Prabhavananda observed that "none of the monks of the Ramakrishna Order regards himself as a humanitarian." He insisted that the monk's one goal in life was to know God, and that "worship and meditation" offered the "means to that end."[30] Supporters of humanitarian aid to others, the swamis have been unwilling to justify humanitarian work for its own sake. In this respect, the Ramakrishna Order has remained true to the spirit of traditional Hinduism.

Swami Vivekananda once remarked that every religion needed to include three key elements: a philosophy, a ritual, and a mythology. The function of the philosophy was to distill the "essence" of the religion; the ritual should embody the philosophy in "more concrete form"; and the mythology should illustrate the philosophy by focusing on the "legendary lives of great men."[31] Though most Western followers were originally attracted by the movement's philosophic doctrines, many went on to embrace its devotionalism and religious rites.

Despite his statement that ritual was needed, Swami Vivekananda at first discouraged introduction of any form of devotionalism in the West, convinced that rationalistic Westerners would prefer a more philosophic approach. He soon changed his mind, however. As he reported to his English disciple E. T. Sturdy, his eyes were suddenly opened in late 1895 while conversing with a student in London who asked him to explain the rituals of his creed. Convinced on the spot that Western followers needed a "church" after all, he urgently requested Sturdy to join him at the Asiatic Society's library to search out sources from which the desired rites could be drawn. Apparently, he hoped to create instant rituals. "We will fix something grand, from birth to death of a man," he explained to his English disciple, expressing confidence that, once introduced, the rituals would endure.[32] Though the swami apparently abandoned the scheme, perhaps because of the pressure of his lectures, subsequent swamis rapidly introduced devotionalism, which now plays a significant role both in India and the West. Indeed, the Ramakrishna movement today promotes worship of a central God-figure and veneration of associated saints, including a mother-figure, a chief apostle, and a body of inner disciples.

Christopher Isherwood aptly described the focus and central feature of the movement's devotional practices as the "cult of Ramakrishna." The teachings come from Vedanta, but worship centers on Ramakrishna. The fundamental tenet of the movement is the conviction that Ramakrishna is no less than God, or, to use the Hindu term, an avatar and incarnation of Brahman.[33] According to Hindu belief, the gods have repeatedly incarnated in human form from earliest times in order to renew understanding that life's goal is spiritual realization. Entirely free of maya, avatars are reputed to be able instantly to awaken spiritual understanding in others. In the Ramakrishna Order, Rama, Krishna, Buddha, Jesus—and Ramakrishna—are all regarded as avatars.

Following Swami Vivekananda's example the movement has always permitted individual choice concerning Ramakrishna's divinity, and apparently no explicit requirement exists that a follower must avow such a belief.[34] "About doctrines and so forth I have to say only this," the swami once wrote: "if anyone accepts Paramahamsa Deva [Ramakrishna] as Avatara etc., it is all right; if he doesn't do so, it is just the same." The swami particularly resisted claims of miraculous acts that contradicted normal laws of causation, warning his fellow monks against making too much of their guru's supernatural powers. He clearly feared, as he said, that "fools" would "make a mess of the whole thing." Since Ramakrishna "had a whole world of knowledge to teach," he suggested that devotees should avoid talk of miracles which "do not prove anything."[35] Though he personally accepted Ramakrishna's divinity, he urged that no one be forced to accept the claim that he was an avatar.

Despite such admonitions, the "cult of Ramakrishna" has steadily grown in importance, and today worship of Ramakrishna has become nearly universal in centers everywhere. Now regarded as a sacred shrine, his small room at the Dakshineswar temple attracts tens of thousands of pilgrims from all over the world each year. Meanwhile, the story of his life has been reworked, with growing emphasis on supernatural events and the birth of a modern deity.[36] Despite frequent statements of universalism, followers often treat the Bengali visionary not as just another avatar but as the culmination of all previous avatars and the synthesizer of all religions. "His life and varied spiritual experiences," Swami Prabhavananda wrote in 1938, "afford a basis for harmonizing not only the teachings of the scriptures and philosophies of India, but also . . . the truths taught by Christ and Mahomet."[37] The publication of *Sri Ramakrishna Upanishad* in 1953 marked a final step in his sanctification, as his teachings were placed on the same level as India's most ancient scriptures.[38] In the case of the Ramakrishna movement, *The Gospel of Ramakrishna* has achieved the status of a work viewed by most followers as the final, authoritative source of truth concerning Ramakrishna's teachings, to be consulted for answers on all spiritual questions.

Like other scriptures, statements in the *Gospel* do not always conform to tenets accepted by the movement. Tensions arising from Ramakrishna's frequently expressed opposition to humanitarian works and Vivekananda's fervid advocacy of social service provide an excellent example of how such discrepancies have been handled. (Followers, of course, assume that Ramakrishna and Vivekananda taught the same message.) In an article entitled "The Origin of Swami Vivekananda's Doctrine of Service," Swami Ashokananda attempts to prove that Ramakrishna was positive toward relief work by citing a number of minor incidents in the *Gospel* which suggest a sympathetic outlook. The problem is that Ramakrishna frequently questioned humanitarian activity, a fact Ashokananda ultimately has to concede. Indeed, he confesses that, if "explicit utterances" were the measure, one could hardly deny that Ramakrishna "did not expressly preach the doctrine of service." Despite contrary evidence, the swami surmounted the difficulty by claiming that, if not overtly, such a doctrine could be found in Ramakrishna's teaching in "subtle and potential form"; and that Swami Vivekananda had "only developed" the idea handed on by Ramakrishna.[39]

Ramakrishna's deification has inevitably led to a reevaluation of his close associates, who have also come to be seen as divine agents and participants in a larger plan. The elevation of his closest disciples may be seen in the following quotation, which appears in the preface to *The Disciples of Ramakrishna*:

> Immeasurably great was Sri Ramakrishna, and so too were his disciples. The Divine Power that became embodied and worked as the Master was also channeled through his disciples, making them Its blessed instruments. Sri Ramakrishna may be likened to a gigantic banyan tree. . . . His disciples symbolize the many offshoots, branches and limbs of that mighty tree, each one unique, expressing a particular phase of the Master's multiple personality.[40]

In due course, all who had direct contact with Ramakrishna came to be regarded as saints who deserved special veneration. Among the direct disciples, Swami Vivekananda clearly stands highest, hailed as Ramakrishna's special favorite and anointed successor. His picture almost always stands alongside Ramakrishna's on Vedanta society altars. Swami Brahmananda, who succeeded Vivekananda and served as president of the Ramakrishna Order until his own death in 1922, ranks as the next most venerated disciple. Indeed, Brahmananda is treated more and more as Vivekananda's equal, the disciple who trained a new generation of monks and consolidated the movement in the difficult decades after the passing of the two founders. One leading swami has commented that, except for Brahmananda's critical stabilizing influence, the movement could easily have degenerated into an Indian version of "good-works Protestantism," as a result of Vivekananda's preoccupation with organization.[41] Most Vedanta societies now celebrate Brahmananda's birthday, along with Ramakrishna's and Vivekananda's, and a special temple dedicated to his memory has been erected near the Vivekananda temple at the Belur Math. Other direct disciples have also begun to attract special attention, including birthday celebrations and publication of eulogistic biographies.[42]

One other figure in the sacred pantheon of the Ramakrishna movement remains to be considered, namely, Sarada Devi, or, as she is usually known, the "Holy Mother," the modest, self-effacing wife of Ramakrishna. For a Westerner unacquainted with Indian religious tradition, her gradual elevation to a spiritual position of near equality with her husband must appear as one of the most amazing developments in the history of the movement. As one commentator explained, "Her place is next, if not equal, to that of the Master himself." Another writer testifies: "There was no difference between Sri Ramakrishna and Sri Sarada Devi. . . . The same divinity, the same supreme spirit manifested itself in two bodies."[43]

Examination of the early record suggests that the Holy Mother was to a large extent ignored in the movement's first decades. As the wife of their spiritual teacher, Sarada Devi was naturally treated respectfully by Ramakrishna's disciples, but certainly not with the veneration she would inspire later. She was betrothed to Ramakrishna at the age of five, but did not join her husband until she was eighteen. A shy, unassuming country girl of deep piety, she remained on the sidelines throughout the critical years when her husband was attracting disciples and laying the foundations for the future movement. She returned to the obscurity of her native village of Jayrambati for several years after Ramakrishna's death, surviving her husband by more than three decades. She died finally in 1920.[44] And yet, today, followers of the movement around the globe venerate Sarada Devi as a religious figure of incalculable power and significance.

Followers trace Sarada Devi's special role in the Ramakrishna movement to an incident in 1872, when, in a state of high ecstasy, Ramakrishna is said to have seated his wife on a throne-chair and proceeded to worship her as the Mother of the Universe. Little was made of the event at the time, but Ramakrishna's disciples later cited the event as an indication that Ramakrishna wished his wife's divinity recognized.[45] Though official accounts routinely present Sarada Devi as a major figure throughout the history of the movement, contemporary sources do not support such a view. Swami Gambhirananda declares in his official history that "from 1890, her rightful place as the spiritual guide in succession to the Master began to be increasingly recognised." Yet Swami Vivekananda advised one of his monks in 1894: "You have not yet understood the wonderful significance of Mother's life—none of you." He went on to explain her role: "Without Shakti (Power) there is no regeneration for the world. . . . Mother has been born to revive that wonderful Shakti in India."[46] Though Vivekananda's comments demonstrate his own perception of Sarada Devi's special role, they at the same time emphasize that such recognition was not yet widely shared. If Sarada Devi's spiritual significance was, indeed, recognized from 1890 on, one must wonder why her name was almost never mentioned in the movement's writings and periodicals until after 1920. Volumes such as Swami Gambhirananda's have already largely obscured the halting steps in Sarada Devi's transformation from village woman to Holy Mother.

On the other hand, Sarada Devi's elevation might have been predicted by any student of Indian religion. In contrast to Judaism and Christianity, in which the deity is traditionally portrayed as a male and indeed a Hebraic patriarch, Hinduism has always featured female deities. From time immemorial, Hindu avatars have had their consorts, led by Rama, who was paired with Sita; Brahma, who was joined to Sarasvati; and Shiva, who alternated with Parvati, Durga, and Kali. Devotees of Shaktism go even further, making the feminine principle the dominant feature in their religious observances by worshiping Shakti as the Mother of the Universe. Ramakrishna undoubtedly found the acceptance and worship of a mother god natural, as Shaktism was particularly strong in northeastern India where he spent his life. As we have seen, he became a devoted follower of Kali, passing much of his later life at the Dakshineswar temple, which was dedicated to worship of the goddess. Placed in such a context, no one should be surprised by the worship of Sarada Devi. From the perspective of traditional Hinduism as well as that of contemporary followers, Ramakrishna may be viewed as a modern avatar and the Holy Mother as his consort. Worship of Sarada Devi is the logical corollary of the worship of Ramakrishna.

The impressive celebrations held throughout India during the centenary of her birth in 1953 underscored Sarada Devi's emergence as a religious figure second only to Ramakrishna in the modern movement. Aside from her role as Ramakrishna's consort, she has increasingly been held up as the ideal woman. Her modesty, self-sacrifice, devotion to her husband, and piety are recommended as virtues to be sought by all women. "There can be no greater purifier of the mind and heart than meditation on the significance of the Mother's life," one writer has testified.[47] The swamis all recommend that their women devotees study her life and emulate her actions.

It must be noted that the combination of a Vedantic philosophy with veneration of Ramakrishna and the Holy Mother seems strange and even contradictory. On one hand, the Ramakrishna movement affirms a universalistic message;

but, on the other, it promotes the "cult of Ramakrishna" and worship of the Holy Mother. Apologists for the movement, of course, insist that there is no contradiction. Emphasizing a philosophical approach, they argue, Vedanta clearly is the path for the advanced spiritual seeker. But if unable to make such an arduous choice, the devotee may seek enlightenment through worship of a personal god. Confronted with contradictory choices, Hinduism has tended to incorporate rather than exclude religious options.

In the United States at least, the movement emphasizes its philosophic message much more heavily than the "cult of Ramakrishna," particularly in lectures and publications intended for the general public. Apparently, this represents a conscious policy that traces all the way back to Swami Vivekananda, who was convinced that Americans would immediately reject the movement if they identified it with devotionalism. When a pious Indian supporter mailed rosaries to the United States for distribution to Western devotees, the swami sharply rebuked him, observing that "religion of the type that obtains in our country does not go here." "If you ask them to become Hindus," he warned, "they will all give you a wide berth and hate you, as we do the Christian missionaries." In a subsequent letter, he was even more explicit about his concern, confessing that "What I am most afraid of is the worship-room."[48] Despite his own intense personal devotion to Ramakrishna, the swami practically never mentioned his name publicly during his American lectures, a practice generally perpetuated by the swamis who succeeded him.

The policy seems to have changed in recent decades, however, as a growing prominence of the "cult of Ramakrishna" and devotional practices at American Vedanta societies testify. The turning point was the centennial celebrations of Ramakrishna's birth in 1937, marked by widely publicized public lectures devoted to Ramakrishna's life and teachings at all the Vedanta societies. At present, the American centers all maintain altars and worship rooms where Ramakrishna is worshiped, while public classes on *The Gospel of Sri Ramakrishna* are regularly offered. The movement's public stance should not be confused with the private practice of devotees. An inner group of American followers undoubtedly heard much of Ramakrishna from the outset, and many of these adopted Hindu devotional practices. Today most serious American devotees maintain small altars in their homes and participate regularly in the special devotional observances of their Vedanta societies.

Finally, notice should be taken of the Ramakrishna movement's attitude toward Christianity—certainly a key factor in its American work. In attempting to introduce Hinduism into an overwhelmingly Christian country, the order has understandably devoted a good deal of attention to Christian doctrines and practices. In general, the swamis have approached Christianity with sympathy and appreciation, a view one would surely expect considering Ramakrishna's position that all religions equally provide paths to God. Examples of the movement's broad, universalistic attitude abound throughout its literature. To illustrate, in a lecture presented in 1900 to a California audience, Swami Vivekananda argued that the various world religions were "not contradictory" but rather "supplementary," with each religion contributing "one part of the great universal truth." Suggesting that the "watchword" must be "acceptance" and not "exclusion," he went on, rather flamboyantly, to proclaim his readiness to join in "worship with them all": "I shall go to the mosque of the Mohammedan; I shall enter the Christian's church and kneel before the crucifix; I shall enter the Buddhistic temple, where I shall take refuge in Buddha and in his law. I shall go into the forest and sit down in meditation with the Hindu."[49] The Ramakrishna movement certainly has not abandoned this ecumenical spirit. Most, and perhaps all, Vedanta centers in America today prominently display pictures or statues in their worship rooms of Jesus and Buddha alongside Ramakrishna and Vivekananda.

Though the movement embraced a positive attitude toward all religions, including Christianity, individual swamis have not hesitated to criticize Christian failings. This was particularly true during the movement's first decades in the United States. Aside from criticisms of the Western missionary effort in India—a favorite target—the sharpest attacks were leveled at Christianity's dogmatic and institutional excesses. Typically, the swamis distinguished between Jesus and his teachings, which they praised, and the Christian church's organization and dogma, which they condemned. Swami Abhedananda neatly encapsulated the position in the subtitle of one of his books: "Why a Hindu Accepts Christ and Rejects Churchianity." In the volume Abhedananda suggested the necessity of distinguishing between the pseudoreligion found in many churches, or "Churchianity," and the "true Christianity" taught by Jesus, which "had no dogma, no creed, no system, [and] no theology.[50] Christianity's most serious shortcomings, according to the swamis, were its claim to exclusive truth, aggressive missionary style, frequently expressed contempt for other religions, and undue emphasis on miracles rather than reason. Without exception, these failings were attributed, not to Christianity's founder, but to the church that had violated his teachings. The distinction between Christianity's founder and the church formed to promote his teachings has permitted the swamis to lambaste Christian failings freely without compromising their universalistic claim to honor all religions.

The attack on "Churchianity" once again underscores the depth of the Ramakrishna movement's feelings of ambivalence toward institutional organization, be it Christian or Hindu. As noted earlier, the swamis have revealed profound doubts about such organization since the time of Vivekananda, apparently unwilling to recognize that the Ramakrishna Order, after all, has always been as much a religious organization as a spiritual movement. In modern India the movement has become famous for its efficiency and mastery of organization, and its antiorganizational bias seems the more remarkable considering that much of its own success has stemmed from close attention to such concerns.

It must be added that the Jesus honored by the Ramakrishna movement bore less resemblance to the Jesus worshiped in most Christian churches than to a Hindu holy man. Indeed, the swamis claimed that Jesus might be best understood as an "Oriental Christ"—a man whose preoccupation with spirituality, ascetic practices, and renunciation of the material world captured the Asian ideal. Swami Akhilananda's *Hindu View of Christ* offers an excellent example of such an interpretation. Featuring chapters on "Christ, an Oriental" and "Christ, a Yogi," the swami characterized Jesus as the "Oriental of Orientals," who embodied the "ideal of typical Oriental life."[51] Akhilananda argued that Jesus deserved to be viewed as an avatar as much as Krishna or Buddha, and that the only serious difference between Hinduism and Christianity concerned their disagreement over whether God had incarnated only once, as Christians insisted, or whether he had incarnated numerous times, as Hindus believed. Walter G. Muelder, dean of the School of Theology at Boston University, penned a warm introduction for the book in which he lauded the swami's "inside" view of Jesus.

In a variation, the swamis portrayed Jesus as a great yogi whose highly developed spiritual powers and self-mastery suggested the famous yogis in India. At one point, Swami Abhedananda actually characterized Jesus as a great yogi, "born in a Semitic family"; and he went on to suggest that the surest way to comprehend the various miracles spoken of in the New Testament was to study the "science of Yoga." The swami insisted that all of Jesus' gospel miracles—including his ability to walk on water, feed the multitude with a few loaves of bread, and raise the dead—could be easily duplicated by a master yogi.[52] The San Francisco Vedanta Society advertised sale of a picture of Jesus in lotus position, with the caption, "He was a great Yogin." An accompanying statement proclaimed: "He knew all Yoga-practices to perfection. All psychic powers were extremely developed in Him. He came to this world and practiced Yoga systems for the sake of humanity; so that those who would not be able to understand and follow His teachings, might learn from His practical life."[53]

In explaining the surprising similarities between Christianity's founder and India's holy ones, several swamis promoted the theory that Jesus had spent the crucial period between his twelfth and twenty-eighth years in Asia, studying yoga and other Eastern religious practices. This widely discussed explanation achieved surprising acceptance in late nineteenth-century America as the result of the popularity of Russian journalist Nicholas Notovitch's *The Unknown Life of Jesus*. Though repeatedly discredited by scholars in the years since 1900, the theory has remained popular among groups on the fringe of mainstream religion.[54]

The swamis did not restrict their efforts to portraying Jesus in Indian dress; they also undertook a reinterpretation of Christian doctrines to conform to Hindu conceptions. A good example was Swami Prabhavananda's rendering of "The Lord's Prayer" in 1953. Analyzing the prayer's familiar phrases a few words at a time, the swami in effect recast it as "The Hindu's Prayer." Thus, he explained that the "Our Father," with which the prayer begins, should be understood as an appeal to the personal god of bhakti yoga, of whom Jesus had taught his disciples, instead of the higher concept of an impersonal God, which he had recognized as too abstract for them to comprehend. The "Which art" affirmed that God was a reality that could not be proved through reason—just as the Vedanta taught; the words "In heaven" must be understood, not as an indication of place, but as a reference to transcendental consciousness, or what Hinduism called *samadhi*. Again, the swami explained that the phrase "And forgive us our debts as we forgive our debtors" should be interpreted as a "reference to what the Hindus and Buddhists call the law of karma."[55]

Joan Rayne's interpretation of the Christian Trinity provides a second example of such reconceptualization. A devotee at the Hollywood Vedanta Society in 1957, Rayne explained that the notion of "God the Father" might be better understood as a reference to Brahman, the all-pervading spirit; that "God the Son" might be viewed as a Christian version of "divine incarnation," with Jesus playing the same avatar role that Buddha, Ramakrishna, and other great figures had played in other times; and, finally, that "God the Holy Ghost" could be better understood as the "God within each one of us," who is "identical with God the Father," or Brahman.[56] Rayne's analysis suggests just how strained such interpretations could be. However well intentioned, the efforts of Ramakrishna swamis to draw out the parallels between Hinduism and Christianity clearly did little to enhance understanding of either religion.

Western commentators have sharply differed over the nature of the message presented by the Ramakrishna movement and its conformance to tradition. In a pioneering 1915 study entitled *Modern Religious Movements in India*, John Farquhar classified the movement as one of several nineteenth-century groups that championed a "Full Defence of the Old Religions." (By contrast, he categorized the Brahmo Samaj among those "Movements Favoring Serious Reform.") Though he conceded that Swami Vivekananda's emphasis on humanitarianism represented a new emphasis and significant break with past tradition, Farquhar argued that both Ramakrishna and Vivekananda looked much more to a restoration than a reformation of Hinduism. "Ramakrishna's indiscriminate acceptance and uncritical defence of everything Hindu," he observed, "expanded in his disciple into unbounded laudation of everything Indian." Farquhar largely confined his analysis to the movement's Indian work, but Wendell Thomas apparently reached much the same conclusion about the body's Western message, as indicated by the chapter on the Ramakrishna movement in his 1930 study *Hinduism Invades America*. While he noted evidence of Western and Christian influence, Thomas argued that the Ramakrishna movement's American message and methods were extremely conservative, a fact emphasized when it was compared with other Hindu groups active in the United States. Indeed, Thomas claimed that the Ramakrishna movement was "on the whole more medieval and otherworldly" than "many of the conservative Hindu groups in India itself."[57]

By contrast, later commentators such as the well-known French writer on Vedanta philosophy, René Guénon, fiercely attacked Ramakrishna and Vivekananda for abandoning traditional Hinduism to teach what the Frenchman contemptuously dismissed as "Vedanta Westernized." Convinced that there was little difference between the Ramakrishna movement and other nineteenth-century Hindu bodies such as the Brahmo Samaj and Arya Samaj, Guénon complained that a "Western propensity for proselytism" had penetrated all of them with the result that they were "Eastern in nothing but the name." Dismissing the Ramakrishna movement's "so-called Vedanta," he declared that its brand of Hinduism had "practically nothing" in common with Vedantic metaphysical doctrines.[58]

Any final judgment concerning the conformance of the Ramakrishna movement's presentation of Hinduism to tradition depends a good deal on the comparison made, particularly if one is speaking of the American scene. Compared with most other Hindu religious groups that have labored in the United States, it has been quite conservative in its transmission of the Hindu message. The emphasis placed on Vedanta and the four yogas, the frequent appeals to the teachings of the Upanishads and Bhagavad Gita, the obvious concern with accurate translations of the major Hindu writings—all emphasize a desire by the movement's swamis to present the teachings of Hinduism as faithfully as possible. The fact that most scholarly bibliographies on Hinduism now routinely include the swamis' translations and expositions indicates the acceptance their interpretations have achieved. Every Ramakrishna swami dispatched to the United States has had years of instruction and training in the traditional teachings and practices of Hinduism carried out under the watchful eyes of senior monks at the Belur monastery.

Several other factors have reinforced the movement's conservative attitude toward message and method of work. Though Swami Vivekananda began as an outspoken reformer, he increasingly assumed the role of apologist in his later years. While his harsh criticisms of Hinduism's corruptions steadily declined, his defense of India's traditional religious practices steadily mounted. The very organization of the American movement has accentuated the conservatism of the message presented in the West. Though in theory Vedanta societies in the United States are autonomous, in fact the teachers and the teaching have always come from India. Unlike most other religious bodies introduced from the outside, which have rapidly assimilated to American ways, Vedanta societies have maintained strong ties to India. In one way at least, American centers may be even more conservative than centers in India. Responding to India's social problems, the Ramakrishna movement in India has stressed humanitarian activity; by contrast, the movement has identified spiritual renewal as the need of the West. To this extent, the Ramakrishna movement may be said to promote reform Hinduism in India while championing traditional Hinduism in the United States.

5 | The Appeals of Vedanta

ONE OF THE central issues that inevitably arises when the impact of Asian religion in the United States is discussed is the question: Who, exactly, is attracted to the Eastern religions? Do followers come from all strata of American society, or do they, perhaps, exhibit special characteristics that distinguish them from other Americans? In the past various answers have been suggested. In the years immediately before World War I, commentators such as Mabel Potter Daggett and Elizabeth Reed tended to identify the typical follower as female and affluent; in addition, converts to Asian religions were frequently stigmatized as unbalanced, alienated, or, at the very least, jaded. Then, during the 1960s, attention shifted to young, middle-class people in rebellion against their conformist parents and an affluent society. Today there is more and more evidence that alienation has dropped into the background and that Eastern spirituality has broad appeal.[1] A second issue frequently debated concerns the appeal of Eastern spirituality. What is it that has drawn Americans in increasing numbers to Asian religion? Is it the actual attraction of the Eastern teachings or, perhaps more important, a rejection of Western values and religion? In the following pages the appeal of the Ramakrishna movement's message for Americans will be considered with particular focus on the issues noted. The questions are: Who was attracted to the Ramakrishna movement, the first Asian religious movement to establish a permanent base in the United States? And second, what seemed to attract Americans to the Ramakrishna movement and its Vedantic teachings?

But before proceeding, notice should be taken of a widespread belief at the turn of the century that has colored all subsequent discussions of the Asian appeal. This was the notion, expressed almost from the first appearance of Eastern teachers in the United States, that rich American society women have been unusually drawn to conversion to Eastern religions. Mabel Potter Daggett's sensational article "The Heathen Invasion," which appeared in the *Hampton-Columbian Magazine* in 1911, offered a classic formulation of the view. The article's subheading starkly summarizes the argument advanced: "American women losing fortunes and reason seeking the eternal youth promised by the swarthy priests of the Far East."[2] Written in emotionally charged language, Daggett warned (1) that increasing numbers of Americans were looking East, (2) that a disproportionate number of such seekers were affluent women, and (3) that most of the women seemed quite unable to resist the charms exerted by Asian teachers. The covert message conveyed was as important as the overt message, as suggested by the language used throughout the article. References to "swarthy" priests would surely have awakened deep anxieties in a period of intense racial sensitivity, while emphasis on the Asian teachers' "gorgeous robes" was clearly intended to suggest that the Asian emissaries were exploiting the opportunity to enrich themselves. The readership of Daggett's article is difficult to gauge, but it unquestionably reached a large audience after it was reprinted in the *Missionary Review of the World* in 1912.[3]

The 1912 publication of Mrs. Gross Alexander's "American Women Going After Heathen Gods," published in the *Methodist Quarterly Review*, and Elizabeth A. Reed's more extended *Hinduism in Europe and America*, which appeared in 1914, undoubtedly increased the general public's concern. Both publications echoed Daggett's charge that "clean-hearted" American women were being lured to their destruction. Further rumblings could be heard as late as 1929, as a result of Mersene Sloan's inflammatory *The Indian Menace: An Essay of Exposures and Warning, Showing the Strange Work of Hindu Propaganda in America and Its Special Danger to Our Women*.[4]

In fact, women *were* more prominent than men in the early history of the Ramakrishna movement—though there is little evidence to suggest that they were being duped as Daggett and other alarmists charged. When one recalls the more recent charges of brainwashing brought against movements such as the Hare Krishnas, the realization dawns that critics have sometimes found it easier to believe that the appeal of Asian religion stems from unfair methods rather than from more substantial attractions.

But what of the Ramakrishna movement in general? Is the gender question the only important one? Unfortunately, there is very little hard evidence as to who became a follower, especially in the movement's first decades in America. Throughout most of the movement's history, the swamis have resisted inquiries concerning their followers' backgrounds as a waste of time.[5] Inspection of the movement's periodicals and extensive published works also fails to supply information. In the absence of more empirical data, the only alternative possible has been an examination of the backgrounds of leading American followers, whose important roles and contributions to the movement led to published sketches concerning their lives. Almost by definition such prominent followers could hardly be considered representative; nevertheless, their biographies may at least suggest some limited generalizations concerning the backgrounds of Americans attracted to the movement.

Vivekananda's leading disciples offer a good beginning point, since they have received considerable attention in the movement's literature. In 1895, following months of strenuous lecturing, the swami summoned his closest followers to a spiritual retreat at Thousand Island Park in upstate New York. In addition to spiritual instructions, he apparently hoped to use the opportunity to select and train the leaders who could carry on the American work after he departed. One of the participants later recalled, "It was a strange group." "No wonder the shop-keeper to whom we went for direction upon our arrival, said, 'Yes,' there are some queer people living up on the hill."[6] Among the twelve who responded to Vivekananda's call, the two most memorable figures were an intense man named Leon Landsberg and a French-born woman known only as Marie Louise. At the close of the retreat, both took the vows of a sannyasin, which qualified them as the first two Western-born swamis in American history.

Born a Russian Jew and educated in Germany and France, Landsberg had apparently been living in the United States for several years before his first en-counter with Vivekananda. He was a journalist by vocation who had operated a newspaper in the South and later worked for one of the major New York dailies. "I have always been a seeker for truth," he once remarked, explaining that he had "studied many religions" finding "some truth in all." He had passed through several other religious organizations, including the New York Theosophical So-ciety, before discovering Vedanta.[7] He served for several years as Vivekananda's chief lieutenant and constant companion, often going ahead of the swami to make arrangements for lectures and conducting classes during the swami's fre-quent absences. Marie Louise Burke, one of the movement's chief historians, has described Landsberg as "hypersensitive," "self-centered," "subject to fits of black depression," and "inclined to self-pity and delusions of persecution."[8] In-deed, Landsberg broke away from the movement in anger, driven by feelings of jealousy toward Vivekananda's other disciples.

Marie Louise (not to be confused with Marie Louise Burke) also revealed an immigrant background. A naturalized citizen, she had resided in New York City more than twenty years prior to her first encounter with Vivekananda. She was well known in radical circles, identified as a socialist, a friend of Emma Gold-man's, and the champion of liberated womanhood. She was approximately fifty at the time of the Thousand Island retreat. One of her contemporaries described her as a "tall, angular woman" with short-cropped hair who was "so masculine in appearance" that one had to look twice before determining that she was a woman.[9] Strong willed and self-confident, she characteristically announced that her path would be jnana yoga, the highest and most difficult form of yoga. Vive-kananda was obviously impressed by her potential, as demonstrated by his deci-sion to give her the *sannyas* vows (the final vows taken by one who has re-nounced all worldly attachments in favor of a life of asceticism and contemplation) soon after she joined his work. Vivekananda's act of granting *sannyas* to a foreign woman created a stir in India.[10]

Throwing herself into the Vedanta work, Marie Louise directed classes in New York while the swami lectured in England. She quickly opted to initiate a work of her own, however, founding an independent "Advaita congregation" in

Brooklyn and subsequently moving to Chicago, where she established a body known as the Advaita Society. Proceeding to consolidate her work, she held a "Sannyasin Ordination," raising one of her female disciples to swamihood before an altar adorned by pictures of Ramakrishna, Jesus, and Vivekananda.[11]

Marie Louise's independence clearly troubled the leaders of the Ramakrishna movement, with tensions rapidly escalating after she launched a strenuous lecture tour across India in 1899. Apparently, she made a considerable impression; Indian audiences were intrigued by the novelty of a Western woman dressed in a sari proclaiming the truths of Hinduism.[12] Her relations with the authorities of the Ramakrishna movement continued to deteriorate, however, leading to a complete rupture. After her return to the United States, she briefly renewed her Vedanta work, but subsequently moved toward New Thought, establishing the School of Mind and Soul Culture in New York City.[13]

Vivekananda's selection of Leon Landsberg and Marie Louise as America's first swamis obviously proved disappointing. One of his close disciples later explained his choice of the two followers as the result of his belief that "fanaticism is power gone astray."[14] Both certainly revealed intensity and zeal, which he hoped to channel; pressured to locate assistants to carry on his work, the swami understandably chose people who revealed energy and enthusiasm. Subsequently, he became much more cautious about granting *sannyas* vows, ordaining only one other American swami, an obscure man identified only as "Dr. Street," whom he initiated as "Swami Yogananda." Described by Vivekananda as a "genuine American" and "religious teacher of some standing," Street had apparently studied hatha yoga for many years and written a book on Egyptian mysticism before taking up Vedanta.[15]

Vivekananda's other leading American disciples seem steadier than either Landsberg or Marie Louise. Few proved more steadfast than Christine Greenstidel, who became known as "Sister Christine." Another immigrant, she came to America from Germany as a child of three. She was a Christian Scientist when she first heard Vivekananda in 1894. Apparently, she dreamed of undertaking women's educational work in India but did not feel free to leave until her mother had died and her younger sisters could care for themselves. Finally departing for India in 1902, for more than a decade she managed the Nivedita School, founded by Vivekananda's disciple Margaret Noble, for the education of Hindu women. Like many other Western devotees, she experienced serious health problems in India which forced her home. She lectured on Indian religion in the Detroit area for the next ten years, then returned to India a second time; but the deterioration of her health again forced her return home. Today, Greenstidel has come to be regarded in the movement as a model Western devotee because of her willingness to fully adopt the dress and lifestyle of an orthodox Hindu woman.[16]

Despite appearances to the contrary, not all of Swami Vivekananda's American disciples were foreign-born. Ellen Waldo, said to be a distant relation of Ralph Waldo Emerson, had been a "religious seeker" who had "wide experience in teachers" before embracing Vedanta.[17] She was a member of the Brooklyn Ethical Association when she first heard Vivekananda lecture in 1894. She quickly became one of the swami's most trusted assistants, shouldering responsibility for his housekeeping duties during his New York classes and recording his remarks at Thousand Island Park, which were subsequently published as *Inspired Talks*. It is worth noting that all four of the people so far considered— Leon Landsberg, Marie Louise, Christine Greenstidel, and Ellen Waldo—reveal relatively modest socioeconomic backgrounds.

Vivekananda's most important American disciple was Sara Bull. She was a woman of broad culture, and her home in Cambridge, Massachusetts, became something of an intellectual salon, where one might encounter such luminaries as William James, Josiah Royce, and Thomas Wentworth Higginson. She had discovered the attractions of Asian religion as early as 1886, attending readings of the Bhagavad Gita offered by an Indian Theosophist named Mohini Chatterjee, who briefly lectured in the United States in the eighties. She had also dabbled in New Thought, a frequent link among future Vedantists. Turning to Vedanta, in 1898 she joined a group of select disciples under Swami Vivekananda's personal direction for a pilgrimage across northern India.[18]

Bull's well-publicized role as a benefactor of Hinduism undoubtedly helped create the stereotype of the vulnerable society woman, who was believed to be particularly susceptible to the mystic spell of Hindu holy men. As one of Swami Vivekananda's major financial backers, she underwrote much of the expense incurred in erecting the Ramakrishna movement's headquarters in Belur. She willed the movement a large sum of money at her death in 1911, but her daughter contested the will and was able to get the endowment nullified. Boston newspapers closely followed the legal battle, portraying Vivekananda's disciple as a gullible victim who had fallen under the unhealthy influence of Eastern yogis.[19] The Ramakrishna movement had to confront the unfavorable publicity arising from the case for years afterward.

One other name must be mentioned to complete the list of Swami Vivekananda's most important American followers. Though she insisted that she was the swami's "friend" rather than his "disciple," Josephine MacLeod nevertheless stands out as one of his most devoted supporters. Descended from a socially prominent family, she and her sister had both been studying the Bhagavad Gita and practicing meditation for years before meeting Vivekananda. She journeyed across northern India with the swami in 1898 and accompanied him on a European tour in 1900. In later years she also resided for extended periods at the Belur headquarters. She was instrumental in the establishment of a Ramakrishna society in France and is credited with awakening Romain Rolland's original interest in Ramakrishna, which led to the famous French writer's *Prophets of New India*. She became a disciple of Swami Prabhavananda's in her final years, thus spanning the Ramakrishna movement's entire history from Swami Vivekananda to the post-World War II era.[20]

Though a tiny sample, the examples so far considered suggest that generalizations concerning the typical American Vedantist need to be formulated with care. Followers such as Sara Bull and Josephine MacLeod conform to the upper-class stereotype, but Christine Greenstidel certainly does not. Marginal figures such as Leon Landsberg and Marie Louise, who obviously rejected many of the values of contemporary American society, would seem to have little in common with an individual such as Ellen Waldo, whose roots reached deeply into native soil. That being said, Vivekananda's close disciples do suggest three important similarities: a disproportionate number were women, a good number were foreign-born, and most seem to have had contact with groups on the fringe of the American religious mainstream before affiliating with Hinduism.

If we turn to four later followers of the Ramakrishna movement, whose lives are sufficiently well documented to allow comparison with Swami Vivekananda's disciples, we find that the pattern is fairly consistent. Cornelius Heyblom, a Dutch-American who became one of the first Western-born Ramakrishna swamis, may be considered first. His recollections of life in the movement in *Atman Alone Abides* provide one of the best records of a Western devotee's adjustments to modern Hinduism. Born in 1870, Heyblom was the son of a prosperous Amsterdam merchant; he immigrated to the United States after his graduation from college. Apparently, he turned to Asian religion in part as a reaction against a very strict Protestant upbringing.[21] He was dabbling in New Thought and Theosophy in New York City when he heard Swami Abhedananda speak and became a devoted disciple. After a time he took first monastic vows (*brahmacharya*). He briefly lived in a community known as the Lord's Farm, which practiced Christian communism, but soon transferred to the Ramakrishna retreat near San Francisco, where he remained for the next six years. He finally reached India in 1906 and spent the next half-century there.[22]

Heyblom represents one of a very small number of Westerners who completely adapted to the life of a Hindu ascetic. Though numerous American devotees have gone to India over the years, few have remained very long or successfully accommodated to India's food and living conditions. A notable exception, Heyblom survived the rigorous monastic training at the movement's Belur monastery and rose to become a full swami in the Ramakrishna Order. We are told that he observed Hindu customs as fully as possible—living under the Spartan conditions usual among Indian monks and conducting pilgrimages about the country in the simple garb of a sannyasin. (Such a life took its toll. On two occasions breakdowns in his health forced his return to the United States, but the third attempt proved successful and he never again returned to the West.) Known in the movement as Swami Atulananda, in later years he referred to himself as a Hindu.[23] He died in 1966 at the age of ninety-six.

While Heyblom found his way into the Ramakrishna movement as a relatively young man, many devotees have been middle-aged and older before discovering Vedanta. A woman known only as Sister Avabamia offers a typical exam-

ple. Since she has been largely ignored in movement literature, only a few frag-
ments concerning her background may be cited. She was Swedish, had resided in
Seattle some years, and had authored a number of metaphysical books, including
Internal Breathing as Body Builder and an intriguing volume entitled *Soul Travel
among the Flowers*. The books as well as other writing clearly indicate influence
by the New Thought movement. Middle-aged and already an experienced
teacher at the time of her acceptance of Hinduism, she claimed to have delivered
more than 3,000 lectures before audiences in Europe, Canada, and the United
States.[24]

Though converted to Hinduism, Sister Avabamia remained quite Western
and evangelical in her approach to Vedanta. She launched a strenuous campaign
of lectures and classes in Australia and New Zealand in 1908, delivering more
than 1,200 addresses over the next several years. Drawing on the methods of
American business, she announced a "Ladies Only" class, where women could
learn about health and beauty. She also promoted contests between "Vedanta
clubs," with prizes given to the best speaker, the most energetic worker, and the
society which recruited the largest membership.[25] Unfortunately, contemporary
sources do not comment on the success or failure of these initiatives. In 1911,
she moved on to Sri Lanka and India, where Avabamia again launched a whirl-
wind of lectures and announced the founding of new schools and Vedanta centers. Aware that she needed to make some effort to accommodate her presentation to Asian audiences, she adopted the *pranam*, the Indian greeting in which
one places one's palms together, and *tilaka*, the dot applied to the forehead by
orthodox Hindu women. Newspaper reports headlined her as the "first white
Hindu from the West."

The strict silence of Ramakrishna journals concerning Sister Avabamia's
wide-ranging activities suggests that Belur officials were not pleased. Though the
specific causes remain obscure, we know that soon after reaching India, Avabamia broke with the order. Ramakrishna leaders clearly disapproved of her unau-
thorized work and as a result refused to recognize the Vedanta societies she organized. Departing India soon after, Avabamia charged that, however admirable
in other respects, the Ramakrishna Order's subordination of women and concentration of power in the hands of its president were undemocratic and intolerable
in an organization that claimed to be international.[26] Avabamia's difficulties
with officials at Belur parallel the troubles Vivekananda's disciple Marie Louise
had experienced some years earlier and suggest that independent women leaders
have not fared well in the movement.

By contrast, Laura Glenn, who assumed the name of Sister Devamata, was
far more successful than Marie Louise or Sister Avabamia, ranking as one of the
most notable American Vedantists so far produced. The daughter of well-to-do
parents, she graduated from Vassar College and subsequently lived in Europe for
ten years; she also spent a period in an Anglican convent. Apparently, such works

as Edwin Arnold's *Light of Asia*, the Upanishads, and the Bhagavad Gita ignited her original interest in Hinduism. She attended Swami Vivekananda's lectures in New York for two years, but despite a strong attraction to Vedanta held back, apparently immobilized by a sister's disapproval. "She had no sympathy with my Oriental studies," Glenn later recalled, "and often said she wished I 'could get salvation nearer home.' "27 Her father obviously opposed her Asian interests as well, at one point threatening to disinherit her if she continued her Eastern associations. Despite disapproval, she steadily became more deeply involved, assisting Swami Abhedananda for several years and finally embracing Swami Paramananda as her spiritual teacher.

At Paramananda's urging Glenn moved to India in 1907 to learn Hinduism at first hand, taking up residence in a monastery in south India. During two years in India she came to know most of the movement's leading figures, including Ramakrishna's wife, Sarada Devi, and Swami Brahmananda, who assumed leadership of the order after Vivekananda's death. Explaining her decision to go to Asia, she later observed that, in the same way that students in the past had "gone to Paris to study art" or "to Germany to study music," in the future they would "turn to India" to acquire the "most efficient method" of developing their "religious consciousness."28 Despite strong philosophic interests, Glenn came to prefer the devotional path of bhakti over the more intellectual approach of jnana yoga.

Glenn's experiences in India removed any remaining doubts she harbored about devoting herself completely to Hinduism. Returning to the United States in 1909, she threw herself into Swami Paramananda's work, rapidly emerging as his chief lieutenant. Acting as a "one-person staff," according to a recent history, she "assumed the roles of housekeeper, laundress, and cook, as well as secretary, publicist, and administrator of the new Centre."29 She also developed into a competent platform speaker, regularly lecturing at the Boston Vedanta Society and Ananda Ashrama in California during Paramananda's absences. However, her literary activities constituted her most lasting contribution to the Ramakrishna movement's work in America. She recorded and published a number of Paramananda's works and for many years edited the Boston and Ananda Ashrama journal, *The Message of the East*. Though declining health forced her to suspend her career as a public speaker in the early 1920s, Glenn remained heavily involved in literary work right up to the time of her death in 1942. Her published works include *Days in an Indian Monastery*, one of the earliest Western reports of Hinduism from the inside; *Swami Paramananda and His Work*, a two-volume history of the Boston and California centers; and a long list of other imprints, including such works as *Habit of Happiness* and *Building Character*.

All of the individuals so far noted are now dead. A new generation of Ramakrishna devotees has come of age, but few contemporary followers have written of their experiences. The exception is John Yale, for many years a member of the

Vedanta Society of Southern California and presently an assistant at the Centre Vedantique Ramakrichna near Paris. In describing his religious evolution, Yale comments that he had attended church as a child but ceased going in his late teens. He subsequently tried business but found himself feeling strangely unfulfilled. Searching for a belief system, he now embraced Episcopalianism, dabbled in psychoanalysis, and, finally, turned to Vedanta after reading Swami Prabhavananda's and Christopher Isherwood's translation of the Bhagavad Gita. He has subsequently chosen a monastic life and is today known as Swami Vidyatmananda.[30]

Yale has made a major contribution through publication of two of the most revealing inside accounts yet produced about the modern Ramakrishna movement and its Western impact. *What Vedanta Means to Me* presents first-person statements by a wide assortment of Western followers, suggesting the modern attractions of the Ramakrishna movement. The second volume, *A Yankee and the Swamis*, recounts Yale's impressions of the Ramakrishna movement's work in India as a result of a two-year journey during 1951–1952, when he visited thirty-eight Ramakrishna centers. Though the portrait of the Ramakrishna movement reveals his ability to view the movement with considerable detachment, Yale leaves little doubt about his own commitments.

> Suppose someone present in the area of the Mediterranean Sea in A.D. 100 had noted down impressions concerning the direct disciples of Christ—what they were like, their memories of the old times, the concerns that moved them. Such information would be of inestimable value. My position is that these are comparable times, and that I have met and written of equally significant men.[31]

This statement embodies the belief of many contemporary followers of Ramakrishna.

Scrutiny of the backgrounds of key followers may reveal some sense of the types of Americans attracted to the Ramakrishna movement, but one cannot be sure how representative they were. Indeed, the very fact that they attracted notice and played leadership roles suggests that they were exceptional and atypical. The obvious need is a systematic study based on quantitative data that can be verified. Since the movement's original followers have died, such an examination is out of the question for earlier decades, but a contemporary quantitative study is feasible. To be successful, such an enterprise would require the full cooperation of Ramakrishna authorities as well as competence in the use of quantitative methods. One of the first requirements of such a study would be to clarify the meaning of membership in the movement, since the definition seems to vary from center to center.

Wendell Thomas attempted to offer a quantitative analysis of membership in his pioneering 1931 volume *Hinduism Invades America*. Though very imperfect, his findings are nevertheless worth noting. He reports that he mailed a questionnaire to all five American Vedanta societies then extant and that four of the five responded. The breakdown for the thirty-seven members who returned their questionnaires revealed that most were native-born Americans, three-fourths were women, and more than one-half came from Protestant homes; further, two-thirds of the respondents from religious homes had had some connection with sects or religious movements on the perimeter of American religion before turning to Vedanta. Thomas concluded that in the United States the Ramakrishna movement seemed to attract "interesting" personalities, "mostly women" and "mostly of foreign extraction" who had "done rebellious thinking" in their youths.[32] Obviously, no modern social scientist could accept Thomas's methodology: the sample is too small; the investigation relies entirely upon written responses, without follow-up interviews; and the reporting of results is imprecise ("about two-thirds," "more than three-fourths"). Still, the survey is in some ways instructive.

Until a more adequate quantitative study appears, however, analysis of the backgrounds of American followers of the Ramakrishna movement must rely on the evidence at hand. The following generalizations are based upon examination of the movement's literature, scattered interviews with contemporary Vedanta society members, responses to an informal questionnaire circulated among selected members of the movement, and a review of the conclusions of other scholars. (For the moment, the influx of Asian Indians since 1965 will be ignored, a recent infusion that has significantly altered the movement's profile.) The evidence suggests that Western converts to the Ramakrishna movement *do* reveal certain commonalities of background.

First, the typical member tends to come from a middle- or upper-middle-class background. To reverse the generalization, members of the lower and lower-middle class have rarely indicated much interest in the Ramakrishna movement, viewing Hinduism as too "other," and even "un-American," for serious consideration. Disproportionate numbers of professional people, successful businesspeople, and white-collar workers—most of them college-educated and a surprising number descendants of prominent families—do indicate strong interest. Few religious movements of such size have attracted so many writers. Though there are notable exceptions, the typical Vedantist has tended to be better educated, better traveled, and better off economically than a typical member of America's mainstream churches. The cultured and fashionably dressed people who attend Vedanta society services today cannot be very different from the middle- and upper-class Americans Swami Vivekananada attracted in the 1890s. Appropriately, most Vedanta societies are located in older, more affluent neighborhoods.

Second, the typical member tends to be female. Outside observers and inside informants almost invariably agree on this point. Female members tend to outnumber males in most American religious bodies, of course, but the proportion—running as high as two to one—remains higher in the Ramakrishna movement.

The 1936 *Census of Religious Bodies*, one of our only sources for pre–World War II membership figures, reported a total of 365 female versus 163 male members in that depression year.[33] Obviously, the greater role women in the movement have played as assistants and leaders simply reflects their prominence as followers. At the same time, the pattern does seem to be changing in recent decades, with a more even balance between the sexes. Presumably, as the Asian religions achieve greater American acceptance, the distribution should more closely approximate the composition of mainstream religious bodies.

Third, the typical member is an adult. There have always been some young people in the movement, but the number has been much smaller proportionately than in mainline churches. Though children's classes have occasionally been offered, most Vedanta classes and activities are directed toward adults. When I called the matter to the attention of a contemporary follower, he countered that Vedantists did not ignore their children's spiritual needs but preferred to provide religious instruction in their homes. In the relatively rare cases in which children were involved, the children appeared to be embracing Vedanta as easily as a child raised in a Christian or Jewish home accepts Christianity or Judaism.

Fourth, the typical member has been a "spiritual seeker." Almost without exception, the future member comes to Vedanta only after a period of intense and sometimes prolonged search among various alternatives. In the first decades of the century, an extraordinary number of followers revealed some connection with Theosophy, New Thought, Spiritualism, or Christian Science—and sometimes all four—before becoming Vedantists. After World War II, a significant number of devotees had previously explored "culture-religions": Freudian or Jungian psychology, existentialism, or Marxism. To put the point differently, few members have been born Vedantists.

Fifth, the typical member has been Protestant in background. There have also been numerous Vedantists with Roman Catholic, Orthodox, and Judaic backgrounds, particularly in the period before World War II; but the large majority of followers were raised as Protestants. Reacting against what they often describe as a narrow religious background, Protestant informants repeatedly confess that they find Vedanta's universal message especially liberating. Followers of all religious backgrounds had usually ceased to attend church or synagogue years before their discovery of the Ramakrishna movement.

Finally, a disproportionate number of members have been foreign-born. The very process of migration seems to have undermined Old World ties and encouraged greater openness to new religious choices. The foreign presence was particularly large in the Ramakrishna movement's first years, but after World War II a much smaller but still significant flow of new European immigrants appeared, somewhat reviving the role of foreign-born members. Then, passage of the Immigration and Nationality Act in 1965 finally opened the doors to Asian immigrants, which has led to large increases in Indian-born members. Eager to maintain their cultural and religious identities, Indian Americans have recently flocked to the Ramakrishna movement because of its ties to their mother land. As a nation largely populated by European immigrants, the foreign-born have, of course, played a large role throughout American history. At no point, however, have foreign-born members constituted a majority in the Vedanta societies.

A number of qualifications are in order. The most obvious is the reminder that we are considering a movement of very small size, which makes any generalization risky: In 1991 the total membership numbered no more than 2,500 individuals.[34] While followers from upper-middle-class backgrounds have certainly been prominent, significant numbers of Vedantists in each era have been average people from the lower-middle and lower class. Though many followers have completed college educations and gone on to advanced degrees, many others dropped out of school early. There are more women than men in the movement, to be sure, but the ratio has shifted over time toward greater balance; meanwhile, families are becoming more prominent, and an increasing number of children are raised as Vedantists. Though many converts have been "spiritual seekers," many have not. Protestants may have predominated in the movement, but there have always been significant numbers of members from other religious backgrounds. Finally, despite their high visibility, the foreign-born have never really dominated the Vedanta societies. In short, if we may speak of a typical American Vedantist, we also should recognize that there are many variations within the type.

What precisely have been the attractions of the Ramakrishna movement's teachings for American followers? What is it that has led individuals raised in a Judeo-Christian religious tradition to look toward a religion as seemingly alien as Hinduism? Fortunately, there is some prospect of answering these questions, thanks to a revealing series published in the 1950s in the journal *Vedanta and the West*. Entitled "What Vedanta Means to Me," the series presents the testimonials of a wide spectrum of American followers and sympathizers who attempt to explain what had originally attracted them to Hinduism and the Ramakrishna movement.[35] Clearly intended to suggest that Vedanta is for everyone, the series features contributors who include businesspeople and intellectuals, native-born Americans and recent immigrants, farmers and famous writers. To cite individual examples, there are statements from a Beverly Hills advertising executive, a society woman, a college professor, a medical researcher, an unhappy wife, a playwright, a recent high school graduate, and a Washington fruit-grower. The prominence of European-born contributors among the series participants presents some difficulty, but since practically all resided in the United States for a decade or more, with a number becoming naturalized citizens, I conclude that their responses may be grouped with those of Americans. Though the participants hardly constitute a cross-section of American society, followers of the Ramakrishna movement have never represented all sections of American society.

The disproportionate number of middle-class, college-educated, professional people among the contributors accurately reflects the disproportionate number of such people in the Ramakrishna movement.

Apparently, Vedanta's greatest attraction to Americans has been its perceived breadth and universalism. Series contributors repeated the universalist claim again and again. John van Druten, a well-known playwright, explained, "I think that this, to me, is the greatest significance of Vedanta: its all-embracingness, and its assertion that all religions are paths, some more and some less direct, to the same end." Cornelius Heyblom, a Dutch-born immigrant, emphasized what he saw as Vedanta's tolerance and ability to reconcile religious differences. "It breaks down all barriers of sectarianism and dogmas," he observed, and "establishes absolute freedom of thought."[36]

Contributors frequently contrasted Vedanta's universalism to the dogmatic sectarianism and narrow intolerance they found in Christianity, a contrast they used to justify their preference for Hinduism but that at the same time misrepresented both traditions. No participant seemed to recognize that while Christianity has often been seen as characterized by intolerance, it has also been known to preach universalism and love for one's neighbor; or again, that the Vedantic message presented in the West sharply diverged from the more sectarian Hinduism found throughout India. Indeed, the contributors ignored Hinduism's problems almost entirely.

Vedanta's practical, experiential approach is a second appeal frequently mentioned by contributors. In addition to a universalistic metaphysic that made it possible to reconcile religious differences, series writers claimed Vedanta provided an empirical perspective true to experience that anyone might test. Christopher Isherwood confessed that Vedanta "made me understand, for the first time, that a practical, working religion is experimental and empirical." It had taught him that "you are always on your own, finding things out for yourself in your individual way." Isherwood's friend Gerald Heard, another English expatriate writer, emphasized Vedanta's peculiar *combination* of universalism and an experiential methodology. According to Heard, it was the Indian philosophy's "particular blend" of empiricism and metaphysic—the "width of its cosmology" combined with the "immediate practicalness of its advices and practices"—that made it an ideal perspective for twentieth-century people who sought a "world view" consistent with "modern knowledge of the cosmos."[37]

In more familiar words, contributors repeatedly asserted that Vedanta's special appeal resided in its modern reaffirmation that one might still know God. According to Ruth Folling, the teachings not only provided a "chart of the spiritual realm," which had been discovered centuries earlier by the "explorers of the Upanishads," but offered the reassurance that "in our time" Ramakrishna and his disciples had "actually journeyed to that realm." Folling had already begun to investigate Hinduism while still in high school and subsequently entered the

Santa Barbara convent. She confessed that the "enthusiastic reports" of the founders of the Ramakrishna movement "made the idea of travelling there myself conceivable and desirable."[38]

For a number of contributors, Vedanta's special attraction was its psychological power. According to this view, the Indian philosophy provided an ideal therapeutic perspective, similar to psychoanalysis, for the removal of tensions, resolution of conflict, and reintegration of personality. Marianna Masin, a research associate at the Mt. Sinai Clinic in Los Angeles, clearly believed that Vedanta had saved her life. Born into a liberal Jewish family and driven from her home in Czechoslovakia by World War II, she declared that the war had left her and her family "with body, mind, and spirit broken." Vedanta had healed her psychic wounds, however, bringing "at last peace of mind and heart, integration, and a new understanding of life and its complexities." Joan Rayne, who spent several years as a monastic at the Hollywood convent, attributed Vedanta's success to its reliance on yoga: "I have seen far more drastic and desirable personality changes effected through the practice of yogic meditation," she observed, "than I have through psychoanalysis."[39] She spoke with some authority, having undergone psychiatric treatment for a year. Such testimonies are not unique to Vedanta, of course; they do suggest that acceptance of Hinduism led some followers to an abiding sense of personal security and happiness.

Curiously enough, acceptance of Vedanta seems to have frequently contributed toward reconciliation with Christianity—or at least to a more sympathetic view of Christian ideals. A surprising number of "What Vedanta Means to Me" contributors confessed that, after years of rejection and alienation, contact with Hinduism had renewed their respect for Christianity. Playwright John van Druten remarked that, following his embrace of Vedanta, he could "turn back" to Christianity, now finding "much more" than he had previously suspected. Ruth Folling discovered that accepting Vedanta did not mean "turning away" from Christianity but rather an "exciting discovery" of its virtues. She confessed that "reading the teachings of the Bible" "in the context of Vedanta" had made the biblical account more meaningful.[40] Suffering from a general "semantic block" against words associated with his Christian upbringing ("God, savior, comforter, soul, heaven, redemption, love, salvation, etc. etc."), Christopher Isherwood also arrived at a new understanding as a result of his study of Vedanta. He noted that Sanskrit had supplied a "brand new" vocabulary that allowed him to approach mysticism sympathetically and to recognize that his earlier hostility to Christianity was irrational.[41] Since he was an author, it seems fitting that the very words used in speaking of God proved crucial in Isherwood's return to religious belief.

Significantly, most of the articles in the "What Vedanta Means to Me" series emphasize rational appeals. John Yale perhaps expressed the attitude best: "What I have been saying is that Vedanta appealed to me because it is attractive rationally. It allows one to be cosmopolitan, permissive, broad. . . . Its tenets square with reason and with the discoveries of modern science."[42] In fact, a number of nonintellectual factors, and particularly the personality of the swami, also seem to have played a significant role in the attraction to Hinduism. In Christopher Isherwood's case, the guru-disciple relationship loomed much larger than Vedanta's philosophical profundities. Following a drawn-out attempt to explain Vedanta's appeal, the English-born writer abruptly paused, confiding that he had "written all this" and "yet I have really said nothing." He suggested that, in the end, religion hinged much less on ideas than on the influence of one personality upon another. He confessed: "I only know that, as far as I am concerned, the guru-disciple relationship is at the center of everything that religion means to me."[43] Interviews with a variety of devotees underscore the validity of Isherwood's statements. Devotion to a particular swami is the central fact in many followers' lives.

If that is so, then the individual who most influenced series contributors was Swami Prabhavananda, for many years the head of the Vedanta Society of Southern California and one of the Ramakrishna movement's most successful Western workers. A steady stream of troubled seekers came to him for spiritual counseling. Jane Molard, who was experiencing problems in her marriage, described the impression of her first interview. When she and her husband confessed their "considerable personal problems," she noted that the swami had not seemed to "find them at all upsetting or unusual," nor had he admonished them to "do this, or that" as everyone else had.[44] As his local fame spread, increasing numbers flocked into his classes and sought permission to become his students. Christopher Isherwood was not alone in regarding him as the most important figure in his life.

At times the close attachment of American devotees to particular swamis confronted the movement's authorities with a serious problem. On several occasions, following the death of their guru, American followers have actually refused to accept a new swami dispatched from India to carry on the work. Indeed, one informant characterized the general phenomenon as a "guru cult." Though a central attraction for American Vedantists, the relationship to a guru has carried the potential of becoming a disruptive influence.

The "What Vedanta Means to Me" series emphasizes that quite frequently the first step toward Vedanta hinged upon eliminating previous negative stereotypes about the Eastern religions. Though public attitudes have changed significantly since World War II, Americans have generally viewed the Asian religions with considerable skepticism. Claiming to speak for one of the world's great religions, the Ramakrishna movement has often found itself viewed as merely another "Oriental cult." Fruit-grower J. Crawford Lewis confessed that he originally looked into Vedanta, not as a possible path to enlightenment, but out of profound concern for his daughter who had joined a Vedanta society. "Yoga, to me, had always suggested sleight-of-hand tricks, self-inflicted torture, and idols with four arms and two heads," Lewis revealed. Apparently, the negative associations often persisted for an extended period. "It took a long while to find out and be able to appreciate Vedanta," John van Druten remarked. Vedanta connotated a "ritualistic Oriental religion, full of Sanscrit words," which suggested "a kind of exotic mumbo-jumbo."[45] Needless to say, the series articles reveal as much about each contributor as they do about the American appeal of Vedanta teachings.

Finally, the "What Vedanta Means to Me" series points to the crucial role played by printed materials and published books in the American discovery of Vedanta. A small movement with centers located in only a dozen or so American cities, the Ramakrishna movement has always maintained a low profile. Unlike most other Asian teachers who have opened work in the West, the swamis have rejected advertising and other forms of media publicity to get their message out. Instead, they have mainly relied on word-of-mouth and distribution of publications. The frequency with which Aldous Huxley's *The Perennial Philosophy* is mentioned suggests that, at least in the 1940s and 1950s, many seekers found their way to Vedanta originally through the English writer's anthology. Gerald Heard, Christopher Isherwood, and John Yale also published key works that allowed the movement to reach a wider audience.

Though the "What Vedanta Means to Me" series suggests the philosophical attractions of Vedantic teachings, the articles disclose little about the direct impact of the Ramakrishna movement on the inner lives of followers. The movement's swamis have offered Americans Hindu philosophy, but they have also introduced distinctive Hindu rituals and practices, which devotees may adopt. Several questions arise: What is the attitude of American followers toward image-worship and daily meditation? To what extent have rituals and ceremonies been modified to meet Western conditions? Much must be read between the lines because of the swamis' reticence about speaking publicly on such matters, but there is sufficient evidence to suggest that, for many Americans, Vedanta has been a matter of practice even more than of intellectual belief.

The "cult of Ramakrishna" obviously flourishes in all the Vedanta centers, though the degree of emphasis on devotional practices, image-worship, and special ceremonies seems to vary with the particular swami. Some members reject any suggestion of Ramakrishna's divinity, but most American followers now appear to worship Ramakrishna as an avatar and accept him as their spiritual master. Image-worship of Ramakrishna has become standard, with food, flowers, and other traditional offerings placed before his image daily or on special occasions. In addition to the large altar at each of the centers, many American devotees have also established small altars in their homes for private devotions. Most followers also prominently display portraits of Ramakrishna, Sarada Devi, and Vivekananda in their quarters.

Though clearly regarded as a matter not to be discussed publicly, several American followers have testified to deep religious experiences involving Ramakrishna, suggesting the role of devotionalism in their lives. The report of Swami Paramananda's close disciple Laura Glenn will be quoted at length because of the rarity of such published testimonies. Her mystical encounter with Ramakrishna occurred on the anniversary of the Bengali saint's birth, which is always regarded as an especially auspicious day by members of the movement. According to Glenn, devotees had been fasting, meditating, and listening to the reading of sacred texts throughout the day. She proceeds:

> The atmosphere was charged with fervour. The last hour of prayer had come. We had been told that whatever we asked for in this culminating moment of the day would be granted. . . . No desire entered my thought, or rather only one,—to see Sri Ramakrishna once again. The stillness in the room was breathless. Something impelled me to open my eyes and there on the platform amid the masses of flowers, which had been brought in as offering, stood the living Presence. . . . It was clothed in a single long white garment and both body and robe were so shining, so transparent that I could discern through them the faint outline of the flowers behind. . . . The figure stood there for a few seconds with hands outstretched in blessing, then was gone. I looked about. All eyes were closed. Had no other seen?

In the same published account, the American woman describes an even more dramatic encounter on another occasion, which would permanently change her life:

> I took my place before the altar, went through my exercises, and was just beginning my meditation when Sri Ramakrishna stood before me—not the Ramakrishna of Boston or of the birthday, but a colossal figure made of pure light, with glistening garments. Over-awed, I fell on my face before it, crept slowly nearer and laid my forehead on the feet. I knew no more. When I returned to normal consciousness, I found I had been lying in front of the altar for more than an hour. What transpired in that hour I shall never know; but it left me with a new outlook on life, a new vision in my heart.[46]

Paralleling the practices of Western mystics, Glenn pursued a course of "intensive spiritual training" prior to her visions, including a carefully restricted diet, fixed hours for meditation practice, and a demanding regimen of breathing exercises. Though published descriptions of extraordinary encounters such as Laura Glenn's are rare, a number of followers hint at similar experiences.

An informal questionnaire circulated among monastics at the Vedanta Society of South California revealed that all regularly practice meditation, which usually includes use of a rosary and repetition of a mantra provided by the swami.

Most monastic devotees at the Los Angeles center also recite Vedic chants, sing Sanskrit hymns, participate in daily worship (*puja*), and engage in scriptural study. With less time and opportunity to follow a full schedule, lay Vedantists have to restrict their devotional practices largely to meditation and private devotions, participating in image-worship and other forms of devotionalism at the temple only on special occasions.

Beyond the cult of Ramakrishna, the public worship of Sarada Devi as the Holy Mother has emerged among American followers since the 1940s. Rarely mentioned in the movement's first decades, her public recognition in the West may be dated to 1953–1954 when special celebrations in honor of her birth centenary were held at all the American centers.[47] Writing in 1954, Swami Nikhilananda remarked that many American women had begun to "contemplate the Holy Mother as their spiritual ideal"; and he noted that her photograph adorned the altars of numerous American families. In the same year a devotee at the Hollywood center remarked that Sarada Devi was "worshipped daily" and that the number of followers who viewed her "as Mother" had steadily grown.[48]

Until recent years American followers undoubtedly found it difficult to accept the idea of Sarada Devi's divinity. As Joan Rayne pointed out in 1954, Westerners have traditionally viewed the deity either as a male or as a principle. Consequently, the statement that "God, the Divine Mother" had "incarnated Herself as Sri Sarada Devi" was bound to strike the average Westerner as somewhat "fantastic."[49] Rayne confessed that, in the beginning at least, Sarada Devi had struck her as parochial and insignificant compared to Ramakrishna. (Two years in India transformed her outlook.) Today, swamis encourage devotees to view Ramakrishna's wife as the ideal woman, whose attributes of piety, modesty, and devotion deserve wide acceptance. Most contemporary feminists, of course, argue that acceptance of such virtues will not liberate but continue to enslave women.[50]

For a small but significant handful of American devotees, contact with Vedanta has led to lifetime commitments as monks and nuns. The procedures and training for such a choice have been standardized only in recent decades. Male renunciates (*brahmacharis*) in India must spend at least two years at the monastic training center at Belur; female renunciates (*brahmacharinis*) receive their training at the Sri Sarada Math in Dakshineswar. The training divides into two stages: *brahmacharya*, extending over five years, during which the novice fulfills first vows; and *sannyas*, or final vows, which the renunciate formally embraces after four additional years. Upon successful completion of the training, the *brahmachari* assumes the title of a "swami," while the *brahmacharini* becomes a "pravrajika"—which may be translated as "woman ascetic." Symbolizing commitment to a life of renunciation, "ananda" ("bliss") is added to the last part of the male's name and "prana" ("whose life is in") to the woman's name.[51]

Though closely following the Indian model, Western monastic requirements vary somewhat from their prototype. Whereas Indians normally advance from initiation through *sannyas* in nine years, American monastics must spend at least two years longer (one year of preprobation, five years of probation, and five years as a *brahmacharya*). In India the president and two vice-presidents of the Ramakrishna Math alone may initiate new monastics, while in the United States any Vedanta society head may conduct initiations. Training in India tends to be more standardized than in America. In the absence of a formal training center, in America the disciplines followed are largely left up to the individual swami. American monastics are encouraged to spend time in India, but this is not required.[52]

Age restrictions have presented a special problem for American monastics. Though Swami Vivekananda granted vows to middle-aged and even elderly aspirants during his years in the West, strict age limits are now enforced throughout the Ramakrishna movement. With occasional exceptions, a postulant must be at least seventeen and no older than thirty years of age at the time of acceptance into the monastic program. Apparently, the difference in age between Indian and American monastics has been marked, with Indian probationers averaging as much as "ten years younger" than Westerners, according to John Yale. In India individuals move more or less directly into the order from high school or college. Most Westerners, however, enter the Ramakrishna movement considerably later and as adults, with the result that the thirty-year restriction has prevented a number of interested American students from pursuing monastic vows. According to Yale, the movement's leadership has come to view the more advanced ages of Westerners as a serious impediment, since "too much contact with the world" tends to promote "appetites and memories hard to efface later."[53]

Today, most American monastics are affiliated with one of three centers: the Vedanta Society of Northern California in San Francisco; the Vedanta Society of Southern California, headquartered in Hollywood; or the Vivekananda Vedanta Society in Chicago. All three maintain rural retreats (ashramas) where monastics can pursue spiritual life in relative isolation from the distractions of the outside world. Though there are small variations in their rules, the regimen followed at the three centers is much the same. While unusual austerities are discouraged, all monastics are expected to remain celibate and to practice renunciation. Daily sustenance at the ashramas maintained by the three centers is simple but sufficient. The rooms of the monastics seem pleasantly furnished, and the food appears varied and plentiful. The daily schedule at the Ramakrishna Monastery in Trabuco, California, is fairly typical, emphasizing a balance between private meditation, group worship, work, and satisfaction of daily needs. Rising at 6 A.M., the monks observe morning and midday meditations, which punctuate a workday extending from 8:15 to 11:30 A.M. and 3:00 to 6:00 P.M. (5:30 P.M. in winter). Simple meals are served three times a day, with a rest period each afternoon between 2:00 and 3:00 P.M. A Vespers service and spiritual reading close the day, with retirement at 10:00 P.M.[54]

There is some doubt whether the Ramakrishna movement will be able to continue its commitments in future years. The ashramas provide the opportunity for a more intense spiritual life for a tiny minority of followers, but they also deplete resources that might be used more effectively elsewhere. Though all monastics live frugally, the overhead required to support even a small number of residents places heavy financial pressure on the local society. So far, the small number of Americans who have chosen a monastic life has not overwhelmed the available resources; however, if the number increased even slightly, this could create major economic problems for the movement.

In conclusion, it seems clear that the Ramakrishna movement has sufficiently adapted its message to Western conditions to transplant a modern version of Hinduism to American shores successfully. Its message has attracted middle- and upper-class Americans who have broken away from more conventional religious commitments. Though extremely small in total membership, the movement has certainly attracted followers whose educational and vocational levels rank well above the norm for comparable movements. The basis of the Ramakrishna movement's appeal has been its combination of a universal philosophic message with practical methods of pursuing spiritual growth under the guidance of a swami.

6 | The Movement since the 1920s

DESPITE ITS MODEST success in our own time, at the end of the 1920s the Ramakrishna movement's American work seemed stagnant. After nearly four decades of strenuous effort, the only secure Vedanta societies were in New York City, San Francisco, Boston, and Los Angeles. The original sensation created by Asian religious teachers at the Parliament of Religions had clearly worn off. And yet a period of rapid expansion that would mark the two decades after 1930 as one of the most dynamic periods in the movement's history was beginning. Significantly, much of this growth occurred before the 1960s, when Eastern spirituality and Asian religious movements achieved unprecedented attention. Though Vedanta societies occasionally attracted members of the counterculture, they never enjoyed the close ties to youth that one finds in other Asian groups that emerged during this period, such as the Hare Krishnas. To members of the counterculture, the Ramakrishna movement always seemed old-fashioned.

Some indication of the Ramakrishna movement's remarkable turnaround in the 1930s may be had by comparing membership figures in the 1936 *Census of Religious Bodies* with the number of members reported in earlier censuses in 1906, 1916, and 1926. Tabulated by decade, the results are as follows:

	1906	1916	1926	1936
Number of Churches	4	3	3	10
Number of Members	340	190	200	628
Percent of Increase	—	-44.1	5.3	214.0[1]

In short, comparison of the various censuses reveals that the membership of American Vedanta societies more than tripled between 1926 and 1936 (200 to 628), rebounding from a severe decline in the previous decade (340 to 190). The membership has continued to increase at a steady rate since the 1930s, as indicated in the *Yearbook of American and Canadian Churches*, which reported growth to 856 members in the 1951 edition and 1,200 members in the 1956 edition. In 1991 the *Yearbook* lists the membership at 2,500.[2]

Though these totals must be judged miniscule by comparison with other religious bodies, the numbers do not fairly represent the Ramakrishna movement's probable influence. In fact, few other religious bodies of such Lilliputian size have equaled the movement's impact or historical significance. Membership has been small, but the outward reach of the movement has been fairly wide. Actual attendance at Vedanta society functions has always been much larger than reported membership figures, since many people who attend the lectures and classes do not join the societies. Indeed, the movement's outreach can only be adequately judged by including its extensive published literature, the many outside lectures presented annually by the swamis, the repeated visits of high school and college classes to Vedanta temples, and the frequent participation of Ramakrishna swamis as spokespersons for Hinduism at national and international meetings.

Despite a record of impressive growth during the 1930s and 1940s, the movement stabilized in the 1950s and, aside from a second spurt in membership during the 1970s and 1980s, has remained largely unchanged for decades. (This hardly seems surprising in view of the Indian body's historic conservatism and long domination by elder leaders.) The dominant trend since World War II has been cautious expansion along previous lines with membership growth largely confined to existing societies. This seems the more remarkable in view of the fact that there was a major infusion of Indian-born members during the 1970s and 1980s as a result of the increased Asian immigration following the passage of the Immigration and Nationality Act of 1965. Rather than founding new centers, facilities have been expanded at previously established societies; or, in the cases of the more dynamic centers (San Francisco, Los Angeles, and Chicago), branch centers have been established in neighboring areas. Though new swamis appear from India from time to time, they almost always assume duties as assistants in existing societies rather than attempt to inaugurate new Vedanta societies. In practically every case the head swamis now in charge of the Vedanta centers have been in place since the 1960s and 1970s. Most would have to be classified as elderly men.

The pages that follow will offer brief sketches of the recent histories of each of the American Vedanta societies and will conclude with a more detailed description of life at one center, which will perhaps suggest how Vedanta societies function in modern America. In tracing the recent history of individual Vedanta societies, it seems appropriate to organize the discussion by regions of activity, beginning with the Northeast and proceeding to the Middle West and Pacific Coast. Hence, our survey commences with the Ramakrishna movement's work in New York City, Providence, and Boston.

Following Swami Abhedananda's split with his supporters, Swami Bodhananda assumed leadership of the New York Vedanta Society in 1912, a charge he would quietly oversee for the next four decades. Bodhananda managed to keep the New York society alive, but just barely. An Indian correspondent who interviewed him during a 1923 visit to India described the swami as a "pure, simple and sincere old-type Indian monk."[3] The most important event in his long tenure at New York was the acquisition of a permanent home in 1921, in which the society has ever since been housed. A devoted follower, Mary Morton, daughter of Levi P. Morton (the vice-president of the United States under Benjamin Harrison), donated the property to the Ramakrishna movement. While not remembered for bold initiatives, Bodhananda tended to his duties conscientiously, conducting classes, presenting lectures, periodically addressing outside groups, and, for a few years (1931–1933), editing the *Vedanta Darpana*, which served as the New York Vedanta Society's official organ. He also produced a book entitled *Lectures on the Vedanta Philosophy*, which offered a very traditional presentation of Vedanta based on lectures he had delivered in 1924–1925. Transported by a strange fate to one of the world's most bustling cities, Swami Bodhananda worked unspectacularly until his death in 1950 at nearly eighty years of age.[4]

Swami Pavitrananda, who succeeded Bodhananda, was better equipped to carry on the Vedanta work in New York. Before coming to the United States, he had served in India as president of the Advaita Ashrama for more than a decade and had edited the Ramakrishna movement's leading English-language journal, the *Prabuddha Bharata*. He led the New York Vedanta Society for a quarter of a century. Author of such books as *Common Sense about Yoga* (1946) and *Modern Man in Search of a Soul* (1947), the swami's major strength was his proficiency as a writer. Despite titles suggesting modern presentations adjusted to a Western audience, both works present a fairly traditional interpretation of Hindu philosophy. Upon Pavitrananda's death in 1977, Swami Tathagatananda became the New York Vedanta Society's new head, and he has continued in that position down to the present. The large concentration of Indian-born professionals in the New York area has led to an increasing prominence of Asian Indians in the congregation.[5]

In view of its huge population, New York easily justified more than one Vedanta society, an addition made in 1933 with the founding of the Ramakrishna-Vivekananda Center by Swami Nikhilananda. The swami's background suggested his energy. As a young man, he very nearly became an Indian revolutionary rather than a holy man, spending two years in prison because of his association with an anti-British revolutionary group. In the end, however, he turned from revolution to religion, working in the publications department at the Advaita Ashrama for several years before coming to the United States in 1931.[6]

During Nikhilananda's forty-year tenure, the Ramakrishna-Vivekananda Center emerged as one of the movement's most dynamic Western centers. Demonstrating effectiveness as a speaker and explicator of Hinduism, the swami quickly became a familiar figure on the New York intellectual scene, regularly accepting invitations to address such disparate groups as the Indian Academy of America, Roerich Society, Hindustan Association, Fellowship of Faiths, All Soul's Unitarian Church, and St. Paul's Chapel at Columbia University. He also participated in several meetings of the East-West Philosophers' Conference, organized by Charles A. Moore at the University of Hawaii, which brought together many of the world's best-known Eastern and Western philosophers.[7] The swami not only reached out to Westerners but also cultivated close ties with the Asian Indian community in the New York metropolitan area at a time when Indian nationals played almost no role in the Vedanta societies. In the late 1930s he organized an Indo-American Association to sponsor lectures by visiting Indian scholars, and after World War II he offered the facilities and resources of the Ramakrishna-Vivekananda Center as a home base for visiting Indian students, professors, and government officials.

As head of the Ramakrishna-Vivekananda Center, one of Nikhilananda's major undertakings was the establishment of a Vedanta retreat at Thousand Island Park, the site in upstate New York where Vivekananda had briefly lived and conducted classes during his first trip to the United States. Now known as "Vivekananda Cottage," the house in which Vivekananda stayed was restored as nearly as possible to its original condition. The site has become a popular summer retreat for American devotees and, interestingly, is increasingly viewed as a place of pilgrimage as well. In fact, the practice of making pilgrimages to sacred shrines has been a feature of Hinduism in India for thousands of years; now under Nikhilananda, American Hinduism rapidly embraced the same practice in the United States.

Perhaps in part because of his location in America's most dynamic city, in part because of his impressive qualifications, Nikhilananda attracted a number of prominent American followers into the Ramakrishna movement's work. These included such well-known people as Margaret Wilson, President Woodrow Wilson's eldest daughter, who served as the swami's editorial assistant and subsequently moved to India, where she joined the ashrama of Aurobindo Ghose; Joseph Campbell, the eminent authority on comparative mythology, who at one point served as president of the Ramakrishna-Vivekananda Center; Malvina Hoffman, an internationally acclaimed sculptor, whose busts of Vivekananda now grace the grounds of several American Vedanta societies; and poet John Moffitt, who served as Nikhilananda's editorial assistant for many years and eventually became a swami himself.

Nikhilananda was one of the most talented Ramakrishna monks to come to America, and no swami has made a larger literary contribution or equaled his scholarship. To mention only a few works, his long list of publications includes the most reliable English translation of the *Gospel of Sri Ramakrishna*, the best short life of Swami Vivekananda, and one of the most widely used introductions to Indian religion, *Hinduism: Its Meaning for the Liberation of the Spirit*, published in the World Perspective Series. (Other series contributors included Jacques Maritain, Sarvepalli Radhakrishnan, Lewis Mumford, Erich Fromm, Paul Tillich, D. T. Suzuki, and Gunnar Myrdal.) Nikhilananda's most scholarly production was a two-volume edition of the Upanishads, which has been praised as one of the most dependable English translations of that ancient classic. Following his death in 1973, Nikhilananda was succeeded by Swami Adishwarananda, who continues to direct the Ramakrishna-Vivekananda Center today. The society continues a quiet work in a city in constant turmoil.

At the moment of Swami Paramananda's sudden death in 1940, the Boston Vedanta Society clearly ranked as one of the Ramakrishna movement's most successful and securely established American centers. In continuous operation since its founding in 1907, no one could have anticipated that, within a year of the swami's death, it would break away to become an independent Vedanta organization. The Indian leadership responded to the crisis by designating Swami Akhilananda, who had once served as Paramananda's assistant, to organize a new society to carry on the Ramakrishna movement's work in Boston. Located just across from the Massachusetts Institute of Technology, the Ramakrishna Vedanta Society opened within the year.[8] Akhilananda, who was already the leader of the nearby Vedanta Society of Providence, which he had founded in 1928, henceforth divided his time between Boston and Providence. In the 1950s he added the Sarada Ashrama, thirty miles south of Boston, providing a spiritual retreat for both the Providence and Boston congregations.[9]

Like Swami Nikhilananda, Akhilananda enjoyed unusually close contacts with mainstream leaders of the nearby intellectual and religious community, an indication of the growing public acceptance of the Ramakrishna movement in the United States. Among other individuals, he established friendships with Edgar S. Brightman, Pitrim Sorokin, Gordon Allport, Harlow Shapley, Walter Houston Clark, and F. S. S. Northrop—all figures of national prominence in their respective fields. They in turn lauded the swami's personal warmth, openness to new ideas, and vigorous intellectuality.[10] Akhilananda attracted the attention of the Christian community by his warm appreciation of Jesus and Christianity, disclosed in his 1949 book *Hindu View of Christ*. Paul E. Johnson, a professor in psychology of religion at the Boston University School of Theology, commented that if "obviously a devout Hindu," Akhilananda was also "one of the best Christians I have known."[11] Elected to membership in the Minister's Union of Rhode Island and the Rhode Island Council of Churches, the swami frequently spoke at mainstream Christian churches. Akhilananda also excited the interest of psychologists and mental health workers by his books *Hindu Psychology* (1946) and *Mental Health and Hindu Psychology* (1951), both of which outlined the important contributions Hindu conceptions could add to Western understanding. Both books were widely reviewed in psychological journals. Then, following Akhilananda's death in 1962, Swami Sarvagatananda assumed direction of the Boston and Providence centers. Like Akhilananda in the years before, Sarvagatananda rotates back and forth between the Boston and Providence centers on a continuous schedule, regularly delivering the Sunday morning lecture at the Boston society and the Sunday evening lecture at the Providence center. Children's classes are conducted during the summer at a newly opened retreat in Marshfield, Massachusetts.[12]

Though Swami Vivekananda had sought to propagate the seeds of Vedanta in the Middle West as early as the 1890s, the Ramakrishna movement was slow to establish itself in America's heartland. There are undoubtedly several possible explanations for this, including the more rural, more homogeneous, less cosmopolitan population in much of the Middle West; the fact remains that the only two Ramakrishna movement successes in the entire region have been in Chicago and St. Louis.

Since Vivekananda achieved his earliest recognition and fame there during the Parliament of Religions, the Ramakrishna movement has always viewed Chicago as a special place. Several swamis lectured in the city in the decades following Vivekananda's death, but it was not until 1930 that Swami Jnaneshwarananda finally succeeded in establishing a permanent Vedanta society. Apparently, the timing was right, as Jnaneshwarananda did well almost from the outset. In the first six months, average attendance increased from sixty to ninety at Sunday morning services and from fifty to seventy at the evening classes. Only six years after its founding, the United States government's *Census of Religious Bodies* reported the Vedanta society's total membership as 105 people, establishing Chicago as one of the movement's largest centers outside India.[13]

One of Swami Jnaneshwarananda's chief distinctions was his role in introducing music into Ramakrishna society services. Though Vedanta centers now routinely include both choral and instrumental pieces in their services, music plays little or no role in traditional Hindu worship. Since most religious music available in the West carried a Christian message, distinctive Hindu compositions had to be created. An adept musician himself, Jnaneshwarananda personally instructed classes in the playing of traditional Asian instruments, and he regularly scheduled Indian concerts at the center. But Jnaneshwarananda suddenly collapsed and died of a heart attack in 1937 at forty-four years of age.[14]

A year later, Swami Vishwananda assumed leadership of the society, carrying on a quiet work until his own death in 1965. During his thirty-year stewardship, the center changed its name to the Vivekananda Vedanta Society, and a permanent home was acquired in 1955; but measured by reports in the journals, little else worth noting seems to have transpired. However, the Chicago society has again emerged since 1965 as one of the movement's most dynamic Western centers under the energetic leadership of Swami Bhashyananda. Bhashyananda's most ambitious initiative was the founding of the Vivekananda Monastery and Retreat, quartered in a sprawling collection of buildings in rural Michigan, which today offers the only American residential facility for Ramakrishna monastics outside California. Eager to spread Vedanta's message to a wider audience, in the early 1980s Bhashyananda dispatched American-born swamis to Atlanta, Houston, and West Palm Beach. Branch centers flourished until 1987 when the movement's Indian leadership ordered that the new societies be suspended until further notice. Like Swami Nikhilananda, Bhashyananda has made special efforts to reach the rapidly increasing Indian population in the area to the extent that Asian Indians now make up a majority of the Chicago society's members. Successive strokes have nearly incapacitated the swami, leaving much of the society's daily work in the hands of his associate, Swami Chidananda, who came from India in 1991.[15]

The Vedanta Society of St. Louis stands out as the only other successful Ramakrishna center in the Midwest. Perhaps because swamis regularly crisscrossed the area on their frequent journeys back and forth between the Atlantic and Pacific coasts, the city early attracted interest as a possible site for a new center. Splitting his energies between Boston and Los Angeles, Swami Paramananda had begun stopping over in St. Louis for lectures before World War I; however, he never left enough time to create a permanent center. Swami Prabhavananda established a short-lived society in 1928—which went so far as to adopt bylaws and elect officers—but it quickly lapsed.

Swami Satprakashananda finally established a permanent Vedanta society in St. Louis in 1938, which he directed for the next forty years. A graduate of Calcutta University, before coming to the United States Satprakashananda had been an associate editor of *Prabuddha Bharata* and directed the Ramakrishna Mission Center in New Delhi for six years. He continued his interest in writing, publishing, among other works, *Ethics and Religion* and *The Goal and the Way: The Vedantic Approach to Life's Problems*, in which he sought to adapt Vedanta's message to appeal to Western concerns.[16] Swami Chetanananda assumed leadership of the society in 1979 following Satprakashananda's death and continues in that position down to the present. One of the American movement's most scholarly swamis, he is the author of several books, including *They Lived with God: Life Stories of Some Devotees of Sri Ramakrishna*, published in 1989. An informant recently described the St. Louis Society as small but "thriving."[17]

If St. Louis has thrived, the region where the Ramakrishna movement has enjoyed greatest success has been the Pacific rim and, more particularly, the state of California. Indeed, no state has offered more fertile ground for Vedanta or Asian religious movements generally.

Things, however, were not always thus. The shaky first decades of Ramakrishna work in San Francisco gave little evidence to support hope of future success. Originally founded by Swami Vivekananda in 1900 and carried on by Swami Trigunatita, the San Francisco Vedanta Society seemed to stagnate under

Swami Prakashananda, who assumed leadership of the society following Trigunatita's death. Prakashananda had come to the United States in 1906 to serve as
Trigunatita's assistant. He briefly headed a second San Francisco center known
as the Pacific Vedanta Center before succeeding Trigunatita in 1915.[18] Despite
an upbeat 1920 report that the San Francisco society's membership was the
"largest in many years," retrenchment was the dominant motif during Prakashananda's tenure: over the course of a few years, the Pacific Vedanta Center
closed; the society's journal, *Voice of Freedom*, suspended publication; and the
Concord colony, which had been flourishing at the time of Trigunatita's death,
was abandoned.[19]

In the interim after Prakashananda's death in 1926, one swami followed another at the San Francisco Vedanta Society, but for various reasons none remained more than a few years. Swami Madhavananda, who briefly headed the
society from 1927 to 1929, returned to India and eventually became general
secretary of the Order; Swami Dayananda, who presided from 1929 to 1931,
resigned his duties because of illness; illness also forced the retirement of Swami
Vividishananda, who shouldered the work from 1931 to 1932.[20] It hardly seems
surprising that the San Francisco work seemed to stall.

The man who turned the work around—who within a few years transformed the San Francisco Vedanta Society into one of the Ramakrishna's most
vital Western centers—was Swami Ashokananda. The swami appeared in 1932,
with a background resembling that of most monks dispatched to America. A
graduate of the University of Calcutta, he had spent six years working in the
publication department of the Ramakrishna Math in Madras, and he had subsequently served several years as editor of *Prabuddha Bharata*.

Immediately after Swami Ashokananda's arrival, attendance at lectures and
classes began to rise, on occasion running over 100 people. Unlike his contemporary coworkers Swamis Paramananda and Nikhilananda, Ashokananda apparently chose to focus all of his energies within the society, and there are few reports in the movement's journals of outside lectures. In the thirty-seven years he
directed the work, the San Francisco Vedanta Society emerged as one of the
movement's largest and most dynamic centers. Two new ashramas were added to
the retreat already existing at Shanti Ashrama; monasteries were opened at
Olema and in San Francisco; and when the main Hindu Temple could no longer
handle the expanding audience that crowded the society's services, a larger temple was erected. Meanwhile, branch centers were inaugurated in Sacramento and
Berkeley.[21]

Ultimately, the San Francisco Vedanta Society's operations have had to be
divided in order to meet the growing demands of the work. Following Ashokananda's death in 1969, the centers at San Francisco, Berkeley, and Sacramento
were separated. The parent body, now known as the Vedanta Society of Northern California, was originally assigned to Swami Shantaswarupananda and is

now directed by Swami Prabuddhananda. It remains one of the movement's most successful centers. Located strategically near the campus of the University of California, the Vedanta Society at Berkeley has had a succession of leaders. Swami Swahananda, who took up his duties in 1970, served as the body's first head following separation from the San Francisco center; next came Swami Swananda, who assumed the leadership role in 1976, after Swahananda was transferred to head up the Hollywood center; and, more recently, Swami Aparananda has led the society, taking over in 1985 after Swananda returned to India. Despite an excellent location, the Berkeley society has not attracted the support achieved by other societies and today remains one of the American movement's smallest centers. The Vedanta Society at Sacramento has been more successful, led by Swami Shraddhananda throughout its existence. The swami began to conduct classes in Sacramento shortly after his arrival in northern California in 1957 and has been the Sacramento society's official head since a permanent center was opened in 1970. He has recently recovered from a series of health problems.[22]

Though a slight exaggeration, one might almost say that Ashokananda and his coworker Swami Prabhavananda, who for many years directed Ramakrishna work in southern California, singlehandedly created the Vedanta movement in California. At almost the same moment that Swami Ashokananda inaugurated work in San Francisco, Swami Prabhavananda opened lectures to the south in Los Angeles. In time, the Vedanta Society of Southern California would challenge the Vedanta Society of Northern California as the West Coast's most dynamic center. Ramakrishna officials in India allowed both swamis an independence of action that no subsequent swami has enjoyed.

Recognition that the Los Angeles area offered a promising field for Vedanta may, of course, be traced all the way back to Swami Vivekananda. Several subsequent swamis lectured in the area in the first decades of the century, with Swami Paramananda finally capitalizing on the interest generated to found the Ananda Ashrama in 1923. As head of the Vedanta society in Portland, Swami Prabhavananda also began to focus on the area in 1928, to culminate in the establishment of a Vedanta center in Hollywood. Apparently, the area's attractions generated feelings of jealousy and resentment among some Vedantists. According to recent biographer Sara Ann Levinsky, Swami Paramananda's followers viewed Prabhavananda's initiation of work in Hollywood as territorial invasion. Levinsky claims that, in turn, Prabhavananda disapproved of Paramananda's methods and that, as a result of these feelings, relations between the two swamis "would always be touchy."[23]

The very idea of a Vedanta society in the movie capital of America seems incongruous. In reality, the location of the new society was fortuitous, the result of an elderly woman's memory of lectures which she had heard Vivekananda deliver many years earlier. Grateful for Vedanta's message, she decided to offer her home and modest savings to Prabhavananda for a center. The resulting Hollywood society was tucked away on a quiet street and at first attracted little attention. An early follower reported that Prabhavananda often found himself addressing a "handful" of people scattered among "empty seats," with many of the visitors qualifying not as serious students of Vedanta but as "mystery-mongers" and "metaphysical shoppers."[24] The work took off in the later 1930s, however, and over the next decade a large auditorium was added for Sunday services, the Sarada Convent for women was opened near Santa Barbara, and a Ramakrishna monastery was inaugurated at Trabuco, sixty miles south of Los Angeles. The association of famous writers Gerald Heard, Aldous Huxley, and Christopher Isherwood with the society in the early 1940s attracted national and international attention.

Swami Prabhavananda's success as a translator and popularizer made the work of the Vedanta Society of Southern California known throughout the country. During his life, his books sold hundreds of thousands of copies. Among the most popular was his readable translation of the Upanishads, which he prepared in association with Frederick Manchester, and a translation of the Bhagavad Gita, a product of his collaboration with Christopher Isherwood. The Gita sold 227,000 copies in the first two years after its publication in a paperback edition.[25] Indeed, today practically every bibliography on Hinduism lists one or more of Prabhavananda's works as recommended reading.

Since the swami's death in 1976, the Vedanta Society of Southern California has been directed by Swami Swahananda, who has perpetuated the society's reputation as a leader of Vedanta in America. In 1977 a new Vedanta center was opened in San Diego and a permanent home was purchased in 1983. American-born Swami Atmarupananda oversees the San Diego congregation, but the society remains closely tied to the Hollywood center. Swami Swahananda makes regular monthly visits to the San Diego, Santa Barbara, and Trabuco centers. In truth, the separate units represent one work.[26]

Though California attracted greatest attention, during the 1920s Ramakrishna swamis also inaugurated Vedanta work in the Pacific Northwest, an effort that would lead to permanent societies in Portland and Seattle. Swamis had occasionally stopped off in Portland to lecture, but the area was practically untouched when Swami Prabhavananda opened a Vedanta society there in 1925. After shifting his major concern to the Hollywood center, Prabhavananda turned direction of the Portland work over to Swami Vividishananda. Shortly afterward, the center suspended operations due to rising financial problems and Vividishananda's poor health; but Swami Devatmananda revived it in 1932 and the society has flourished ever since.[27] Under Devatmananda, a permanent home was acquired and the Sri Ramakrishna Ashrama opened twenty miles outside Portland. Demonstrating a flair for innovative leadership, Devatmananda established the Vedanta Society Women's League to sponsor study groups and to provide assistance to needy persons. He also staged dramatic performances acted by society members. Swami Aseshananda assumed direction of the Portland Vedanta Society in 1955, and he continues to direct the center today more than thirty-five years later. The extent to which the leadership of the Vedanta societies has remained almost unchanged over decades is surely one of the movement's distinguishing characteristics. In his nineties, Aseshananda is venerated in the movement as one of the last living disciples of Sarada Devi, the Holy Mother.[28]

The Vedanta Society of Western Washington provides the Ramakrishna movement with a second base of operations in the Northwest. The center was originally established in 1938 in Seattle by Swami Vividishananda, who had already spent a decade in Vedanta work in San Francisco, Portland, Washington, D.C., and Denver. As the society matured, it acquired a permanent home and added a 200-acre retreat overlooking the Columbia River. Swami Bhaskarananda assumed leadership of the Washington center in 1980 following Vividishananda's death and has continued as its head down to the present. Bhaskarananda has been instrumental in establishing the Vedanta Society of Western British Columbia in Vancouver, Canada, which he visits on a regular basis. Indian-born devotees tend to dominate both the Seattle and Vancouver centers.[29] This pattern is not wholly typical, for the contemporary role of Asian Indians in the Vedanta societies varies a good deal. For example, there are very few Indian-born members in the St. Louis and Sacramento centers, while Indians now tend to dominate the Chicago, New York, and Seattle centers.

Though Ramakrishna swamis have succeeded in establishing Vedanta centers in more than a dozen American cities, it would be a serious mistake to assume that success always crowned the movement's efforts. History seems to be forever recording victories and ignoring defeats, despite the fact that the failures often reveal more than the successes. In fact, the Ramakrishna movement suffered several notable failures. If nothing else, the frequency of failure underscores the obstacles Asian spiritual movements have had to overcome in putting down roots in the United States.

Philadelphia has represented one major disappointment for the movement. Swami Raghananda attempted to inaugurate a work in Philadelphia in 1924, at first commuting daily from New York, where he was an assistant to Swami Bodhananda. Apparently, he found enough encouragement to justify renting a room in the Pennsylvania city, so that he might devote full time to the venture. But three years of hard effort only produced audiences that varied from twenty to forty people, and membership in the Philadelphia society never exceeded a dozen. Hence, the swami began to schedule extra meetings and to invite inquirers to his room to meet with him directly. Nothing seemed to work, however, so he finally retreated to India in 1927, citing ill health as the reason for his return. Raghavananda's impressive credentials suggest that his failure had little to do with his intellectual qualifications, although other personality characteristics are hard to know. At Calcutta Presidency College, he had passed his M.A. and law examinations with distinction, and he had been a successful editor of *Prabuddha Bharata* before coming to the United States.

Later initiatives were no more successful in establishing a Philadelphia society. Swami Akhilananda made several lecture trips to the city in 1937 but soon abandoned the effort; and Swami Yatishwarananda renewed the campaign in 1942, but once again the ending was the same.[30]

The most spectacular Ramakrishna movement failure, however, has been at Washington, D.C., where repeated attempts have been made going back as far as the turn of the century. Swami Abhedananda probed the area first in 1898, followed a decade later by Swami Paramananda, who managed to create a center that survived several years under the direction of his lieutenant, Sister Devamata. Buoyed by the warm reception of his lectures, Swami Akhilananda mounted still a third effort in 1930. He remained long enough to rent quarters for a center, then summoned Swami Vividishananda from San Francisco to take charge. Over the next four years, Vividishananda tried everything—including illustrated lectures, radio talks, and special programs—but once again the effort collapsed. Unwilling to accept defeat, Akhilananda tried still one more time in 1936, but again he failed.[31] These failures seem all the more surprising in view of Akhilananda's subsequent career as a highly successful leader at the Providence and Boston centers. There is still no Vedanta society in the nation's capital.

Denver offers a final example of the frustrations the Ramakrishna movement has frequently confronted in the United States. Swami Vividishananda, who failed at Washington, D.C., also made a major effort at the Mile-High City. Attempting to build a base of support, he launched the usual round of lectures, classes, and outside speaking engagements that seemed to work in other cities. When these measures failed, he experimented with special programs intended to pique general interest—including slide shows on India, illustrated lectures, appearances before University of Denver classes, and evenings built around readings from the writings of such famous Indian writers as Sarojini Naidu and Rabindranath Tagore. Swamis Akhilananda and Jnaneshwarananda both made hurried trips to Denver to lend their support, but to no avail. Conceding defeat, Vividishananda finally abandoned the field in 1938.[32]

Philadelphia, Washington, D.C., and Denver are not the only instances where the movement failed. Two other cities where the swamis frequently lectured without producing centers are Detroit and Cincinnati. More recently, branch centers opened in Atlanta, Houston, and Austin have also been suspended. The reasons for failure vary to a considerable extent from swami to swami and from center to center, but several factors stand out. These include a lack of continuity because of a shortage of Indian monks to fill slots once new centers have been launched; complete dependence upon local sources for the financial support required to underwrite costs, a particular problem in the early stages of a new society; the need for special talents, particularly English fluency and organizational skills, in attracting and holding an American audience; and the movement's steadfast resistance to the use of any form of advertising to spread news of its work.

Although the Ramakrishna Order has persistently sought control over all Western centers which propagate Ramakrishna's teachings, insisting on leadership by Indian monks authorized by the president of the Ramakrishna Math and Mission, on several occasions independent organizations have appeared. The most important of such bodies in the United States have been the Ananda Ashrama and Boston Vedanta centers, which split away from the movement in 1940 after Swami Paramananda's death. Under the name of "Order of Ramakrishna Brahmavadin," the two centers remain active today. They are largely ignored by movement historians, but their continuing effort to spread Ramakrishna's teachings deserves inclusion in any comprehensive account of the Ramakrishna movement in America.

The "defection" of the two centers was obviously viewed as a very bitter defeat by the movement's leadership.[33] At their peak under Swami Paramananda's leadership, for a time the two bodies ranked among the movement's most successful American centers. Apparently, the split was equally traumatic for the rebel leaders, and particularly for Paramananda's niece Gayatri Devi, who ultimately assumed direction of the independent centers. Recalling the break a quarter of a century later, she confessed that "without exaggeration I can say that this was the most difficult, challenging, and painful period of my entire life." Gayatri Devi would steadfastly insist that the two centers "did not separate happily," but rather "obeyed the order issued by the authorities whom we revered."[34]

The desire of members of the Boston and Ananda Ashrama communities that Paramananda's lieutenants, Gayatri Devi and Sister Daya, carry on the work after the swami's death apparently sparked the explosion. Throughout its history, the Ramakrishna Order has always insisted on its sole right to choose society leaders, and, in times of change in leadership, it has always named an Indian monk trained at Belur as the successor. Clearly, neither Gayatri Devi nor Sister Daya met the Order's requirements. However, supported by most of the Boston and Ananda Ashrama members, the two women refused to step down. The result was that after months of anxious negotiations, including a direct appeal to Swami Virajananda, who had succeeded to the Ramakrishna Order's presidency in 1938, the women assumed leadership themselves.

Gayatri Devi reveals much about the deeper causes of the split in a remarkable letter, dated October 15, 1940, reproduced in its entirety in Devi's autobiographical *One Life's Pilgrimage*.[35] The letter was apparently drafted in response to an earlier communication from Swami Virajananda, in which the president inquired whether Swami Paramananda had left instructions concerning the future of the two societies. Unless written instructions from Paramananda could be produced which clearly designated Sister Daya and Gayatri Devi as successors, Virajananda argued that the two women should immediately abandon their posts. In her October 15 letter, Devi responded that though no "written documents" existed specifying his views, the swami's "unwritten wish" had been that the two women carry on the work. Apparently, the Ramakrishna Order's president also demanded to see a copy of the two societies' constitutions and bylaws, which normally specified that a "Sannyasin representative of the Math" was to "direct the work" and "be the supreme local authority in spiritual matters." Devi's reply was that Paramananda was "not a great believer in organization."[36]

The letter sheds light on the role of women in the Ramakrishna movement. The fact that Gayatri Devi and Sister Daya were both female undoubtedly intensified the objections of the Order's Indian leadership, who held conservative views concerning the proper role of women. In her letter Devi suggested that the two centers might be recognized as a "sisterhood." "We humbly ask you that you give us sanction to carry on Swami Paramananda's entire work as a Sisterhood," she wrote Swami Virajananda. "Your recognition of us as ordained sisters, authorized to spread the Gospel of Ramakrishna and Swami Vivekananda would solve our problem."[37] (In fact, during Paramananda's life, female devotees had filled most of the centers' leadership positions.)

The Ramakrishna Order's president responded in February 1941, dismissing Devi's "sisterhood" proposal and announcing that, henceforth, Paramananda's Boston and California centers would no longer be recognized as part of the Ramakrishna Math and Mission. As regards the role of women, in later years the Order has accepted the establishment of Ramakrishna convents in both India and the West, but to date no woman has been authorized to lead a Western society. The growth of feminism in Western societies promises to keep the issue of the role of women in Vedanta alive in the decades to come.

Before we consider the history of the independent Boston and Ananda Ashrama centers, a word needs to be said about the backgrounds of Sister Daya and Gayatri Devi, the two key figures in the breakaway movement. Following a familiar upper-class pattern, Sister Daya was the daughter of a United States senator from Nevada. Prior to her association with Swami Paramananda, she had been a committed Theosophist, writing and lecturing on theosophical teachings under her given name of Georgina Jones. Then, she was ordained as a Vedanta minister in 1921, rapidly claiming a leadership role as one of Paramananda's most trusted lieutenants.[38] If Sister Daya had to search out Vedanta, Gayatri Devi might be said to have been born to accept it, as one of Swami Paramananda's nieces. She was married at an early age and came to the United States in 1926 shortly after her husband's death. Soon after her arrival she began to present Vedanta lectures and was apparently groomed by Paramananda to succeed him.[39]

Externally at least, the Boston and Ananda Ashrama centers seem to have changed very little since Swami Paramananda's passing. Until her death, Sister

Daya continued to divide the work with Gayatri Devi, with the American woman overseeing the ashrama and the Indian woman in charge of the Boston center. In the half-century since Paramananda's death, the swami's personal influence has continued to pervade the two centers: his teachings and writings are constantly invoked, his birthday has been added to Ramakrishna's and Vivekananda's for special observance, and his picture is displayed with those of Ramakrishna, Vivekananda, and Jesus on the temple altar for worship. Already apparent during the swami's life, a "cult of Paramananda" has been superimposed on the traditional Ramakrishna teachings.

The two independent centers have managed to survive to the present, but there have obviously been strains. One of the major difficulties has been the lack of sufficient staff to keep the widely separated enterprise going. In response to the problem, in 1952 the Boston center was closed, with its activities shifted to a retreat twenty miles outside Boston; and in 1962 the society's journal *The Message of the East* was also suspended. The independent movement confronted its most severe challenge in 1955 with Sister Daya's death, which forced Gayatri Devi to adopt the same exhausting pattern of cross-country journeys that had hastened Paramananda's death. She was barely able to cope and at one point attempted to recruit an assistant from India, a monk from Assam named Swami Puragra Parampanthi. However, the two soon fell out, and the swami abruptly departed to open a separate work. As a result of declining health, Gayatri Devi has been forced in recent years to greatly reduce her movements between the Massachusetts and California centers. Discussions with members of the Ramakrishna movement emphasize that Devi's split from the movement remains a sensitive issue.[40] The survival of the independent centers seems doubtful. Unlike the Ramakrishna Math and Mission, which is able to recruit new workers to continue the work from generation to generation, the "Order of Ramakrishna Brahmavadin" seems almost certain to suspend operations upon its leader's death.

This brief sketch may suggest how the Ramakrishna movement has widened its reach in the United States since the 1930s but does little to explain the role of Ramakrishna in the lives of contemporary American followers. In order to have a close-up view of the way Vedanta societies operate and how Vedanta influences the lives of modern Americans, we now turn our focus to the Vedanta Society of Southern California, which will serve as a case study.[41] The admonition should be added that each Vedanta society is to some extent unique as a result of the differing personality of its swami as well as each society's distinctive history. In fact, according to my informants, the Vedanta Society of Southern California's major claim to distinctiveness has been its liberalism. Obviously, the term "liberalism" allows for widely different interpretations, but in the context of the Ramakrishna movement the southern California society may be classified as more "liberal" because it has generally followed a more relaxed policy toward observance of traditional rules and regulations than other Vedanta societies, with greater emphasis on personal choice. To cite one example, where monastics at the San Francisco Vedanta center observe a strict vegetarian diet, monastics at the southern California centers normally eat fish and fowl. Relations between male and female monastics provide a second example. In sharp contrast to the policy of strict separation of sexes enforced by the Indian leadership at most centers, monastics at the southern California centers have considerable daily contact.

For a half-century the dominant influence at the Vedanta Society of Southern California was Swami Prabhavananda, the center's founder and charismatic leader. Though he died in 1976, Prabhavananda's presence still pervades the society today, kept alive by the society's older members who continue to revere his memory. In *My Guru and His Disciple*, Christopher Isherwood recounts an anecdote that seems to typify the swami's leadership and liberalizing influence. According to the famous English writer, Belur officials at one point sought to enforce a stricter observance of rules among American devotees by transmitting copies of the Order's rules and regulations to each center. Prabhavinanda's response was to ask Isherwood to draft a reply to India, explaining that their "Indian rules couldn't possibly apply to the American centers."[42] Few other swamis could have responded to a Belur communication so casually. His stature as a direct disciple of Swami Brahmananda and his great success in southern California gave him a degree of independence and power unusual among swamis in America.

As a result of that success, the Vedanta Society of Southern California, which was originally housed in a modest home deeded to the society in 1929, today has mushroomed into a complex of buildings that covers much of a city block. The major units at the Hollywood headquarters include a small but striking Hindu temple, whose white Taj Mahal dome may be glimpsed by motorists passing by on the Hollywood Freeway; an impressive bookshop, which stocks a wide range of Eastern and Western religious works; the Vedanta Press, which publishes a steady stream of books on the movement and its teachings; a monastery where male devotees are housed; the Sarada Convent, located in a separate dwelling a block away, where female devotees reside; a hillside garden; and an adjoining apartment complex where lay members and friends of the movement live. Outside Hollywood, the society also operates the Ramakrishna Monastery at Trabuco; the Sarada Convent, 100 miles north in Montecito, a Santa Barbara suburb; the Vivekananda House in South Pasadena (now officially a historical monument), where the famous swami stayed in 1900; and, finally, a newly opened branch center in San Diego.

The Vedanta Society of Southern California's public work consists primarily of lectures and classes scheduled weekly throughout most of the year. Public services are held Sunday mornings at 11 A.M. at all four locations (the Hollywood headquarters, Santa Barbara temple, Trabuco monastery, and San Diego center) and are well attended. The usual Sunday program consists of meditation, chanting, and music, culminating in a lecture in which the teachings of the movement are presented. In order to meet the needs of the various centers, a rotation system has been devised in which Swami Swahananda, the present leader of the society, regularly alternates as the day's speaker with American-born swamis. Midweek classes open to the public are also offered, and in them passages from the Upanishads, Bhagavad Gita, and *Gospel of Ramakrishna* are explicated. The general atmosphere at the lectures and classes is serious, and the intellectual level of the presentations high.

The society reaches out to a wider audience through a variety of publications and a journal. The Vedanta Press, based at the Hollywood center, regularly publishes works on the Ramakrishna movement, Hinduism, and Eastern spirituality generally; it also distributes many of the books published by Ramakrishna presses in India. Until suspended in 1970, the society's journal *Vedanta and the West* also reached out to a national and international audience. The journal is arguably the best-edited Eastern spiritual periodical published in the West to date, and its readable presentation of Vedanta and Hinduism has established a new standard among such publications. Indeed, for several years Aldous Huxley and Christopher Isherwood were regular contributors.

No area of the southern California society's work more clearly reflects Swami Prabhavananda's abiding influence than the prominence given to devotionalism. Though all Vedanta centers in the United States maintain shrines where the image of Ramakrishna and other spiritual leaders are displayed, perhaps no Vedanta society exceeds the southern California society in the prominence given to worship and ritual. Strongly attracted to bhakti devotionalism, Swami Prabhavananda instituted a number of traditional Hindu rites at the Hollywood center, brushing aside the warnings of his fellow swamis that Americans would never accept such practices.

The Hollywood and Santa Barbara temples are open daily from 6:30 A.M. to 7:00 or 7:30 P.M., allowing devotees to engage in meditation and worship throughout the day. As in India, food and flower offerings are placed on the altars daily; special vespers services, including traditional Hindu rites and chanting, are also regularly celebrated. "The shrineroom in the temple is the most important place at the Hollywood center, and all our activities center around it," a devotee reported in 1956. There is no evidence in the years since that devotionalism has lost its centrality. Photographs of Ramakrishna, Sarada Devi, Vivekananda, and Brahmananda dominate the temple altar. One-hour meditations are held in the early morning and at noon, and a Vespers service is observed at 6:00 or 6:30 P.M. each evening. One writer who was attempting to describe such worship for outsiders suggested that people should visualize a "number of men and women with eyes closed, wrapped in shawls, sitting cross-legged on the shrineroom floor."[43]

Built in the distinctive style of a kiva, the circular room used in religious rites by the American Southwest's Pueblo Indians, the Trabuco monastery worship room is particularly striking. It is windowless and centered around a pit area where devotees sit on cushions during meditation and Vespers. The atmosphere is both solemn and impressive. On key days such as the birthdays of Rama-krishna, Sarada Devi, Vivekananda, or Brahmananda, special *pujas* are cele-brated in which more elaborate rites are observed, usually followed by dinners featuring traditional Indian dishes for all who wish to participate. The Holly-wood center may be the only Vedanta society in the West that celebrates a full-scale Kali *puja* in a ceremony that lasts through the night.

Obviously, the Vedanta Society of Southern California offers both Vedanta philosophy and Ramakrishna devotionalism. Vedanta largely dominates the lec-tures and writings, while Ramakrishna is central in the meditations and *pujas*. The combination has led critics to charge that the devotionalism undermines the commitment to Vedantic nondualism; in response, defenders claim that the wor-ship is actually nondualistic, focusing on one of the divine forms merely as a means of reaching Brahman.

Though lectures, classes, and worship play important roles in a follower's daily life, much of the Vedanta student's spiritual effort is pursued privately un-der the guidance of his or her swami. Anyone, apparently, may request private instruction; those who are serious about it undergo special initiation. The so-ciety's *Guidebook* describes the procedure as follows:

> Strictly speaking, an aspirant's life really begins when he or she is given initi-ation by the guru. Each swami in charge of a Western center is empowered to give initiation to those aspirants who request it and whom he considers suit-able. . . . Initiation is a private ceremony held, at the Hollywood center, in the shrineroom of the temple. The guru officially, so to speak, accepts the devotee as his disciple, to whom he gives the name of his or her Chosen Ideal in the form of a short Sanskrit prayer of a few syllables. This prayer, called a man-tram, is not invented by the guru; it has been handed down to him by his guru, and is charged with spiritual power. . . . Usually a rosary is given to facilitate the counting of the mantram.[44]

The procedure varies very little in any of the Eastern spiritual groups active in America.

Apparently, no Vedanta follower is required to observe the rituals, engage in the worship, or accept a guru. Several monastics interviewed at the Vedanta So-ciety of Southern California insisted that their only commitment was to the Ve-danta philosophy. One senses, however, that practically all students sooner or later embrace the full round of devotional practices. The Hollywood society *Guidebook* declares: "Surprising as this may seem, most Westerners, once they have overcome their initial prejudices and misconceptions, find that the way of devotion is at once the most satisfying and most practical approach to the Truth."[45] In fact, the more complete the American follower's immersion in the Ramakrishna movement, the more traditionally Hindu the follower's religious life has seemed to be.

The Vedanta Society of Southern California, like the Vedanta societies in San Francisco and Chicago, plays a leading role in the training of American monastics. During the decade of the 1980s the number of renunciates at the southern California centers has varied between twenty and forty, with as many as ten quartered at the Sarada Convent in Santa Barbara, ten at the Ramakrishna Monastery in Trabuco, and a somewhat larger number assigned to the monastery and convent in Hollywood. It is difficult to see how the associated Vedanta centers could conduct their daily round of activities without the monastics. The monastics contribute much of the work force needed to carry on the society's daily activities. They conduct the meditation and Vesper services, prepare the food, maintain the grounds and buildings, manage the bookshops and publication program, perform most of the repairs, and do the shopping—all fairly demanding tasks in an organization as large as the Vedanta Society of Southern California. The monastics' age range varies from newly recruited *bramacharis* and *brahmacharinis* in their late twenties to elderly devotees who have been connected with the southern California work since the 1940s. Renunciates at Santa Barbara and Trabuco live much more secluded lives than monastics at Hollywood, who must spend many hours weekly engaged in the center's public work.

Though Vedanta societies have traditionally avoided any form of advertising or overt effort to recruit converts, the Vedanta Society of Southern California does reach out to the general public through bookstores at Hollywood and Santa Barbara. Open weekdays and before and after Sunday services, the shops seem to attract a steady flow of browsers. Volumes on Vedanta and the Ramakrishna movement compete for attention with numerous works on Christianity, mysticism, comparative religions, and the major religious traditions. But the only tangible evidence of the society's desire to attract outsiders is a brief notice inserted inside the cover of each Vedanta Press publication, inviting interested persons to write the secretary of the Vedanta Society for further information. It is difficult to say how effective such a low-key policy has been in attracting new followers.

In recent years all Vedanta societies seem to interact with local groups and in community affairs much more actively than earlier. Most swamis are regularly invited to address outside service and professional organizations, and they accept. At the Vedanta Society of Southern California Swami Swahananda delegates much of the outside lecture work to his American assistants. A steady stream of visitors also seek out the centers, including students in high school and university classes engaged in the study of world religions. The earlier climate of hostility and suspicion has been replaced by one of friendship and cooperation. Practically all Vedanta societies now participate in ecumenical undertakings on a regular basis. One of the Hollywood center's most important community links has been its active participation in the Interreligious Council of Southern California. Made up of representatives from Hinduism, Buddhism, Sikhism, Islam, and Judaism, as well as a variety of Christian organizations, the council sponsors interreligious conferences and retreats and encourages dialogue between the world religions. The southern California society fully participates in the council.

Clearly, for a small but significant body of American devotees, the Vedanta Society of Southern California now satisfies the need Christianity formerly satisfied in their lives—and more. Because most followers have had to search out their new commitment, the average American Vedantist is likely to be more committed than a conventional believer who has not so much chosen but grown up in a religious tradition.

Still, although the Vedanta societies have gone a long way to accommodate to Western conditions, problems remain. Rites of passage such as marriage present special difficulties. As renouncers of the world, the swamis' participation in marriage ceremonies presents a certain dilemma, since marriage clearly entails commitment to live in the world. Upon request, the swamis do offer modest "marriage blessing" services, usually limited to small groups. (In India, in contrast, swamis do not normally conduct marriage ceremonies, which are assigned to priests.) Death, the final renunciation, offers no such conflict; and the swamis regularly officiate at memorial services for members who have died.

If we look back on the history of the Ramakrishna movement in its first century in America, several observations may be offered. Perhaps the most obvious is that, from the very beginning, the movement has always been urban in orientation and membership. Historically, students of Vedanta have periodically retreated to ashramas for spiritual renewal, but only for brief periods. The swamis frequently lectured in smaller cities and even villages, but urban centers of population have always been the preferred sites for Vedanta societies. The reasons for such an urban preference are easy to understand and include the more cosmopolitan spirit to be found in cities, the greater population and resources from which to draw, and the xenophobic conservatism of many small towns. As foreigners in a strange land, the swamis naturally looked to the large cities where Indian families were and where some contact with India and Hindu tradition was feasible. The great increase in Asian Indian immigration in recent decades, with a strong concentration in larger cities, can only increase the urban attraction. The corollary may be added that more populous coastal cities such as New York, San Francisco, and Los Angeles have proven more hospitable to Vedanta than such interior cities as Chicago, St. Louis, and Denver.

On the other hand, the Ramakrishna movement has made almost no inroads in the South, despite nearly a century of activity in the United States. Though swamis have regularly visited and lectured in the upper South since the 1920s, no permanent Vedanta center has taken root anywhere in the region right down to the present. The absence of Vedanta in the South may be partially explained as a result of the region's dominant rural background; however, there are other possible explanations peculiar to the region. To begin with, historically the South has been more homogeneous ethnically than other regions of the United States, attracting fewer immigrants and, until the 1960s and the reform of immigration laws, almost no Asian settlers (even though there are fairly large South Asian communities in Dallas, Houston, and Miami today). As a result, religious views have inevitably been more uniform than in other regions. Perhaps most important, since the Civil War Southerners, more than Americans from other regions, have been more preoccupied with race and, specifically, more obsessed by the large number of black people living in their midst. Swami Vivekananda confronted racial prejudice on a number of occasions, and, though the record is largely silent, we may assume other swamis did as well. Swamis from south India especially faced the risk of racial slurs because of the darkness of their skin. Aware of the South's reputation, swamis apparently made less effort there than in other regions, assuming that they would not be welcome. As the South becomes more urban and as more non-Southerners migrate to the Sunbelt states, the pattern may be expected to change. In fact, already between 1979 and 1983 Swami Bhashyananda dispatched several of his assistants to open Vedanta work in the South with considerable success, and directed by American-born swamis, Vedanta groups were soon meeting in Atlanta, Houston, and West Palm Beach. However, the centers were suddenly suspended in 1987 by direct order of Belur, apparently because Indian officials believed that the movement lacked qualified swamis to oversee such expansion.[46]

For the most part, the level of education and training of the swamis dispatched to America has been impressive. Based on a cross-section of all monks who have served in the United States since 1893, the profile of a typical swami might be described as follows: he has been relatively young (early to middle thirties upon arrival from India); well educated (college graduates in most cases, with special training in both Indian and Western religious and philosophical studies); experienced (almost all had served several years at Ramakrishna centers in India); and nearly always fluent in English, with a large number who had served on the editorial staff of *Prabuddha Bharata*, the movement's major English-language journal. Most of the swamis are Bengali in background, which is hardly surprising in view of the fact that the Ramakrishna Math and Mission is headquartered just across the river from Calcutta and that the movement has always been most successful in Bengal.

Comparisons with American missionaries who have propagated Christianity in India are revealing. There are obvious differences between them—for example, Ramakrishna swamis consistently disavow any missionary intention, while Christian missionaries have often proclaimed the desire to convert. But the challenge to be overcome in presenting alien religious conceptions to people of a very different culture seems similar. The most pressing need in both cases was some understanding of the language and culture of the host peoples. The validity of the generalization will vary somewhat with the denominational group, but it seems clear that the typical Ramakrishna monk sent to the United States has been better educated and better equipped by language skills and training than the typical American missionary dispatched to Asia. Frequent references to health ailments emphasize that the swamis faced many of the same problems of physical and dietary adjustment experienced by American missionaries in Asia.

Finally, as with American missionaries abroad, it seems clear that, from the very beginning, the Ramakrishna movement has never had the personnel to cope with the demands of the American work. Requests for additional swamis reverberate throughout the century the movement has labored in the West. That Belur has sent as many talented monks to the United States as it has emphasizes how highly the Western work has been regarded. But the shortage of Indian teachers seems to be growing more urgent, as evidenced by a recent order from the Belur headquarters that no further expansion in the American work be initiated until further notice. For the movement to survive in the West, American-born swamis will have to be trained and entrusted with leadership. Native-born swamis would have the major advantage of already possessing the language skills and cultural understanding needed to present Hinduism to Americans successfully.

7 | The Ramakrishna Movement in History

Past, Present, and Future

So FAR WE have looked at the Ramakrishna movement in the United States without reference to other Asian Indian religious movements. Now, however, it seems appropriate to attempt to link the history of its work with that of other Indian movements that have sought to propagate Hinduism in the West. Similarities to and differences from other Asian groups should emerge from such a comparison. At the same time, the fact that the history of Hinduism in America remains to be written makes such an undertaking difficult. Indeed, with the exception of Wendell Thomas's now dated *Hinduism Invades America*, published sixty years ago, there is no general history of Hinduism in the United States. Raymond Brady Williams's *Religions of Immigrants from India and Pakistan* partially meets the need for such a volume, but the work largely focuses on the period since 1965, when the passage of the Immigration and Nationality Act for the first time opened the gates for significant Asian Indian immigration to the United States.[1] By contrast, in the last decade alone three major historical surveys have traced the American impact of Buddhism: Emma Layman's *Buddhism in America*, Charles Prebish's *American Buddhism*, and Rick Fields's *How the Swans Came to the Lake*.[2] Parallel works on the history of Hinduism are badly needed.

It is clear that in the years since 1893 a surprising number of Indian swamis and teachers have found their way to the United States to lecture and conduct classes. One of the earliest of these was Virchand Gandhi—no relation to Mahatma Gandhi. Gandhi shared the stage with Swami Vivekananda at the 1893 Parliament of Religions, remaining in the United States for more than a year after the parliament's close to lecture and hold classes; he returned for a second tour in 1895.[3] Though a Jainist, he resembled Vivekananda in defending India against missionary attacks and expounding Hindu religious ideals. Swami Rama Tirtha was another early visitor, appearing a few years after Gandhi. Abandoning a position as professor of mathematics at an Indian college, he became a monk and set off across the United States to preach a universalistic Vedantic message. He also attempted to raise scholarship money for Indian students to attend American colleges. The record suggests that he made little effort to win disciples or organize societies.[4]

While Hindu visitors in the 1890s emphasized Vedanta, it is interesting that as early as 1902 a more sectarian form of Hinduism was also being offered to Americans. The man responsible was a former Indian journalist named Baba Bharati. A proponent of Vaishnavism, Bharati founded a Krishna temple in Los Angeles where he introduced devotional worship of Krishna and Chaitanya. He lectured in the United States several years, returning to India in 1907 accompanied by six American disciples.[5] Both Rama Tirtha and Baba Bharati were almost certainly influenced by Vivekananda, whose appearance at the Parliament inspired their attempt to emulate his success.

During the 1920s the flow steadily increased. Now quite forgotten, the new arrivals included Yogi Hari Rama, who came in 1925 and for several years offered beginning and advanced courses in yoga; Rishi Singh Gherwal, who founded a journal called *India's Message* and taught yoga in the western United States; Sant Ram Mandal, who offered correspondence lessons on Indian philosophy and inaugurated the Universal Brotherhood Temple and School of Eastern Philosophy; a teacher known as Swami Omkar, whose disciples planted branches of his movement in Philadelphia and Los Angeles; and Dr. Bhagat Singh Thind, a Sikh who traveled about the country lecturing on yoga and Hinduism.[6]

The point is that the swamis of the Ramakrishna movement have not been unique. Since the 1890s, Asian teachers have made their way to the United States, where they have lectured, conducted classes, founded societies, gathered disciples, published books—and, almost always, disappeared from view as suddenly as they appeared. Clearly, Americans have not embraced every Eastern spiritual movement introduced in the country. In fact, as the first authentic Asian religious body to bring its teachings to the United States directly, the Ramakrishna movement is one of the very few to survive more than a few years.

The Self-Realization Fellowship, founded by Paramahansa Yogananda in 1920, is the only other Hindu religious movement of any size that has endured from the pre–World War II era. Yogananda came to the United States at the beginning of the 1920s to participate in a religious congress sponsored by the American Unitarian Association. Staying on, in subsequent years he lectured widely in American cities. He promoted a version of kriya yoga which he termed "Yogoda" and promised that practice of it would energize the centers of consciousness (*chakras*) located at various points along one's body.[7]

Yogananda's emphasis on yoga and a universal religious outlook paralleled the Ramakrishna movement's teachings, but his methods of propagating Hinduism in the United States diverged sharply from those of the Vedanta societies, for he adopted Western-style techniques to increase the appeal of his teachings. Thus, he publicized his message in the mass media, introduced divine healing into his services, and headlined testimonials of cures in his journal. He also advertised correspondence courses in yoga. Insisting that Yogoda was "not a new religion, nor a new cult, nor a new interpretation," Paramahansa Yogananda claimed that it simply offered an "exact technique" for "widening the channel of human consciousness."[8] His promise that the body need not be denied and that regular practice of Yogoda would surely bring success undoubtedly enhanced his appeal. He assured his audiences that one might remain a good Christian while practicing Yogoda and demonstrated his fraternalism by including the Bible, along with the Bhagavad Gita and his own *Scientific Healing Affirmations*, as recommended readings. His message was intensely practical throughout. Moreover, the message and methods worked if one measures their success by the size and enthusiasm of the response evoked. As early as 1937, *Self-Realization*, the organization's journal, reported that Yogananda had initiated over 150,000 persons into Yogoda since arriving in the United States in 1920; and, at one point, the movement claimed as many as 150 centers.[9]

Yet, though once the most popular Hindu movement in America, the Self-Realization Fellowship has rapidly faded from the scene since the 1950s. Yogananda's death in 1952 was a critical event. Though the fellowship has managed to survive, to a large extent Yogananda's work has been carried on by disciples who have founded parallel but independent movements. Several of these offshoots explicitly call attention to kriya yoga in their names. The spin-offs include the Self-Revelation Church of Absolute Monism, directed by Swami Premananda in Washington, D.C.; the Temple of Kriya Yoga in Chicago, which includes an ashrama and the College of Occult Sciences; a yoga ashrama headquartered in Virginia known as Prema Dharmasala, which offers classes, mails cassettes, and sponsors workshops on kriya yoga; and the Ananda Meditation Retreat in California founded by Swami Kriyananda (J. Donald Walters), a prolific author of books and pamphlets on yoga.[10]

The Self-Realization Fellowship certainly demonstrates the popular success possible through the adoption of aggressive methods; it also suggests the limitations. Many of the tens of thousands drawn into the movement by such methods quickly fell away. The Self-Realization Fellowship reached hundreds of thousands of Americans, but it retained only a tiny number of members. By contrast, the Ramakrishna movement has been more conservative in its methods and has attracted many fewer devotees but has succeeded in holding a greater percentage of its members.

But the larger story is the more recent one. As we come closer to the present, and especially since the 1960s, new Eastern spiritual movements have appeared. Among others, these include the Divine Life Society, founded by Swami Sivananda, notable for its Forest Academy in Rishikish, India, where numerous American seekers go to study yoga; the International Society for Krishna Consciousness, emphasizing Krishna worship, first brought to the United States by Swami A. C. Bhaktivedanta in 1965; Transcendental Meditation, introduced into the United States by Maharishi Mahesh Yogi in 1959, which teaches a form of mantra meditation; the Ananda Marga Yoga Society, founded in India by Prabhat Ranjan Sarkar and first propagated in America in 1969; the International

Yoga Institute, transplanted to America in the 1960s by Swami Satchidananda, emphasizing hatha yoga; Siddha Yoga, brought to the United States by Swami Muktananda during his 1970 world tour; the Divine Light Mission, introduced into the country by teenage guru Maharaj Ji in 1971; and, finally, the Rajneesh Meditation Center, led by Bhagwan Shree Rajneesh, which attracted national and even international attention after the Bhagwan transferred the headquarters of the movement to Oregon in 1981. The large number of other Hindu and Buddhist groups listed in a work such as J. Gordon Melton's *Encyclopedia of American Religions* leaves little doubt of the continuing receptiveness of contemporary Americans to Eastern spiritual movements.[11]

To understand the Ramakrishna movement's special role and distinctive place in the history of Hinduism in the United States, consider two other Hindu movements that have appeared in the United States since 1960—the International Society for Krishna Consciousness and Transcendental Meditation.

Among recent Indian movements, perhaps none has attracted a wider American following than the International Society for Krishna Consciousness (ISKCON), founded by Swami A. C. Bhaktivedanta. Bhaktivedanta was born in Calcutta in 1896 and worked for many years for a chemical company, embracing the life of a sannyasin only after retirement. Persuaded that he had a divine mission to introduce Krishna worship in the West, he arrived in New York City in 1965. He was seventy years old; his total resources consisted of a suitcase, umbrella, dry cereal, and less than ten U.S. dollars in currency.[12]

From the first Bhaktivedanta made few concessions to Western ways: he wore the cotton dhoti (a cloth wrapped around one's lower body worn by traditional Hindus) of a sannyasin and appeared in public with his head shaved and forehead prominently marked in the fashion followed by Vaishnavite believers. We are told that at their first meeting, Swami Nikhilananda, the respected head of the Ramakrishna-Vivekananda Center in New York, advised the elderly Vaishnavite that he would have to abandon both his Indian dress and strict vegetarianism if he wished to remain in the West.[13] (Most swamis of the Ramakrishna movement regularly wear Western clothing.) Characteristically, Bhaktivedanta rejected Nikhilananda's suggestion and insisted on an almost literal acceptance by his American disciples of traditional Hindu practices. All American followers were expected to adopt a strict lacto-vegetarian diet (no meat, fish, or eggs), to avoid use of intoxicants (not only alcoholic beverages and narcotics but also coffee, tea, and tobacco), and to accept complete subordination of women members. As long as Bhaktivedanta lived, the policy of no compromises defined the key difference between the Ramakrishna movement and the Krishna Consciousness movement.[14]

In the West as in India, the ISKCON movement has centered its teaching on the Bhagavad Gita as interpreted by the eleventh-century Vaishnava philosopher Ramanuja and sixteenth-century Bengali saint Chaitanya. The goal is Krishna consciousness, achieved through recitation of the *mahamantra* ("Hare Krishna, Hare Krishna / Krishna Krishna, Hare Hare / Hare Rama, Hare Rama / Rama Rama, Hare Hare"), worship of Krishna as supreme lord, and performance of the *kirtan*, a dance involving rhythmic chanting. At Bhaktivedanta's insistence, all American ISKCON temples observed a rigorous schedule of work and worship, beginning daily with the first offering to Krishna at 4:30 A.M. and ending with the final *kirtan* at 9 P.M. Convinced that he possessed the final truth, Bhaktivedanta refused to cooperate with or engage in dialogue with other religious organizations.[15]

Bhaktivedanta's followers, known popularly as Hare Krishnas, began to attract wide attention in the United States during the 1960s. In 1966 the rapidly growing movement formally incorporated as the International Society for Krishna Consciousness. Hare Krishna missionaries began to appear on street corners and in airports throughout the country, where they sold copies of the movement's magazine, *Back to Godhead*. They made no effort to maintain a low profile, wearing traditional Hindu dress and shaving their heads. Bhaktivedanta and his chosen deputies ruled ISKCON societies autocratically, with no encouragement of democratic participation or local decision making. Following the swami's death in 1977, direction was assumed by a governing board of twenty-two members. According to J. Gordon Melton, by 1984 the American wing of the international movement numbered 3,000 "core community members" and 250,000 "lay constituents," and there were fifty ISKCON centers in the United States.[16] This figure may be inflated. In his 1988 study *Religions of Immigrants from India and Pakistan*, Raymond Brady Williams states that ISKCON membership in the United States has declined to as few as 2,000 members. Indeed, according to Williams, since Bhaktivedanta's death ISKCON has suffered a "general decline" both in membership and income with "many defections" from the movement.[17] Like so many other movements, ISKCON may not long survive the passing of its founder.

The contrast between the International Society for Krishna Consciousness and Ramakrishna movements seems quite dramatic though significant changes in ISKCON since Bhaktivedanta's death have somewhat blurred the differences. While both bodies claim to represent true Hinduism, ISKCON promotes the teachings of Vaishnavism as handed on by Swami Bhaktivedanta, while the Ramakrishna movement stresses the Vedanta as interpreted by Ramakrishna and Vivekananda. The Ramakrishna movement promotes a universalistic outlook in which all major religions are perceived as possible paths to ultimate truth; by contrast, ISKCON has been more sectarian, emphasizing that truth is to be found through worship of Krishna. While swamis of the Ramakrishna movement have always welcomed interaction with other religions, ISKCON officials have generally preferred a policy of religious separation. Despite recent efforts by Indian leaders to establish greater control, Vedanta societies have always been fairly autonomous, with power divided between Belur authorities in India, who designate swamis and determine policy, and local boards of American members who are responsible for financial and administrative concerns. By contrast, under Bhaktivedanta, ISKCON was highly centralized, with all decisions made by the swami. (Since the swami's death ISKCON has become more pluralistic, with power now divided among a series of leaders.) Where Swami Bhaktivedanta demanded that Western devotees strictly observe traditional Hindu rules concerning food, gender relations, and religious observances, the Ramakrishna movement has been more flexible, accepting the need to adjust Hindu practice to Western conditions. In most Vedanta centers, vegetarianism is not compulsory, male-female relationships are relaxed, and observance of Hindu rituals is not mandatory.[18]

The differences noted have lessened since Bhaktivedanta's death in 1977, with the leaders of ISKCON eager to make the movement's message more attractive to both native Americans and Asian-born immigrants. Authority has been somewhat decentralized and more contact between converts and their families has been allowed. Less emphasis is now placed on aggressive fund-raising in public places—a constant source of unfavorable publicity. This "mellowing" of ISKCON has considerably decreased its sectarianism and given the movement some hope of long-term survival based on its greater attraction to Americans.[19]

Transcendental Meditation, the second Hindu movement to be considered, differs radically from the International Society for Krishna Consciousness, emphasizing that Hinduism in modern America has taken many forms. The founder of Transcendental Meditation, Maharishi Mahesh Yogi, was born in central India in 1911. After graduating with a bachelor's degree in physics from Allahabad University, he spent over a decade seeking spiritual enlightenment at the feet of a Hindu master known as Swami Bhahmananda Saraswati. The Maharishi brought Transcendental Meditation to America in 1959, claiming that he had perfected a simplified form of meditation.[20] He was at first ignored. Then, in the 1960s, the Maharishi attracted international attention after the media reported that celebrities such as the Beatles and Hollywood star Mia Farrow had become devotees. "TM," the acronym used both for the method and the movement, became popular among many Americans.

Maharishi Mahesh Yogi has repeatedly stated that Transcendental Meditation offers not a new religion but a new technique that will permit anyone to harmonize his or her inner spiritual and outer material natures. After a brief orientation, the student is given a mantra, instructed for three days in meditation, advised to attend group meetings with other adherents to share experiences, and then sent away to practice, with encouragement to return to a TM center once a month for checking and fine-tuning. TM may perhaps be best characterized as a simplified form of yoga.

It seems safe to say that no Hindu teacher offers a form of meditation better adapted for easy Western acceptance. The traditional warnings concerning slow progress and inevitable setbacks that the practitioner must expect in meditation are notable by their absence. Instead, TM teachers assure their students again and again that practice of Transcendental Meditation is "natural" and should not be forced; unlike most forms of yoga, there is no need to discipline one's thoughts or to seek control of mind. Perhaps most attractive to many Americans, TM users are promised that they do not have to accept any doctrine or religious belief or give up material desires in order to practice meditation. (The Maharishi does request that persons seeking formal initiation refrain from the use of drugs for fifteen days prior to initiation, and that the initiate not eat for several hours before or after receiving his or her mantra.) In TM publications all religious terminology has been systematically eliminated, with the term "Creative Intelligence" replacing references to God and Brahman; similarly, the teaching as a whole becomes the "Science of Creative Intelligence."[21] On the surface at least, the movement and method seem more Western than Asian, with close ties to humanistic psychology and New Age therapies.

Following spectacular growth during the 1960s, Transcendental Meditation has seemed almost sedate in later years. In fact, Maharishi Mahesh Yogi announced in 1968 that TM's strenuous era of expansion had closed. The only real excitement since then has been the controversy surrounding claims by movement officials that advanced Transcendental Meditation practitioners are able to levitate as much as several feet off the floor. Organizational priorities seem to have replaced missionary zeal. Subdivided into separate divisions whose activities are coordinated by a World Plan Executive Council, the TM organization now includes an International Meditation Society, which is responsible for the general public; a Student International Meditation Society, which concentrates on college students; and Maharishi International University, where one may enroll in a full four-year curriculum based on Transcendental Meditation principles. According to J. Gordon Melton, who has published a series of works on the new religions, "over 1,000,000 Americans have taken the basic TM course."[22]

If comparison of the teachings of the Ramakrishna movement with the teachings of Swami Bhaktivedanta might easily convince an outside observer that the Vedantic message presented in America by Ramakrishna swamis has represented a "Westernized" form of Hinduism, a similar comparison of the Ramakrishna movement with Transcendental Meditation might result in the opposite conclusion: that, on the contrary, the Ramakrishna movement presents a fairly traditional Hinduism. Obviously, the judgment one makes depends upon the comparison being made. Placed opposite Transcendental Meditation, the Ramakrishna movement seems quite conservative, offering a traditional Hinduism, based on the Upanishads and other ancient Hindu texts.

The contrasts between the Ramakrishna movement and TM are even more stark than the differences to be found between Ramakrishna swamis and Swami

Bhaktivedanta. Where most Ramakrishna devotees accept image-worship and observe rituals, aside from their initiation, TM practitioners have no connection with Hindu cultic practices. Ramakrishna monks undergo at least nine years of training before they are authorized to guide devotees; Transcendental Meditation teachers initiate students after completing only a three-month course. In the Ramakrishna movement, lectures, classes, and instruction by a guru remain the preferred methods of spiritual instruction and outreach; advertising and the mass media are avoided. By contrast, TM makes heavy use of advertising and the mass media and readily employs Western technology and managerial skills in its work. Where the typical member of a Vedanta society tends to be middle-class and educated, TM practitioners are both young and old, rich and poor, unskilled workers and professionals. Clearly, Hinduism in America has assumed many shapes. The Hindu tradition of transmission of teachings from guru to student guarantees continuity but also allows alterations in the teachings.

The preceding analysis clarifies the Ramakrishna Movement's special place among Indian religious groups in the West. Juxtaposed to ISKCON as taught by Swami Bhaktivedanta and Transcendental Meditation as presented by Maharishi Mahesh Yogi, the Ramakrishna movement clearly stands somewhere between. For nearly a century it has promoted the teachings of Vedanta as found in the Upanishads, the classic philosophical tradition of India; but it has also accommodated the West by its adoption of organized services, emphasis on lectures, and simplification of Hindu rites. The message has remained Hindu, while the methods reveal significant concessions to the West. In sum, the Ramakrishna movement has represented a "middle way" in American Hinduism.

At one time Hinduism was classified in texts on comparative and world religions as an "ethnic" or nonmissionary religion, limited essentially to the Indian subcontinent. As such, it was contrasted to Christianity, Islam, and Buddhism—all missionary religions that had expanded far beyond their country of origin. Obviously, as this study emphasizes, such a generalization is no longer defensible. Led by the Ramakrishna movement, Hinduism has leaped its old boundaries and today may be found in some form in most Western countries, and most prominently in the United States. As the vanguard in the thrust of Hinduism outward, the Ramakrishna movement has played a historic role of world significance.

In conclusion, then, it seems useful to consider both the past and the future, focusing on two final questions. The first concerns why the Ramakrishna movement has survived in the United States for a century, while numerous other Hindu movements have died out. What were the Ramakrishna movement's areas of strength, which permitted it to survive in an unfamiliar and often unfriendly Western environment? Second, what is the Ramakrishna movement's future in the United States? More particularly, what are its problems, past and present, that will determine whether it survives to celebrate a second century in the nation? What issues are most likely to impinge on its American operations in future years?

On close inspection, perhaps the Ramakrishna movement's most important single advantage has been its strong Indian foundation, which has guaranteed a continuous stream of swamis to lead the Western work. With few exceptions, other Asian religious movements that have sought to establish a foothold in the United States have lacked such a support system, with survival heavily dependent upon the ability to create an organization able to continue beyond the leader's death. Few Asian teachers have succeeded in this enterprise. In the 1960s and 1970s Swami A. C. Bhaktivedanta and Maharishi Mahesh Yogi both attracted impressive followings in the United States, but the survival of their movements now appears problematic because of a lack of continuing leadership. Indeed, most new religious movements collapse within a single generation following the death of their charismatic leader. The Ramakrishna movement had lost both of its founders by the opening years of the twentieth century, yet it continues to flourish. Since the movement is known throughout India, new recruits steadily enter the Belur monastery, guaranteeing the supply of new monks needed to maintain the work. No Eastern religious group active in the West today has a stronger base.

The Ramakrishna movement's pragmatic approach has been a second source of its durability. Pursuing the "middle way," it has adopted Western methods and adapted to American conditions but maintained a commitment to Hindu conceptions. The message derives from India, but the manner of operation points to Western influence. Consider Sunday services. Unlike worship in India, where organized group services are rare, services at American Vedanta societies closely approximate congregational services at Protestant churches. The very fact that the most important Vedanta service of the week falls on Sunday morning at the same time as in most churches is significant. As in Protestant services, the lecture (sermon) is central; scriptural readings from the Vedas, Bhagavad Gita, or *Gospel of Ramakrishna* replace readings from the Bible. Concessions to Western preferences have also been made in the areas of diet, dress, and daily lifestyle. The Ramakrishna movement may proffer a Hindu message that dates back thousands of years, but the "packaging" is modern. Western missionaries still debate the need to accommodate Christianity's teachings to other cultures; with its flexible outlook, the Ramakrishna movement embraced a policy of adaptation early on.

Compared to most other Eastern groups, the Ramakrishna movement's American centers also enjoy the advantage of a more secure economic condition. When not immediately undermined by the death of their charismatic leader, new movements have repeatedly foundered as a result of financial difficulties. Practically all of the Vedanta societies own, or are purchasing, their own buildings and land; several are located in exclusive residential areas on land that has become extremely valuable. Expected to be self-supporting from the first, the Vedanta societies learned to live within their means from the first. Grateful devotees have repeatedly willed cash and property holdings to local Vedanta societies. Moreover, American supporters have also given generously to the movement in India; indeed, much of the money needed to construct the impressive Ramakrishna temple at the movement's Belur headquarters came from American donors. The movement's conservative fiscal policies put local societies on a sound financial basis from an early time.

Language competency has been another factor in the movement's ability to survive. Throughout the history of Christian missions, the need to master foreign languages has presented a formidable barrier to missionaries seeking to carry the Gospel to distant nations. Western missionaries in Asia literally spent years developing competency in local languages so that they could proceed with evangelization. Language has never presented a serious impediment in the Ramakrishna movement's American work. Because of their history, the swamis were already proficient in English as a result of their schooling. Since India was ruled by Great Britain until 1947, English remains one of its official languages today. And since the Indian government continues to emphasize English competency, the Ramakrishna movement should be able to replace the present swamis in the United States with a new generation equally proficient in English.

Yet, despite a fairly secure position, the Ramakrishna movement of today faces a number of concerns or issues that will have to be resolved if the movement is to survive and flourish in the twenty-first century. Failure in any area could disrupt and even undermine a century of effort.

The Vedanta societies' relationship to the Ramakrishna movement in India has always been a possible area of conflict. The movement originated in, and has always been headquartered in, India; and all decisions, policies, and regulations flow from India; nevertheless, the movement's Western societies have exercised considerable local autonomy. In theory, the division of responsibilities is quite clear: all spiritual decisions are to be made by the swamis, who look to Belur for direction, while decisions concerning the center's daily operations are delegated to an American board of trustees. In fact, the division of power has never been so clearcut. The great distance between India and the United States and the difficulties in communication caused by separation allowed resident swamis and Western trustees much greater freedom of action than official policy envisioned. The division of functions between a swami and his American board has also frequently diverged from the preferred model. In a number of cases the swami has made all decisions, including economic determinations, which the society's board has automatically approved. Bound to the swami as their teacher and guru, few devotees would dare to object. Democratic in theory, frequently governing arrangements in American Vedanta societies have approached benign dictatorship. In a few cases, disagreement between Indian authorities and a local society has culminated in open rupture, as demonstrated by the secession of the Boston Vedanta Society and Ananda Ashrama following Swami Paramananda's death.

Tensions have mounted in recent years. One cause appears to be the desire of the present Indian leadership—the secretary general and the board of trustees at the Ramakrishna Math in particular—to impose tighter control over the American societies. The status and role of women monastics and the opening of new American centers especially trouble Indian officials. The desire for greater control seems natural; however, growing pressure from India has awakened the fears of some American followers, who prefer the autonomy and informality they have known in the past.

One must suspect that, at the deepest level, the issue of control is tied to Indian assumptions about American culture. Ramakrishna monks from the time of Vivekananda, like most other Indian observers, have viewed the United States as the ultimate embodiment of a materialistic society, while India is held up as the quintessential spiritual society. Asked to state their purpose in propagating Vedanta in the West, many swamis would respond that their goal is to replace Western materialism by Eastern spirituality. Though there is some basis for such a perception, the contrast obviously represents gross simplification,[23] but to some degree, Ramakrishna officials have accepted the need for strong Indian control of American centers as a requirement forced upon them by their perceptions of Americans' materialistic predisposition.

Formulated another way, the basic conflict involves questions of freedom versus authority. In India, few would question the authority of senior Ramakrishna monks. In the same way that a novice is expected to obey his guru, followers as a group are expected to accept the authority of the movement's president and general secretary. Conflict arises because most Americans favor a more individualistic tradition in which the individual chooses for herself or himself. Ironically, a number of Vedantists whom I interviewed explained their Hindu preference as a rejection of Christian dogma and authoritarianism in favor of religious freedom. So far, Belur's drive for greater control has led American followers not to open dissent but to quiet withdrawal.

A growing shortage of monks to carry on the Ramakrishna Order's far-flung operations represents another threat to the movement's future survival. To some extent, the problem has always existed, but pressure has intensified since World War II. As interest in Eastern spirituality has increased, the number of Americans who seek out Vedanta has also grown. Already stretched too thin, the society has no additional swamis to meet the demand. New Vedanta societies could be started overnight in a number of American cities if there were swamis available to lead them. Replacements for swamis now serving in the United States will be difficult to find because of the special skills and background required for success in the West. Today's swami not only should have unusual command of

English but considerable skill as an organizer, public speaker, and spiritual coun-
selor. At present there are barely enough swamis to oversee the extensive Indian
operations without shifting monks to the West.

It must be said that the movement's decision to rely entirely on Indian monks
to direct the American work has compounded the problem. Such a policy was
inevitable at first, since no one else was equipped to provide leadership. American
devotees regularly served on the board of trustees and assisted the swami as requested, but they never assumed leadership roles. Swami Paramananda was the
major exception, as indicated by his heavy reliance on Laura Glenn (Sister Devamata) and Georgina Jones (Sister Daya) to share the leadership burden at his
Boston and California centers. American-born swamis seem to offer the only re-
alistic hope of easing the shortage. Increasing numbers of American devotees have
completed their monastic training, including attendance at the monastic school
at the Belur Math, where Indian monks receive their preparation. They have become swamis in recent decades. American-born monks may conduct classes, deliver lectures, and oversee a wide range of activities traditionally reserved for
head swamis, but as yet no Western swami has been entrusted to head an American center. Though not openly expressed, Belur officials seem to fear that appointment of American swamis to lead the movement's Western societies could
precipitate unacceptable revisions in the Indian organization's work and even
schism.

The Ramakrishna movement's growing conservatism also poses some doubts
about the order's future. Adaptable and open to change in its first decades, the
movement became increasingly rigid in later years as it mostly rejected change.
In almost every way, the Vedanta societies of the 1890s and early 1900s conducted themselves as they do in the 1990s. The order's refusal to employ any
form of public advertising in its American work has guaranteed that, after 100
years, the movement remains relatively unknown. Indeed, it seems symbolic that
Vedanta societies are almost always housed unobtrusively in unmarked structures. My interviews repeatedly emphasized that future devotees had to take considerable pains to discover a Vedanta society and that, almost always, the follower
had to initiate the first contact. In the 1990s study classes employ the same texts
and use the same format as in the early 1900s; the lectures then and now appear
to be almost identical. While American Christianity in the last 100 years has
evolved from one-room country churches into multistory urban complexes and
shifted emphasis from the "old rugged cross" to the electronic ministry, the
Vedanta societies have remained frozen in time. Were Swami Vivekananda to
return today, he would find the movement's message and methods in the 1990s
almost identical with those of the 1890s.

Instead of adapting to the customs and practices of the United States, the
Ramakrishna movement seems to have become even more conservative with the
passage of time. Where changes have appeared, as in the growing "cult of Rama-

krishna" and increasing prominence of devotionalism, the direction is toward a more traditional Hinduism. Comparison with other Hindu movements such as the Self-Realization Fellowship and Transcendental Meditation underscore just how conservative the Ramakrishna movement's methods are. Unlike the Vedanta societies, both the Self-Realization and Transcendental Meditation movements consciously geared their messages to American tastes, built up sophisticated Western-style organizations, and employed the mass media heavily to reach a mass audience. Transplanted to Asia, Christianity has had to become more "Oriental" in order to win acceptance. In the same way, Vedanta will surely need to become "Americanized" before it can hope to make significant inroads in the United States.

Another development likely to affect the future of the Ramakrishna movement in the United States is the increasing role of Asian Indians in the Vedanta societies. Until the 1960s the movement's followers were always primarily "WASPs," that is individuals who were white, Anglo-Saxon, and Protestant by background. There have been black, Jewish, and Hispanic members; but the typical Vedantist throughout most of the movement's history was a WASP. The passage of the Immigration and Nationality Act of 1965 has clearly changed this. By placing Asian immigration on the same footing as European immigration, the law has permitted Indians to migrate to the United States in significant numbers for the first time. Strangers in a strange land, a rising number of these newly arrived Indians are affiliating with Vedanta societies, attracted by the desire to maintain their Indian identities as much as by the Ramakrishna movement's Vedantic message. In some cases Indian members already outnumber non-Indian members in the Vedanta societies.

The increase in Asian-born members is likely to diminish the attraction of Hinduism for native-born Americans if the latter begin to view the Vedanta societies as ethnic enclaves. The position of Buddhism in America may serve as an analogue. Though never more popular intellectually, in the United States today Buddhism is largely the religion of Japanese Americans and an increasing number of Vietnamese, Cambodian, Laotian, and other eastern and southeastern Asian immigrants. To the extent that they become ethnic organizations, the Vedanta societies will be less effective as transmitters of Hinduism to the West. In interviews, swamis both in India and the United States expressed concern that the rising American prominence of Asian Indians would detract from the movement's work in the West. Several expressed the hope that as the numbers of Indian Americans increase, they will prefer to build their own temples. These demographic changes are too recent to evaluate with any certainty.

Finally, the role of women in the Ramakrishna movement and, more specifically, differences between Indian and American attitudes on gender relationships could become a source of conflict in the future. Historically, swamis stationed in the United States have varied widely in attitude regarding women: while

Swamis Vivekananda and Paramananda seem to have treated female devotees much the same as males, tapping several women to serve in leadership positions, other swamis have preferred that their female devotees remain in the background.[24] As most monks grew up in conventional Hindu families where male dominance and female subordination have been the norm, a conservative outlook on gender seems natural. Symbolizing the Ramakrishna movement's recognition of the division between genders, male worshipers sit in the front and women at the back during evening worship at the Ramakrishna temple in Belur.

Attitudes and practices normal in Asia may not be acceptable in the West, however. In conversations with a number of American-born female devotees, I sensed considerable concern that Ramakrishna officials in India would seek to impose traditional Hindu roles on Western women. Most female followers willingly accept subordination as part of their spiritual training but would, in some cases at least, object to subordination to male dominance. Because of the relative autonomy of American Vedanta societies, historically women followers have enjoyed greater freedom than in India. Since 1960 the feminist movement has greatly increased American sensitivity concerning gender relationships. The drive for equality represents one of the major trends in modern America. Will female followers of Ramakrishna in the West embrace the more conservative Indian pattern, or will they insist on equality? Only the passage of time will tell. Widespread perception of the Ramakrishna movement as a male-dominant organization would seriously weaken its appeal for all Western people—male as well as female.

If the future remains dim, the role of the Ramakrishna movement in the history of Hinduism in the United States seems reasonably clear. In its first hundred years, it has already made its mark in three areas.

In the first place, it was the pioneer movement in the introduction of Hinduism in the West. When Swami Vivekananda appeared at the Parliament of Religions in 1893, Hinduism was an idea perhaps, but not a live option. An occasional Indian visitor had lectured on Hinduism before 1893, but Hinduism as a living religion in the West begins with Vivekananda. As already noted, the establishment of Vedanta societies in the United States after 1893 marked a critical moment in the history of Hinduism. While Christianity, Islam, and Buddhism had actively carried their teachings to other nations for many centuries, Hinduism had largely stayed at home. The swamis of the Ramakrishna movement first introduced Hinduism in the West and at the same time undermined older assumptions about its nonmissionary role.

Second, the Ramakrishna movement's efforts induced a number of other Asian religious movements also to open work in the West. Glowing reports of Swami Vivekananda's appearance at the Parliament of Religions and the resulting perception that Americans eagerly looked to Eastern spirituality undoubtedly inspired other Asian teachers to look West. Why has the United States, more than other Western nations, been so attractive to Asian religious groups? A number of answers to the question may be submitted, but one obvious explanation is the example of Swami Vivekananda. The widely reported success of his American lectures encouraged other Asian teachers to look to the United States as an especially fertile terrain in which to broadcast the seeds of Eastern spirituality.

Finally, more than any other group, the Ramakrishna movement has become the "official" voice of Hinduism in the West. The original attitude of distrust toward all Hindu religious groups encouraged by the sensationalistic charges of Mabel Potter Daggett and Elizabeth Reed in the first decades of the century has dissipated. Over the long run, the Ramakrishna movement's obvious commitment to present Vedanta at a high level, the swamis' strong intellectual qualifications, and an ecumenical attitude toward other religious bodies have won over most critics. Evidence of public acceptance has been frequently cited in the preceding pages and includes regular contacts with major American academic and religious leaders; frequent invitations to participate in interreligious dialogue; and wide reference to their books and translations by scholars, theologians, and the general public. At religious congresses and interreligious meetings a Ramakrishna swami is almost certain to be the invited participant when a Hindu religious viewpoint is required. One hundred years in the United States has given the movement a visibility and degree of acceptance unequaled by any other Asian group.

Despite any present and future difficulties, there seems little doubt that the Ramakrishna movement will remain a significant force in Asia and the West for many years to come. In India Ramakrishna and Vivekananda are today hailed as national heroes who not only resurrected and revitalized Hinduism but assisted in India's national rebirth. The Indian government in recent decades has repeatedly singled out the movement for special recognition, streets are named in honor of its founders, and the Ramakrishna Mission Institute of Culture in Calcutta is applauded for its contributions to Indian intellectual life. Nearly 100 centers scattered throughout the Indian subcontinent continue to spread Ramakrishna's and Vivekananda's teachings, manage schools, and engage in extensive medical and relief operations.[25] Though the Order and its leaders have come under increasing attack from critics on the left because of their organization's close relations with the government and defense of traditional Hinduism, the Ramakrishna movement remains one of India's most respected and honored bodies.

Less prominently and on a far smaller scale, the movement's Vedanta societies have also achieved growing recognition and acceptance in the West. Present in the United States since the 1890s and represented today by twelve major centers, several branch centers and ashramas, considerable assets and property holdings, 2,500 active members, and many more sympathetic nonmembers, the Ramakrishna movement also seems certain to remain active in America for decades and, perhaps, centuries to come. Though its conservative methods make rapid expansion unlikely, its well-established centers and nearly a century of Western experience also make its collapse improbable. While its membership in the United States has always been extremely small, the number of followers is, nevertheless, sufficient to assure survival. The emergence of a more sympathetic attitude toward Asian religions since the 1960s enhances the probability of future growth and long-term survival. Considering that we are speaking of a body once dismissed as too "other" ever to take root in America, the Ramakrishna movement's achievement is impressive.

Few movements better illustrate the complexity of cross-cultural interactions. If the Ramakrishna movement has sought to transmit Eastern ideals and practices to the West, it has also sponsored Western conceptions and programs in the East. The movement's acclaimed educational and humanitarian projects in India owe much to the West. Not so many years ago, Western writers proclaimed the imminent Western domination of the world. Today, we recognize that the movement of influence East and West is very much a two-way process. As a pioneer in paving the way for introduction of Asian religious conceptions in the West, the Ramakrishna movement may be said to stand on the edge of one of the "megatrends" of modern world history.

Vedanta Centers

United States

California

Vedanta Society of Berkeley
2455 Bowditch St.
Berkeley, CA 94704
(415) 848-8862

Vedanta Society of Northern California
2323 Vallejo St.
San Francisco, CA 94123
(415) 922-2323

> Vedanta Retreat
> P.O. Box 215
> Olema, CA 94950
> (415) 663-1258

Vedanta Society of Sacramento
1337 Mission Ave.
Carmichael, CA 95608
(916) 489-5137

Vedanta Society of Southern California
1946 Vedanta Pl.
Hollywood, CA 90068
(213) 465-7114

> Santa Barbara Temple
> 927 Ladera Lane
> Santa Barbara, CA 93108
> (805) 969-2903

Ramakrishna Monastery
P.O. Box 408
Trabuco Canyon, CA 92678
(714) 858-0342

Ramakrishna Monastery
1440 Upas St.
San Diego, CA 92103
(619) 291-9377

Illinois

Vivekananda Vedanta Society
5423 South Hyde Park Blvd.
Chicago, IL 60615
(312) 363-0027

Massachusetts

Ramakrishna-Vedanta Society of Massachusetts
58 Deerfield St.
Boston, MA 02215
(617) 536-5320

Michigan

Vivekananda Monastery and Retreat
Route #2, 122nd Ave.
Ganges Township, MI 49408
(616) 543-4545

Missouri

Vedanta Society of St. Louis
205 South Skinker Blvd.
St. Louis, MO 63105
(314) 721-5118

New York

Ramakrishna-Vivekananda Center
17 East 94th St.
New York, NY 10028
(212) 534-9445

Vedanta Society
34 W. 71st St.
New York, NY 10023
(212) 877-9197

Oregon

> Vedanta Society of Portland
> 1157 So. E. 55th Ave.
> Portland, OR 97215
> (503) 235-3919

Rhode Island

> Vedanta Society of Providence
> 224 Angell St.
> Providence, RI 02906
> (401) 421-3960

Washington

> Vedanta Society of Western Washington
> 2716 Broadway East
> Seattle, WA 98102
> (206) 323-1228

Other Centers in the West

Argentina

> Ramakrishna Ashrama
> Gaspar Campos 1149
> Bella Vista 1661 Buenos Aires
> Argentina
> 666-0098

Canada

> Vedanta Society of Toronto
> 650 Meadows Blvd.
> Mississauga, Ontario, Canada L4Z 3K4
> (416) 566-5775

England

> Ramakrishna Vedanta Centre
> Unity House, Blind Lane
> Bourne End, Bucks, SL8-5LG
> England
> 26464

France

> Centre Vedantique Ramakrichna
> Boîte Postale No. 27
> 77220 Gretz, France
> 407-03-11

Switzerland

> Centre Vedantique
> 9 Chemin des Gravannes
> Ch. 1246 Corsier
> Geneva, Switzerland

Notes

1. The Nineteenth-Century Background

1. Percival Spear, *A History of India: Volume Two* (Hammondsworth, England: Penguin Books, 1978), 116. See also Percival Griffiths, *Modern India* (4th ed.; New York: Frederick Praeger, 1965), 63–66.

2. Scholars such as Agehananda Bharati and Eric Sharpe raise serious doubts whether one may any longer speak of the complex practices and conceptions of Indian religion as "Hinduism," a term which conveys the illusion of a more systematic, more unified philosophical tradition than is warranted by the facts. Sharing their misgivings, Robert Minor always refers to "Hinduism" in quotes, as indicated in his "Sarvepalli Radhakrishnan and 'Hinduism': Defined and Defended," in Robert D. Baird (ed.), *Religion in Modern India* (New Delhi: Manohar Publications, 1981), 305–38. Though the point is well taken, such a practice seems awkward. In succeeding pages the term will always be used without quotes—with the admonition that, as much as possible, one must resist the temptation of reconceptualizing the South Asian religion. Particularly see Agehananda Bharati, "The Hindu Renaissance and Its Apologetic Patterns," *Journal of Asian Studies* 29 (Feb. 1970), 267–87.

3. Quoted in Charles H. Heimsath, *Indian Nationalism and Hindu Social Reform* (Princeton: Princeton University Press, 1964), 11. For background, see William T. de Bary (ed.), *Sources of Indian Tradition* (New York: Columbia University Press, 1958); A. L. Basham, *The Wonder that Was India* (rev. ed.; New York: Hawthorn Books, 1963); Heinrich Zimmer, *Philosophies of India*, ed. Joseph Campbell (New York: Meridian Books, 1956); and Kenneth W. Morgan (ed.), *The Religion of the Hindus, Interpreted by Hindus* (New York: Ronald Press, 1953).

4. Stephen Neill, *A History of Christian Missions* (Hammondsworth, England: Penguin Books, 1964); Sushil M. Pathak, *American Missionaries and Hinduism: A Study of Their Contacts from 1813 to 1912* (Delhi: Mushiram Manoharlal, 1967), especially 77–89; and Carl T. Jackson, *The Oriental Religions and American Thought: Nineteenth-Century Explorations* (Westport, Conn.: Greenwood Press, 1981), 85–102.

5. See D. S. Sarma, *Studies in the Renaissance of Hinduism in the Nineteenth and Twentieth Centuries* (Benares: Benares Hindu University, 1944); John N. Farquhar, *Modern Religious Movements in India* (New York: Macmillan, 1915); and Robert D. Baird (ed.), *Religion in Modern India* (New Delhi: Manohar Publications, 1981).

6. De Bary, *Sources of Indian Tradition*, 604.

7. See the sketches in Sivanath Sastri, *History of the Brahmo Samaj*, 2 vols. (Calcutta: R. Chatterji, 1911–12), I, 1–79; Sarma, *Studies in the Renaissance of Hinduism*, 71–116; and Baird, *Religion in Modern India*, 163–77.

8. De Bary, *Sources of Indian Tradition*, 602.

9. David Kopf, *The Brahmo Samaj and the Shaping of the Modern Indian Mind* (Princeton: Princeton University Press, 1979). See also Spencer Lavan, "The Brahmo Samaj:

India's First Modern Movement for Religious Reform," in Baird, *Religion in Modern India*, 1–25, and Sarma, *Studies in the Renaissance of Hinduism*, 17–116.

10. Protap C. Mozoomdar [Majumdar], *The Life and Teachings of Keshub Chunder Sen* (Calcutta: Baptist Mission Press, 1887), and Kopf, *Brahmo Samaj*, 249–86.

11. See Kenneth W. Jones, *Arya Dharm: Hindu Consciousness in 19th-Century Punjab* (Berkeley: University of California Press, 1976), especially chap. 2; Sarma, *Studies in the Renaissance of Hinduism*, 164–92; and Hal W. French and Arvind Sharma, *Religious Ferment in Modern India* (New York: St. Martin's Press, 1981), 46–49.

12. See the discussion in Harold W. French, *The Swan's Wide Waters: Ramakrishna and Western Culture* (Port Washington, New York: Kennikat Press, 1974), particularly 145–85.

13. For the most up-to-date scholarly treatment, see Bruce F. Campbell, *Ancient Wisdom Revived: A History of the Theosophical Movement* (Berkeley: University of California Press, 1980). See also Gertrude M. Williams, *Priestess of the Occult (Madame Blavatsky)* (New York: Alfred Knopf, 1946).

14. See the author's *Oriental Religions and American Thought*, already cited. I have drawn heavily on the book's findings in the pages immediately following.

15. Josiah Quincy (ed.), *The Journals of Major Samuel Shaw* (Boston: William Crosby & H. P. Nichols, 1847), 195.

16. Stuart C. Miller, "The American Trader's Image of China, 1785–1840," *Pacific Historical Review* 36 (Nov. 1967), 375–95, and Jackson, *Oriental Religions*, 6–13.

17. Clifton J. Phillips, *Protestant America and the Pagan World: The First Half Century of the American Board of Commissioners for Foreign Missions, 1810–1860* (Cambridge, Mass.: Harvard East Asian Monographs #32, 1969), and Pathak, *American Missionaries and Hinduism*.

18. For example, see Virchand R. Gandhi, "Why Christian Missions Have Failed in India," *Forum* 17 (Apr. 1894), 160–66, and Purushotam Rao Telang, "Christian Missions as Seen by a Brahmin," *Forum* 18 (Dec. 1894), 481–89.

19. [William Tudor], "Theology of the Hindoos, as Taught by Ram Mohun Roy," *North American Review* 6 (Mar. 1818), 386–93. Quotes on pp. 386 and 389. See Jackson, *Oriental Religions*, 36–40.

20. John T. Rutt (ed.), *The Theological and Miscellaneous Works of Joseph Priestley* (Hackney, England: George Smallfield, 1817), XVII, 161, 166, 204.

21. Adrienne Moore, *Rammohan Roy and America* (Calcutta: Sadharan Brahmo Samaj, 1942).

22. Spencer Lavan, *Unitarians and India: A Study in Encounter and Response* (Boston: Beacon Press, 1977), and Jackson, *Oriental Religions*, 32–36 and 103–22.

23. Bradford Torrey and Francis H. Allen (eds.), *The Writings of Henry David Thoreau*, 20 vols. (New York: AMS Press, 1968), VII, 266.

24. See Arthur E. Christy, *The Orient in American Transcendentalism: A Study of Emerson, Thoreau, and Alcott* (1932; reprint ed., New York: Octagon Books, 1963), and Frederic I. Carpenter, *Emerson and Asia* (Cambridge, Mass.: Harvard University Press, 1930).

25. See Carl T. Jackson, "The Orient in Post-Bellum American Thought: Three Pioneer Popularizers," *American Quarterly* 22 (Spring 1970), 67–81.

26. Clarke, *Ten Great Religions: An Essay in Comparative Theology* (Boston: James R. Osgood, 1871). For biographical details, see Edward Everett Hale (ed.), *James Freeman Clarke: Autobiography, Diary, and Correspondence* (Boston: Houghton Mifflin, 1891), and Arthur S. Bolster, Jr., *James Freeman Clarke: Disciple to Advancing Truth* (Boston: Beacon, 1954).

27. Johnson, *Oriental Religions and Their Relation to Universal Religion: India* (Boston:

James R. Osgood, 1872), 2. See also *Oriental Religions and Their Relation to Universal Religion: China* (Boston: James R. Osgood, 1877). The third volume focused on Persian religion. For biographical details, see Roger C. Mueller, "Samuel Johnson, American Transcendentalist: A Short Biography," *Essex Institute Historical Collections* 115 (Jan. 1979), 9–60.

28. Conway (ed.), *The Sacred Anthology: A Book of Ethnical Scriptures* (5th ed.; London: Trubner, 1876). For biographical details, see Conway's *Autobiography: Memories and Experiences of Moncure Daniel Conway*, 2 vols. (Boston: Houghton Mifflin, 1904), and Mary B. Burtis, *Moncure Conway, 1832–1907* (New Brunswick, N.J.: Rutgers University Press, 1952).

29. Conway, *My Pilgrimage to the Wise Men of the East* (Boston: Houghton Mifflin, 1906), 240.

30. Brooks to Mrs. Arthur Brooks, Jan. 30, 1883, reprinted in Alexander V. G. Allen, *Life and Letters of Phillips Brooks*, 2 vols. (New York: E. P. Dutton, 1900), II, 393.

31. Cited in Arthur E. Christy (ed.), *The Asian Legacy and American Life* (New York: John Day, 1942), 43. See Brooks Wright, *Interpreter of Buddhism to the West: Sir Edwin Arnold* (New York: Bookman Associates, 1957).

32. Clarke, "Affinities of Buddhism and Christianity," *North American Review* 136 (May 1883), 467–77.

33. See the chapter on Notovitch in Edgar J. Goodspeed, *Strange New Gospels* (Chicago: University of Chicago Press, 1931), 10–24. Notovitch's book was published in a new edition as late as 1926.

34. See the author's "The Emergence of the Oriental Scholar," in *Oriental Religions*, 179–99. A full-length study of the origins and history of Oriental scholarship in America is badly needed.

35. Lewis H. Jordan, *Comparative Religion: Its Genesis and Growth* (Edinburgh: T. & T. Clark, 1905); Eric L. Sharpe, *Comparative Religion: A History* (London: Gerald Duckworth, 1975), particularly 97ff. and 136–38; and Joseph M. Kitagawa, "The History of Religions in America," in Mircea Eliade and Joseph M. Kitagawa (eds.), *The History of Religions: Essays in Methodology* (Chicago: University of Chicago Press, 1959), 1–7.

36. Paul A. Carter, *The Spiritual Crisis of the Gilded Age* (DeKalb, Ill.: Northern Illinois University Press, 1971). Arthur M. Schlesinger, Sr., "A Critical Period in American Religion, 1875–1900," *Proceedings of the Massachusetts Historical Society* 64 (June 1932), 523–47, called attention to the special difficulties as far back as the 1930s.

2. The Founders

1. F. Max Müller, *Ramakrishna: His Life and Sayings* (New York: Charles Scribners, 1899); Romain Rolland, *Prophets of the New India* (New York: Albert & Charles Boni, 1930); and Christopher Isherwood, *Ramakrishna and His Disciples* (New York: Simon & Schuster, 1959).

2. *The Gospel of Sri Ramakrishna*, trans. Swami Nikhilananda (New York: Ramakrishna-Vivekananda Center, 1942), vii-viii. See the analysis of the *Gospel* in Isherwood, *Ramakrishna and His Disciples*, 257–82, and Walter G. Neevel, Jr., "The Transformation of Sri Ramakrishna," in Bardwell L. Smith (ed.), *Hinduism: New Essays in the History of Religions* (Leiden: E. J. Brill, 1976), 57–64.

3. *Gospel of Ramakrishna*, 3–5, and Swami Saradananda, *Sri Ramakrishna: The Great Master* (Madras: Sri Ramakrishna Math, 1952).

4. Neevel, "Transformation of Sri Ramakrishna," 69–70.

5. *Gospel of Ramakrishna*, 18.

6. See Saradananda, *Sri Ramakrishna*, 182–203.

7. *Gospel of Ramakrishna*, 20–21. See Herbert V. Guenther, *The Tantric View of Life* (Berkeley: Shambala, 1972), and Agehananda Bharati, *The Tantric Tradition* (Garden City, New York: Anchor Books, 1970). Tantrism has played a large role in Buddhism as well as Hinduism. In the United States members of the so-called hippie generation also indicated strong interest in Tantra during the 1960s.

8. See Walter Neevel, "Transformation of Sri Ramakrishna," 75–78, and Heinrich Zimmer, *Philosophies of India*, ed. Joseph Campbell (New York: Meridian Books, 1956), 560ff. Zimmer was one of the first scholars to call attention to Tantric influence on Ramakrishna.

9. The Vedanta philosophy is more fully discussed in chapter 4.

10. Among these testimonies, the most extreme was Swami Saradananda's claim that, following Tota Puri's departure, Ramakrishna remained almost continuously absorbed in samadhi for six months. See Saradananda, *Sri Ramakrishna*, 246–53.

11. Gupta, "A Day with Ramakrishna Paramahansa," *Prabuddha Bharata* 41 (Feb. 1936), 105, originally published in the May 1927 issue of the *Modern Review*. Gupta had been an editor of the Lahore *Tribune*.

12. Rolland, *Prophets of New India*, 20; Müller, *Ramakrishna*, 94; and Wendell Thomas, *Hinduism Invades America* (New York: Beacon Press, 1930), 59.

13. See the analysis in D. S. Sarma, "The Experience of Sri Ramakrishna Paramahamsa," *Journal of Religion* 7 (Mar. 1927), 186–203. Aldous Huxley popularized the conception that Western and Eastern mystics represented different voices describing a common reality. See his *The Perennial Philosophy* (New York: Harper, 1945).

14. Sastri, *Men I Have Seen: Personal Reminiscences of Seven Great Bengalis* (Calcutta: Sadharan Brahmo Samaj, 1948), 63.

15. Swami Nikhilananda, *Vivekananda: A Biography* (1st Indian ed.; Calcutta: Advaita Ashrama, 1964), 75–76n.1.

16. Saradananda, *Sri Ramakrishna*, 259–60.

17. Ibid., 295–96.

18. Cyrus R. Pangborn, "The Ramakrishna Math and Mission: A Case Study of a Revitalization Movement," in Smith, *Hinduism: New Essays*, 103.

19. See, for example, Freda Matchett, "The Teaching of Ramakrishna in Relation to the Hindu Tradition and as Interpreted by Vivekananda," *Religion* 11 (Apr. 1981), 171–84.

20. Reproduced in Swami Vivekananda, *My Master; With an Appended Extract from the Theistic Quarterly Review* (New York: Baker & Taylor, 1901), 71, originally published in October 1879. In the United States Majumdar was generally referred to in nineteenth-century accounts as "Protap Chunder Mozoomdar."

21. Swami Satprakashananda, "The Image of Sri Ramakrishna: Its Significance," *Vedanta Kesari* 38 (Apr. 1952), 452, and Swami Nikhilananda, "Sri Ramakrishna's Spiritual Experiences," ibid., 41 (Mar. 1955), 387.

22. His Eastern and Western Disciples, *The Life of Swami Vivekananda* (8th ed., Calcutta: Advaita Ashrama, 1974), 3–31, and Swami Nikhilananda, *Vivekananda: A Biography* (1st Indian ed.; Calcutta: Advaita Ashrama, 1964), 1–17.

23. Reported in Bhupendranath Datta, *Swami Vivekananda: Patriot Saint* (Calcutta: Nababharat Publishers, 1954), 154.

24. His Eastern and Western Disciples, *Life of Vivekananda*, 28. See also George M. Williams, *The Quest for Meaning of Swami Vivekananda: A Study of Religious Change* (Chico, Calif.: New Horizons Press, 1974), 10–15.

25. Seal, "An Early Stage of Vivekananda's Mental Development," *Prabuddha Bharata* 12 (Apr. 1907), 64–65.

26. His Eastern and Western Disciples, *Life of Vivekananda*, 24.

27. Nikhilananda, *Vivekananda*, 24.

28. George M. Williams, "Swami Vivekananda: Archetypal Hero or Doubting Saint?" in Robert D. Baird (ed.), *Religion in Modern India* (New Delhi: Manohar Publications, 1981), 204–208.

29. His Eastern and Western Disciples, *Life of Vivekananda*, 151–67, and Nikhilananda, *Vivekananda*, 70–74.

30. Isherwood, *Ramakrishna and His Disciples*, 318.

31. Williams, *Quest for Meaning*, 47–51.

32. His Eastern and Western Admirers, *Reminiscences of Swami Vivekananda* (2nd ed.; Calcutta: Advaita Ashrama, 1964), 38.

33. See his comments in letters dated Dec. 28, 1893, and Mar. 19, 1894, in *The Complete Works of Swami Vivekananda* (14th ed.; Calcutta: Advaita Ashrama, 1974), V, 27, and VI, 254–55. Marie Louise Burke, *Swami Vivekananda in America: New Discoveries* (2nd rev. ed.; Calcutta: Advaita Ashrama, 1966), 365–76, concludes that the idea of a separate Western mission did not crystallize in Vivekananda's mind until late 1894.

34. John Henry Barrows (ed.), *The World's Parliament of Religions* (Chicago: The Parliament Publishing Co., 1893), 2 vols; J. V. Nash, "India at the World's Parliament of Religions," *The Open Court* 47 (June 1933), 217–30; and Kent Druyvesteyn, "The World's Parliament of Religions" (Ph.D. dissertation, University of Chicago, 1976).

35. His Eastern and Western Disciples, *Life of Vivekananda*, 300–26, and Nikhilananda, *Vivekananda*, 116–37.

36. Monroe, *A Poet's Life: Seventy Years in a Changing World* (New York: Macmillan, 1938), 137.

37. Burke, *Vivekananda in America*, 95ff., and His Eastern and Western Disciples, *Life of Vivekananda*, 335–51.

38. Quoted in Burke, *Swami Vivekananda in America*, 159 and 175.

39. Ibid., 289–313.

40. Ellinwood, "A Hindu Missionary in America," *Homiletic Review* 28 (Nov. and Dec. 1894), 400–406 and 494–99; *Missionary Review of the World* 7 (Mar. 1894), 221.

41. Virchand Gandhi, "Why Christian Missions Have Failed in India," *Forum* 17 (Apr. 1894), 160–66. Fred P. Powers answered Gandhi in "The Success of Christian Missions in India," *Forum* 17 (June 1894), 475–83. The debate was continued by Purushotam R. Telang, "Home Life in India: Child-Marriages and Widows," *Forum* 18 (Sept. 1894), 95–106, and J. M. Thoburn, Bishop of the Methodist Episcopalian Church in India, in "Christian Missions in India," *Forum* 18 (Dec. 1894), 481–501. Gandhi responded in the *Arena* 11 (Jan. 1895), 157–66. The debate continued in *The Monist* 5 (Jan. 1895), 264–81, with contributions from Gandhi, Bishop Thoburn, and Paul Carus. In India John Murdoch alerted readers to Vivekananda's charges in *Swami Vivekananda on Hinduism: An Examination of His Address at the Chicago Parliament of Religions* (Madras: Christian Literature Society, 1895).

42. For a fuller discussion of turn-of-the-century missionary thinking concerning the Asian religions, see chap. 1, "Protestant Missionary Attitudes to Hinduism after 1858," in Eric J. Sharpe, *Not to Destroy But to Fulfill: The Contribution of J. N. Farquhar to Protestant Missionary Thought in India before 1914* (Uppsala: Swedish Institute of Missionary Research, 1965). See also Charles W. Forman, "A History of Foreign Mission Theory in America," pp. 69–140 in R. Pierce Beaver (ed.), *American Missions in Bicentennial Perspective* (South Pasadena, Calif.: William Carey Library, 1977).

43. *Letters of Swami Vivekananda* (3rd ed.; Calcutta: Advaita Ashrama, 1970), 115; *Complete Works of Vivekananda*, V, 51.

44. *Complete Works of Vivekananda*, VI, 301.

45. Burke, *Vivekananda in the West*, 367–74.

46. *Complete Works of Vivekananda*, VI, 303; ibid., V, 72.

47. See Sister Christine, "Vivekananda and His Message," *Vedanta and the West* 10 (Sept.–Oct. and Nov.–Dec. 1947), 135–45, 167–72; Mary C. Funke, "Reminiscences of Swami Vivekananda," *Prabuddha Bharata* 32 (Feb. 1927), 71–77; and Marie Louise Burke, *Swami Vivekananda in the West: New Discoveries. The World Teacher: Part One* (Calcutta: Advaita Ashrama, 1985), 104–81. The house where the group stayed has been restored and serves today as a Ramakrishna movement museum and summer retreat.

48. His Eastern and Western Disciples, *Life of Vivekananda*, 359.

49. Ibid., 383.

50. The swami's return to India is analyzed in Gambhirananda, *History of Ramakrishna Math*, 114–40, and His Eastern and Western Disciples, *Life of Vivekananda*, 452–538. Sankari Prasad Basu and Sunil Bihari Ghosh (eds.) trace the swami's Indian reception in *Vivekananda in Indian Newspapers, 1893–1902* (Calcutta: Bookland Private Ltd., 1969).

51. His Eastern and Western Disciples, *Life of Vivekananda*, 456–57; *Complete Works of Vivekananda*, III, 132–33.

52. Gambhirananda, *History of Ramakrishna Math*, 119–21, and His Eastern and Western Disciples, *Life of Vivekananda*, 500–504 and 634–37.

53. His Eastern and Western Disciples, *Life of Vivekananda*, 494.

54. See Marie Louise Burke, *Swami Vivekananda: His Second Visit to the West. New Discoveries* (Calcutta: Advaita Ashrama, 1973); quoted material on 618–19.

55. Burke, *Vivekananda in America*, 642, and *Vivekananda: Second Visit*, 259–60.

56. See chap. 4 for a fuller discussion of the attitude toward science.

57. *Complete Works of Vivekananda*, I, 124.

58. His Eastern and Western Admirers, *Reminiscences*, offers a selection of vivid portraits; see also Burke, *Vivekananda in America*, 631–41.

59. Quoted in His Eastern and Western Disciples, *Life of Vivekananda*, 312.

60. Harold Isaacs, *Images of Asia: American Views of China and India* (New York: Capricorn Books, 1962), 239–302. The volume was originally published as *Scratches on Our Minds*.

61. Isherwood, "What Vedanta Means to Me," *Vedanta and the West* 14 (Sept.–Oct. 1951), 158–59.

62. A California Disciple, "Swami Vivekananda: A Reminiscence," *Prabuddha Bharata* 20 (Feb. and Mar. 1915), 32; Ida Ansell, in *Reminiscences of Vivekananda*, 381.

3. Trials of Survival

1. See Wendell Thomas, *Hinduism Invades America* (New York: Beacon Press, 1930), especially 177–87, 217–18, and 221–22. See also Raymond Brady Williams, *Religions of Immigrants from India and Pakistan: New Threads in the American Tapestry* (Cambridge: Cambridge University Press, 1988), which focuses on developments since the 1965 passage of the Immigration and Nationality Act.

2. Quoted in Burke, *Swami Vivekananda in the West: New Discoveries. The World Teacher: Part One* (Calcutta: Advaita Ashrama, 1985), 326. Reprinted in vol. 7 of *The Complete Works of Swami Vivekananda*, the letter was mistakenly attributed to Vivekananda's Indian disciple Perumal Alasinga. See ibid., 380.

3. Ibid., 373.

4. See Swami Aseshananda, *Glimpses of a Great Soul: A Portrait of Swami Saradananda* (Hollywood: Vedanta Press, 1982), for fuller details. Saradananda is mainly remembered as the

author of *Sri Ramakrishna: The Great Master*, the most authoritative "inside" biography of Ramakrishna.

5. Swami Atulananda [Cornelius Heyblom], "My First Contacts with Vedanta," *Prabuddha Bharata* 59 (Feb. 1954), 71. The most important source is *The Complete Works of Swami Abhedananda, Birth Centenary Edition* (Calcutta: Ramakrishna Vedanta Math, 1967–70), 10 vols. His autobiography appears in "My Life-Story," in X, 595–774. See also Sister Shivani [Mary LePage], *An Apostle of Monism: An Authentic Account of the Activities of Swami Abhedananda in America* (Calcutta: Ramakrishna Vedanta Math, 1947), and the sketch in Swami Gambhirananda (ed.), *The Apostles of Shri Ramakrishna* (Calcutta: Advaita Ashrama, 1967), 252–65.

6. See "Letter of a New York Friend," *Brahmavadin* 3 (June 16, 1898), 769–71.

7. Ibid., 5 (Jan. 1900), 170–71; ibid., 6 (Feb. 1901), 214.

8. Ibid., 5 (Jan. 1900), 166; ibid., 6 (Feb. 1901), 214–15; *Prabuddha Bharata* 5 (July 1900), 111–12.

9. *Brahmavadin* 6 (Dec. 1900), 134–38; "Vedanta Work in New York," *Pacific Vedantist* 1 (Feb. 1902), 19.

10. Marie Louise Burke, *Swami Vivekananda: His Second Visit to the West. New Discoveries* (Calcutta: Advaita Ashrama, 1973), 633, 634.

11. *Pacific Vedantist* 1 (Feb. 1902), 19.

12. See *Brahmavadin* 6 (Dec. 1900), 136–37; ibid., 9 (Mar. 1904), 116–19; *Vedanta Monthly Bulletin* 1 (May 1905), 32; ibid., 1 (July 1905), 61.

13. *Brahmavadin* 6 (Dec. 1900), 134–38, and *Prabuddha Bharata* 5 (Mar. 1900), 5. The children's class is described in a sensationalistic article, "New York's Juvenile Vedantists," originally published in the *New York Herald*, Mar. 4, 1900, and reprinted in *Prabuddha Bharata* 5 (May 1900), 77–78.

14. *Vedanta Monthly Bulletin* 1 (Feb. 1906), 167.

15. *Prabuddha Bharata* 5 (June 1900), 93; *Vedanta Monthly Bulletin* 2 (May 1906), 31.

16. Radhakrishnan and Muirhead (eds.), *Contemporary Indian Philosophy* (2nd rev. ed.; London: George Allen & Unwin, 1952), 49–64.

17. Abhedananda, *India and Her People* (New York: Vedanta Society, 1906), 15–16 and 19.

18. Abhedananda, *Vedanta Philosophy: Religion of the Hindus* (New York: Vedanta Society, 1901), 17–18.

19. Swami Gambhirananda, *History of the Ramakrishna Math*, 178–79, briefly mentions the collapse in his official history, but quickly moves on, dismissing the event as "this rather delicate episode of our history." See also the chapter in Gambhirananda (ed.), *Apostles of Ramakrishna*, 252–65.

20. *Vedanta Monthly Bulletin* 3 (July 1907), 78; ibid., 4 (June 1908), 37; ibid., 4 (Mar. 1909), 118–19; ibid., 5 (July-Aug. 1909), 160; *Prabuddha Bharata* 13 (Apr. 1908), 76, and ibid., 13 (Sept. 1908), 172.

21. *Vedanta Monthly Bulletin* 3 (Jan. 1908), 173; ibid., 3 (Mar. 1908), 208–209; *Brahmavadin* 13 (Oct. 1908), 496.

22. *The Complete Works of Swami Vivekananda, Mayavati Memorial Edition* (14th ed.; Calcutta: Advaita Ashrama, 1973), VIII, 515, 516.

23. A Brahmacharin [Cornelius Heyblom], "With the Swamis in America," *Prabuddha Bharata* 23 (Dec. 1918), 277–78.

24. Despite her partisanship, I have mainly relied on the account of Sister Shivani, *Apostle of Monism*, 151–52. Abhedananda's loyal disciple provides the only detailed description of what happened.

25. Sister Devamata [Laura Glenn], "A Life Picture of Swami Paramananda," *Message of the East* 29 (July–Aug.–Sept. 1940), 145.

26. Gambhirananda, *History of the Ramakrishna Math*, 179.

27. *Prabuddha Bharata* 17 (Oct. 1912), 197, and Sister Shivani, *Apostle of Monism*, 168 and *passim*.

28. *Prabuddha Bharata* 20 (July 1915), 140; ibid., 25 (Apr. 1920), 96; ibid., 26 (Sept. 1921), 216; and Gambhirananda, *History of the Ramakrishna Math*, 259–62 and 352–53.

29. Actually, Swami Turiyananda preceded Trigunatita at San Francisco, leading the society from 1900–1902. One of the most traditional monks to come to the United States, he had difficulty adjusting to American conditions and soon returned to India. See Swami Ritajananda, *Swami Turiyananda: A Direct Disciple of Sri Ramakrishna* (Madras: Sri Ramakrishna Math, 1963), and the chapter in Gambhirananda, *Apostles of Ramakrishna*, 303–23.

30. *Complete Works of Vivekananda*, VI, 297. See the twelve-article series by His Western Disciples, "The Work of Swami Trigunatita in the West," *Prabuddha Bharata* 33 (Jan.–Dec. 1928), and Gambhirananda, *Apostles of Ramakrishna*, 328–49.

31. See *Brahmavadin* 9 (Feb. 1904), 48; "Rules of the Vedanta Society," *Voice of Freedom* 3 (Apr. 1911), n.p.; and *Prabuddha Bharata* 33 (May 1928), 226. The new journal replaced the defunct *Pacific Vedantist*.

32. *Prabuddha Bharata* 33 (Aug. 1928), 356–57; ibid., 33 (Mar. 1928), 131.

33. *Prabuddha Bharata* 33 (Mar. 1928), 131–32; *Voice of Freedom* 1 (Apr. 1909), n.p.; ibid., 1 (June 1909), vii.

34. *Prabuddha Bharata* 33 (Sept. 1928), 407; ibid., 33 (Apr. 1928), 162.

35. Ibid., 8 (Aug. 1903), 148; ibid., 22 (May 1917), 94–96; *Voice of Freedom* 3 (Apr. 1911), 20.

36. See, for example, "Hindu Immigration," *Voice of Freedom* 2 (Sept. 1910), 119–29; and "The World's War," ibid., 6 (Sept. 1914–Feb. 1915), 101–108, 129–38, 148–57, 173–78, 188–95, 207–10.

37. *Vedanta Monthly Bulletin* 1 (Apr. 1905), 12; *Voice of Freedom* 1 (Oct. 1909), 107. Original italics omitted. No author is listed, but internal evidence leaves little doubt that Trigunatita was the author.

38. *Voice of Freedom* 3 (Nov. 1911), 151–52; ibid., 2 (Dec. 1910), 195. The depth of Trigunatita's commitment to socialism may be debated. Apparently, his political sympathies did not foreclose making profits through real estate speculation, since he periodically bought property in San Francisco's expanding neighborhoods in the hope of selling later at a better price. To be sure, he channeled all proceeds back into the Vedanta work. See *Prabuddha Bharata* 33 (Sept. 1928), 409.

39. *Prabuddha Bharata* 33 (May 1928), 230.

40. Ibid., 33 (Apr. 1928), 161–65.

41. Ibid., 33 (May 1928), 227.

42. See *Voice of Freedom* 6 (Feb. 1915), 203; *Prabuddha Bharata* 33 (Oct. 1928), 465–67.

43. *Prabuddha Bharata* 33 (Dec. 1928), 563–68; see also *San Francisco Chronicle*, Dec. 28–29, 1914.

44. See Sister Devamata [Laura Glenn], *Swami Paramananda and His Work* (La Crescenta, Calif.: Ananda Ashrama, 1926–1941), and Sara Ann Levinsky, *A Bridge of Dreams: The Story of Paramananda, A Modern Mystic, and His Ideal of All-Conquering Love* (West Stockbridge, Mass.: Lindisfarne Press, 1984).

45. Levinsky, *Bridge of Dreams*, 118.

46. Devamata, *Swami Paramananda*, I, 110–11.
47. Levinsky, *Bridge of Dreams*, 117.
48. Ibid., 117–18, 163, and 200.
49. See Devamata, *Swami Paramananda*, I, 172–202.
50. Ibid., I, 240–58, 263–84, and II, 35–54.
51. Devamata, *Swami Paramananda*, II, 150–67; *Message of the East* 18 (May 1929), 147; ibid., 27 (Apr.–May–June 1938), 127; ibid., 28 (July–Aug.–Sept. 1939), 187–92.
52. Devamata, *Swami Paramananda*, I, 262.
53. In the Ramakrishna movement the term *sister* usually signifies that the individual has been initiated into *sannyas*, or final monastic vows.
54. Levinsky, *Bridge of Dreams*, 159–60, 186.
55. "Heart of Mankind," *Message of the East* 15 (Mar. 1926), 58–59; "Raja Yoga," ibid., 22 (June 1933), 164–65.
56. See, for example, "From a Disciple's Notebook," ibid., 38 (Oct.–Nov.–Dec. 1949), 242–47; "Healing of Body and Mind," ibid., 11 (Mar. 1922), 50–51.
57. Devamata, *Swami Paramananda*, I, 302.
58. Ibid., I, 87; Levinsky, *Bridge of Dreams*, 198, 343.
59. Thomas, *Hinduism Invades America*, 115.
60. Ibid., 134–76. A detailed scholarly study of this significant Hindu movement is sorely needed.
61. See, for example, Levinsky, *Bridge of Dreams*, 335–36 and 368–69.

4. Vedanta for Americans

1. Sarvepalli Radhakrishnan, *Indian Philosophy*, 2 vols. (New York: Macmillan, 1927), I, 138. In addition to Radhakrishnan's dated but still useful volumes, I have consulted Heinrich Zimmer, *Philosophies of India* (New York: Meridian Books, 1956); René Guénon, *Man and His Becoming According to the Vedanta* (New York: Noonday Press, 1958); Kenneth W. Morgan (ed.), *The Religion of the Hindus: Interpreted by Hindus* (New York: Ronald Press, 1953); Thomas J. Hopkins, *The Hindu Religious Tradition* (Encino, California: Wadsworth, 1971); and Sarvepalli Radhakrishnan and Charles A. Moore (eds.), *A Source Book in Indian Philosophy* (Princeton: Princeton University Press, 1957), an excellent anthology. Guénon's treatment of Vedanta is strongly colored by the author's personal beliefs; Eliot Deutsch, *Advaita Vedanta: A Philosophical Reconstruction* (Honolulu: University of Hawaii Press, 1969), provides a more reliable analysis.
2. See Agehananda Bharati, "The Hindu Renaissance and Its Apologetic Patterns," *Journal of Asiatic Studies* 29 (Feb. 1970), 267–87.
3. Robert Minor, "Sarvepalli Radhakrishnan and 'Hinduism': Defined and Defended," in Robert D. Baird (ed.), *Religion in Modern India* (New Delhi: Manohar Publications, 1981), 305–38. See also Eric J. Sharpe, "Indian Nationalism and Hindu Universalism," *Temenos* 12 (1976), 38–49; Gerald Larson, "The Bhagavad-Gita as Cross-Cultural Process," *Journal of the American Academy of Religion* 43 (1975), 651–59; and Edward Said's far-ranging and seminal *Orientalism* (New York: Random House, 1978).
4. Bharati, "The Hindu Renaissance and Its Apologetic Patterns," 29.
5. *Brahmavadin* 9 (Feb. 1904), 41–43.
6. Satprakashananda, "The Ramakrishna Society," in Vergilius Ferm (ed.), *Religion in the Twentieth Century* (New York: Philosophical Library, 1948), 396.
7. Nikhilananda, *Hinduism: Its Meaning for the Liberation of the Spirit* (New York: Harper, 1958), 18.

8. Swami Prabhavananda, "Samkara's Philosophy of Non-Dualism," *Voice of India* 1 (Nov. 1938), 14; the original italics have been omitted. Radhakrishnan, *Indian Philosophy*, II, 583.

9. Brahmacharini Usha, *A Ramakrishna-Vedanta Wordbook* (Hollywood: Vedanta Press, 1962), 86. Though not officially sanctioned, the small volume provides a handy reference to Hindu and Vedantic philosophic terms as understood in the Ramakrishna movement.

10. For example, see Swami Prabhavananda, "The Limbs of Yoga," *Voice of India* 1 (June 1938), 10n.1. Students of hatha yoga would claim that their goals are as spiritual as the goals proclaimed in meditational forms of yoga.

11. See *The Complete Works of Vivekananda, Mayavati Memorial Edition* (14th ed.; Calcutta: Advaita Ashrama, 1973), Vols. 1–3. *Karma-Yoga* appears in I, 25–118; *Raja-Yoga* in I, 119–313; *Jnana-Yoga* in II, 57–288; and *Bhakti-Yoga* in III, 29–69. Nikhilananda, *Hinduism*, 87–145, and Abhedananda, *How to Be a Yogi* (10th ed.; Calcutta: Ramakrishna Vedanta Math, 1943), provide expositions.

12. Nikhilananda, *Hinduism*, 96.

13. Ibid., 105.

14. *Complete Works of Vivekananda*, III, 37.

15. Nikhilananda, *Hinduism*, 120.

16. See Sarma, *Studies in the Renaissance of Hinduism in the Nineteenth and Twentieth Centuries* (Benares: Benares Hindu University, 1944), 244–51, and "M" [Mahendranath Gupta], *The Gospel of Sri Ramakrishna* (New York: Ramakrishna-Vivekananda Center, 1942), 32–35.

17. Nikhilananda, *Ramakrishna: Prophet of New India* (New York: Harper, 1942), 99. Ramakrishna's emphasis on direct experience has undoubtedly been a key factor in the success of the movement in the United States. From the time of the seventeenth-century Great Awakening, Americans have shown a powerful attraction to such experience, a fact demonstrated by the popularity of revivalistic preachers from George Whitefield to Billy Graham.

18. Sarma, *Renaissance of Hinduism*, 249.

19. Swami Prabhavananda, "Sri Ramakrishna," *Voice of India* 1 (Sept. 1938), 10.

20. Swami Prabhavananda and Christopher Isherwood, "The Yoga Aphorisms of Patanjali," *Vedanta and the West* 13 (Mar.–Apr. 1950), 54.

21. Abhedananda, *How to Be a Yogi*, 23; *Complete Works of Vivekananda*, III, 184.

22. *Complete Works of Vivekananda*, II, 89.

23. Ibid., VII, 60; ibid., I, 134.

24. Nikhilananda, *Hinduism*, chap. 4, 57–86. The quote appears on p. 57.

25. Prabhavananda, "The Wisdom of the Upanishads," *Vedanta and the West* 3 (Mar.–Apr. 1940), 6–7.

26. "Interview with Swami Vivekananda," *Prabuddha Bharata* 3 (Sept. 1898), 19.

27. Abhedananda, "Vedanta in Daily Life," *Vedanta Monthly Bulletin* 1 (Nov. 1905), 114; Nikhilananda, *Hinduism*, 74–75; and Satprakashananda, "The Ramakrishna Society," in Ferm, *Religion in the Twentieth Century*, 396–97.

28. Swami Jnaneshwarananda, "Vitality of Vedanta," *Vedanta and the West* 11 (Sept.–Oct. 1948), 133. (His name is often spelled "Gnaneswarananda.")

29. Pavitrananda, *Modern Man in Search of Religion* (Mayavati: Advaita Ashrama, 1947); Swami Nirvedananda, *Religion and Modern Doubts* (Dhakwia, Bengal: Vidyamandira S. Mandel, 1945); and Akhilananda, *Hindu Psychology: Its Meaning for the West* (New York: Harper, 1946).

30. See Swami Prabhavananda, "Sri Ramakrishna, Modern Spirit and Religion," in Christopher Isherwood (ed.), *Vedanta for the Western World* (Hollywood: Vedanta Press, 1945), 246.

31. *Complete Works of Vivekananda*, I, 72. The order has been altered for purposes of greater clarity. The original formulation lists the elements as a philosophy, mythology, and ritual.

32. Ibid., VIII, 356–57; see also Marie Louise Burke, *Swami Vivekananda in the West: New Discoveries. The World Teacher. Part One* (Calcutta: Advaita Ashrama, 1985), 254–56.

33. Isherwood, "Discovering Vedanta," *Twentieth Century* 170 (Autumn 1961), 70. See also Swami Abhedananda, *Great Saviours of the World* (3rd ed.; Calcutta: Ramakrishna Vedanta Math, 1966), 17–19.

34. However, see the remark of a former follower, Swami Agehananda Bharati [Leopold Fischer], *The Ochre Robe* (London: George Allen & Unwin, 1961), 141–42: "I came to feel, in due course, that the attitude toward Ramakrishna did matter a great deal, though this was not said, and that monks and novices who refused to regard him 'in a very special light' did not last long in the Order."

35. *Complete Works of Vivekananda*, VII, 496; ibid., V, 52.

36. See, for example, "Holy Nativities. Sri Ramakrishna," *Message of the East* 19 (Feb. 1930), 57.

37. Prabhavananda, "Sri Ramakrishna," *Voice of India* 1 (Sept. 1938), 10.

38. *Sri Ramakrishna Upanishad* (Mylapore: Sri Ramakrishna Math, 1953).

39. [Swami Ashokananda], "The Origin of Swami Vivekananda's Doctrine of Service," *Prabuddha Bharata* 33 (Feb. 1928), 60–61. Italics omitted.

40. Preface, [Swami Pavitrananda], *The Disciples of Ramakrishna* (Mayavati: Advaita Ashrama, 1943), ix. The individual lives were originally written by different authors. Swami Gambhirananda, who subsequently became president of the Ramakrishna Order, revised the volume to leave out the treatment of lay disciples, retitling it as *The Apostles of Shri Ramakrishna* (Calcutta: Advaita Ashrama, 1967).

41. Quoted in John Yale, *A Yankee and the Swamis* (London: George Allen & Unwin, 1961), 76. For Brahmananda's life and teachings, see the biography by Swami Prabhavananda, *The Eternal Companion: His Life and Teachings* (Hollywood: Vedanta Society of Southern California, 1944), and the chapter in Swami Gambhirananda (ed.), *The Apostles of Shri Ramakrishna*, 80–117.

42. See, for example, Swami Vividishananda, *A Man of God: Glimpses into the Life and Work of Swami Shivananda. A Great Disciple of Sri Ramakrishna* (Mylapore: Sri Ramakrishna Math, 1957), and Anonymous, *The Story of a Dedicated Life: Being the Biography of Swami Ramakrishnananda, A Direct Disciple of Sri Ramakrishna* (Madras: Sri Ramakrishna Math, 1959).

43. Appendix, *Disciples of Sri Ramakrishna*, 476; T. M. P. Mahadevan, "Sri Sarada Devi and the Mission of India," *Vedanta Kesari* 42 (Jan. 1956), 377.

44. See Swami Gambhirananda, *Holy Mother: Shri Sarada Devi* (Madras: Sri Ramakrishna Math, 1955), and *Sri Sarada Devi, The Great Wonder: A Compilation of Revelations, Reminiscences and Studies* (New Delhi: Ramakrishna Mission, 1984).

45. Gambhirananda, *Holy Mother*, 49–51.

46. Gambhirananda, *History of the Ramakrishna Math*, 61; *Complete Works of Vivekananda*, VII, 484.

47. Mahadevan, "Sri Sarada Devi and the Mission of India," *Vedanta Kesari* 42 (Jan. 1956), 376.

48. *Complete Works of Vivekananda*, VII, 481. "Epistles of Swami Vivekananda," *Prabuddha Bharata* 23 (Mar. 1918), 60.

49. *Complete Works of Vivekananda*, II, 365 and 373–74.

50. Abhedananda, *Vedanta Philosophy: Why a Hindu Accepts Christ and Rejects Churchianity* (New York: The Vedanta Society, 1901), 1.

51. Akhilananda, *Hindu View of Christ* (New York: Philosophical Library, 1949), 46.

52. Abhedananda, *How to Be a Yogi*, 192 and 199. See the whole chapter, "Was Christ a Yogi?" 175–201.

53. *Voice of Freedom* 1 (June 1909), v. Such pictures may still be purchased at Vedanta societies today.

54. See the excellent discussion in Edgar J. Goodspeed, *Strange New Gospels* (Chicago: University of Chicago Press, 1931), 10–24.

55. Prabhavananda, "The Lord's Prayer," *Vedanta and the West* 16 (Mar.–Apr. 1953), 37–42. See also Prabhavananda's "The Sermon on the Mount," in Christopher Isherwood (ed.), *Vedanta for the Western World*, 313–49.

56. Included in John Yale (ed.), *What Vedanta Means to Me: A Symposium* (Garden City, N.Y.: Doubleday, 1960), 191. Charles S. Braden, "Hindu Interpretations of the Bible and Jesus," *Journal of Bible and Religion* 12 (Feb. 1944), 42–47, offers an illuminating evaluation of such interpretations based primarily on Ramakrishna movement writings.

57. Farquhar, *Modern Religious Movements in India* (New York: Macmillan, 1915), 205; Thomas, *Hinduism Invades America* (New York: Beacon Press, 1930), 248.

58. Guénon, *Introduction to the Study of the Hindu Doctrines* (1945), quoted in Harold W. French, *The Swan's Wide Waters: Ramakrishna and Western Culture* (Port Washington, N.Y.: Kennikat Press, 1974), 145.

5. The Appeals of Vedanta

1. See Wade Clark Roof and William McKinney, *American Mainline Religion: Its Changing Shape and Future* (New Brunswick: Rutgers University Press, 1987).

2. Mabel Potter Daggett, "The Heathen Invasion," *Hampton-Columbian Magazine* 27 (Oct. 1911), 399–411.

3. Daggett, "The Heathen Invasion of America," *Missionary Review of the World* 35 (Mar. 1912), 210–14.

4. Mrs. Gross Alexander, "American Women Going After Heathen Gods," *Methodist Quarterly Review* 61 (July 1912), 495–512; Elizabeth A. Reed, *Hinduism in Europe and America* (New York: G. P. Putnam, 1914); and Mersene E. Sloan, *The Indian Menace . . .* (Washington, D.C.: The Way Press, 1929). I have been unable to discover Alexander's given name. See also Cornelia Sorabji's more sober "Hindu Swamis and Women of the West," *Nineteenth Century* 112 (Sept. 1932), 365–73.

5. I speak here from personal interview experience. Whenever I inquired about membership figures or social backgrounds, the swamis always brushed my question aside.

6. Sister Christine, "Vivekananda and His Message," *Vedanta and the West* 10 (Sept.–Oct. 1947), 141.

7. *Brahmavadin* 1 (Apr. 11, 1896), 195; see also Sister Christine, "Vivekananda and His Message," 144–45. His lectures were frequently reported in the early 1890s in leading Theosophical journals. *The Path* 9 (July 1894), 131–32, identifies him as a member of the New York Theosophical Society.

8. Burke, *Swami Vivekananda: His Second Visit to the West. New Discoveries* (Calcutta: Advaita Ashrama, 1973), 127. See also her *Swami Vivekananda in the West: New Discoveries. The World Teacher: Part One* (Calcutta: Advaita Ashrama, 1985), 15–16, 127–29, 318–24, 339, 521–23.

9. Sister Christine, "Vivekananda and His Message," 144; see also *Brahmavadin* 1 (Feb. 29, 1896), 150.

10. Editorial note, *Amrita Bazar Patrika*, Mar. 18, 1896, cited in Sankari Prasad Basu and Sunil Bihari Ghosh (eds.), *Vivekananda in Indian Newspapers, 1893–1902* (Calcutta: Bookland Private Ltd., 1969), 309.

11. Burke, *Vivekananda in the West*, 322–23, and *Brahmavadin* 1 (Aug. 1, 1896), 290–91.

12. *Brahmavadin* 4 (Apr. 15, 1899), 479–80. See also ibid., 4 (June 15, 1899), 624–26.

13. *Unity* 31 (July 1909), 52. *Brahmavadin* 3 (Dec. 16, 1897), 297–99; ibid., 3 (Mar. 16, 1898), 535–37; ibid., 3 (July 15, 1898), 845–47; and ibid., 4 (Jan. 1, 1899), 241–42.

14. Sister Christine, "Vivekananda and His Message," 144. Burke attempts to explain his choice in *Vivekananda in the West*, 128–29.

15. Vivekananda to E. T. Sturdy, Feb. 13, 1896, in *The Complete Works of Swami Vivekananda, Mayavati Memorial Edition* (14th ed.; Calcutta: Advaita Ashrama, 1973), V, 100. Burke, *Vivekananda in the West*, 518–20.

16. Boshi Sen, "Sister Christine," *Prabuddha Bharata* 35 (Sept. 1930), 419–23, and Swami Nikhilananda, "Sister Christine," *Modern Review* 47 (May 1930), 583–87.

17. Sister Devamata [Laura Glenn], "Memories of India and Indians, Part II," *Prabuddha Bharata* 37 (May 1932), 242–44. Quotes on 243. See also Burke, *Swami Vivekananda in the West*, 121–22 and 333–35.

18. Sister Nivedita [Margaret E. Noble], "In Memoriam: Sara Chapman Bull," *The Modern Review* 9 (June 1911), 582–86. See also *Who's Who in America* (1910–11), VI, 263, and Burke, *Swami Vivekananda in America: New Discoveries* (2nd rev. ed.; Calcutta: Advaita Ashrama, 1966), 489–92.

19. For example, see the *Boston Herald*, May 17–June 28, 1911.

20. Sister Amiya [Amiya Corbin], "Josephine MacLeod (1848–1949)," *Vedanta and the West* 13 (Jan.–Feb. 1950), 28–32; quotes on 28. Italics omitted. See also her memoir, Josephine MacLeod, "Reminiscences of Swami Vivekananda," *Vedanta and the West* 13 (May–June 1950), 66–79.

21. Swami Vidyatmananda [John Yale] (ed.), *Atman Alone Abides: Conversations with Swami Atulananda* (Madras: Sri Ramakrishna Math, 1978), "Introduction," vii–viii. See also Brahmachari Prema Chaitanya [John Yale], "The North and the Himalyas," *Vedanta and the West* no. 122 (Nov.–Dec. 1956), 41–43.

22. Swami Atulananda [Cornelius Heyblom], "My First Contacts with Vedanta," *Prabuddha Bharata* 59 (Feb. 1954), 70–72; Gurudusa [Cornelius Heyblom], "A Visit to the Lord's Farm (Reminiscences)," *Prabuddha Bharata* 23 (Aug. 1918), 183–87, continued in ibid., 23 (Sept. 1918), 204–209; and A Bramacharin [Cornelius Heyblom], "With the Swamis in America," *Prabuddha Bharata* 23 (Oct. 1918), 231–35.

23. Brahmachari Gurudas [Cornelius Heyblom], "Why I Became a Hindu and Some of My Indian Experiences," *Prabuddha Bharata* 24 (July and Aug. 1919), 160–63 and 183–86. See also Swami Atulananda, *Vedanta as an Influence on My Life* (Bangalore: Vokkaligara Sangha Press, 1925). His health problems are mentioned in Vidyatmananda, *Atman Alone Abides*, vii.

24. *Star of the East* 8 (July 1, 1912), 410. The *Star of the East* was published from 1905 to 1912 and is the only source for her career as a Vedantist. The journal was subsequently retitled as the *Vedanta Universal Messenger*.

25. See her "The Vedanta Movement in the English Colonies and Its Pioneerage," *Star of the East* 6 (July 1, 1910), 13–15. See also ibid., 7 (July 1, 1911), 208; ibid., 6 (Nov. 1, 1910), 16; and ibid., 6 (Feb. 1, 1911), 8.

26. Ibid., 7 (May 1912), 380–87.

27. Devamata, "Memories of India and Indians," *Prabuddha Bharata* 37 (Apr. 1932), 191. See also ibid., 37 (May and June 1932), 242–44 and 301–304, and the obituary article, "In Memory of Sister Devamata," *Message of the East* 32 (Jan.–Feb.–Mar. 1943), 35–40.

28. Devamata, *Days in an Indian Monastery* (2nd ed.; La Crescenta, Calif.: Ananda Ashrama, 1927), 326.

29. Sara Ann Levinsky, *A Bridge of Dreams: The Story of Paramananda, A Modern Mystic, and His Ideal of All-Conquering Love* (West Stockbridge, Mass.: Lindisfarne Press, 1984), 142.

30. Brahmachari Prema Chaitanya [John Yale], "What Vedanta Means to Me," *Vedanta and the West* no. 116 (Nov.–Dec. 1955), 15–42.

31. Yale, *A Yankee and the Swamis* (London: George Allen & Unwin, 1961), 13.

32. Wendell Thomas, *Hinduism Invades America* (New York: Beacon Press, 1930), 80.

33. See Table 3 of United States Bureau of the Census, *Census of Religious Bodies: 1936. Vol. II, Part 2. Denominations K to Z: Statistics, History, Doctrine, Organization and Work* (Washington, D.C.: U.S. Government Printing Office, 1941), 1662. Not all centers reported their male-female distributions.

34. See Constant H. Jacquet, Jr., and Alice M. Jones (eds.), *Yearbook of American and Canadian Churches: 1991* (Nashville: Abingdon Press, 1991), 264.

35. The series commenced in *Vedanta and the West* with the Jan.–Feb. 1951 issue and appeared irregularly thereafter. John Yale edited a selection of the articles in *What Vedanta Means to Me: A Symposium* (Garden City, N.Y.: Doubleday, 1960).

36. John van Druten, "What Vedanta Means to Me," *Vedanta and the West* 15 (Mar.–Apr. 1952), 60; Swami Atulananda [Cornelius Heyblom], ibid., no. 122 (Nov.–Dec. 1956), 10.

37. Christopher Isherwood, "What Vedanta Means to Me," ibid., 14 (Sept.–Oct. 1951), 157–58; Gerald Heard, ibid., 14 (Jan.–Feb. 1951), 26–27.

38. Pravrajika Saradaprana [Ruth Folling], in Yale, *What Vedanta Means to Me*, 206–207.

39. Marianna Masin, "What Vedanta Means to Me," *Vedanta and the West* no. 125 (May–June 1957), 53–54; Joan Rayne, ibid., no. 128 (Nov.–Dec. 1957), 37.

40. John van Druten, ibid., 15 (Mar.–Apr. 1952), 63; Pravrajika Saradaprana [Ruth Folling], in Yale, *What Vedanta Means to Me*, 207.

41. Christopher Isherwood, "What Vedanta Means to Me," *Vedanta and the West* 14 (Sept.–Oct. 1951), 159–60.

42. John Yale, in Yale, *What Vedanta Means to Me*, 164–65.

43. Isherwood, "What Vedanta Means to Me," *Vedanta and the West* 14 (Sept.–Oct. 1951), 160. For a fuller treatment of the central role Swami Prabhavananda played in his life, see Isherwood's *My Guru and His Disciple* (New York: Farrar, Straus, & Giroux, 1980).

44. Jane Molard, "What Vedanta Means to Me," *Vedanta and the West* no. 131 (May–June 1958), 54.

45. J. Crawford Lewis, ibid., 15 (Sept.–Oct. 1952), 156; John van Druten, ibid., 15 (Mar.–Apr. 1952), 62.

46. Sister Devamata [Laura Glenn], "The Living Presence," *Vedanta Kesari* 22 (Feb. and Mar. 1936), 401.

47. See *Prabuddha Bharata* 59 (July 1954), 400, and ibid., 59 (Aug. 1954), 440; see also *Vedanta Kesari* 41 (Dec. 1954), 279–80, and ibid. 42 (July 1955), 156–57.

48. Nikhilananda, "The Holy Mother, an Ideal of Perfect Womanhood," *Prabuddha Bharata* 59 (Sept. 1954), 461; Ursula Bond, "What Sarada Devi Means to Me," reported in *The Indian Express*, Dec. 6, 1954. For other early appreciations by American followers, see

Dorothy Kruger, "At the Touch of the Mother," *Vedanta Kesari* 23 (July 1936), 100–102; Gwendolyn Thomas, "Ideally Perfect," *Vedanta Kesari* 41 (July 1954), 122–25; Amiya Corbin, "Holy Mother," *Vedanta and the West* 10 (Mar.–Apr. 1945), 34–41; and Elizabeth Davidson, "Snow White," *Vedanta Kesari* 41 (July 1954), 110–15.

49. Rayne, "The Nearing Remote," *Vedanta Kesari* 41 (July 1954), 118.

50. See Rosemary Ruether, *Religion and Sexism: Images of Women in the Jewish and Christian Traditions* (New York: Simon & Schuster, 1974), and *Sexism and God-Talk: Toward a Feminist Theology* (Boston: Beacon Press, 1985). Recent publications that explore the role of women in Asian religions include Rita Gross and Nancy A. Falk (eds.), *Unspoken Worlds: Women's Religious Lives in Non-Western Cultures* (San Francisco: Harper & Row, 1980); Diana Y. Paul, *Women in Buddhism* (Berkeley: Asian Humanities Press, 1979); and Ursula King (ed.), *Women in World Religions Past and Present* (New York: Paragon House, 1987).

51. See Brahmacharini Usha, *A Ramakrishna-Vedanta Wordbook* (Hollywood: Vedanta Press, 1962).

52. Information based largely on interviews conducted during a 1987 visit to the Vedanta Society of Southern California.

53. Brahmachari Prema Chaitanya [John Yale], "May He Illumine Us," *Vedanta and the West* no. 134 (Nov.–Dec. 1958), 36–37. See the entire article on pp. 18–58 for a useful discussion of key differences between Indian and Western practices.

54. Typewritten schedule available at Ramakrishna Monastery, Trabuco, June 1987.

6. The Movement since the 1920s

1. United States Bureau of the Census, *Census of Religious Bodies: 1936. Vol. II, Part 2. Denominations K to Z: Statistics, History, Doctrine, Organization and Work* (Washington, D.C.: U.S. Government Printing Office, 1941), Table 2, 1662.

2. George F. Ketcham (ed.), *Yearbook of American Churches: 1951 Edition* (New York: National Council of Churches of Christ in the U.S.A., 1951), 111; Benson Y. Landis (ed.), *Yearbook of American Churches: Edition for 1956* (New York: National Council of Churches of Christ in the U.S.A., 1955), 106; Constant H. Jacquet, Jr., and Alice M. Jones (eds.), *Yearbook of American and Canadian Churches: 1991* (Nashville: Abingdon Press, 1991), 264. Apparently, the totals represent estimates rather than exact counts, since the numbers reported remain fixed for sizable periods (e.g., at 1,200 from 1957–1983) and the totals are rounded to multiples of 100. For years the Vedanta Society of New York has submitted the annual membership figures for publication in the *Yearbook*.

3. *Prabuddha Bharata* 29 (Jan. 1924), 48.

4. *Vedanta Kesari* 19 (Feb. 1933), 399; *Prabuddha Bharata* 55 (June 1950), 264; and "An Interview with Swami Bodhananda," *Prabuddha Bharata* 29 (Mar. 1924), 126–29. Brahmacharini Bhavani [Nancy Kenny] provides brief sketches of recent developments in all the societies in her "Vedanta Centres in the West," in *Salutations to Sri Ramakrishna: The Post-Centenary Golden Jubilee of Bhagawan Sri Ramakrishna's Advent and the Centenary of the Ramakrishna Math and the Ramakrishna Order. Souvenir 1987* (Mylapore: Sri Ramakrishna Math, 1987), 25–42. Swami Sarveshananda, an American-born swami with many years of experience in the movement, and Pravrajika Bhaktiprana, a longtime nun at the Sarada Convent in Santa Barbara, provided updates on the societies during a series of telephone conversations in July and August 1992.

5. *Prabuddha Bharata* 27 (Aug. 1922), 319–20; ibid., 56 (Feb. 1951), 112.

6. *Prabuddha Bharata* 36 (Sept. 1931), 465–66; *Vedanta Kesari* 18 (Sept. 1931), 200; *Vedanta and the West* no. 127 (Sept.–Oct. 1957), 49–54.

7. *Vedanta Kesari* 34 (June 1947), 79–80; *Prabuddha Bharata* 57 (Dec. 1952), 516; Swami Gambhirananda, *History of the Ramakrishna Math and Mission* (Calcutta: Advaita Ashrama, 1957), 375, 401–402, 430.

8. For the reestablishment of the center, see *Vedanta Kesari* 32 (Mar. 1946), 254, and ibid., 42 (Nov. 1955), 318–19.

9. *Vedanta Kesari* 32 (Mar. 1946), 253–54; ibid., 42 (Nov. 1955), 318–19; Gambhirananda, *History of the Ramakrishna Math*, 370. See also Claude A. Stark, *God of All: Sri Ramakrishna's Approach to Religious Plurality* (Cape Cod, Mass.: Claude Stark Inc., 1974), 162–77.

10. See the testimonials included in Swami Akhilananda, *Spiritual Practices. Memorial Edition with Reminiscences by His Friends*, ed. Alice M. Stark and Claude A. Stark (Cape Cod, Mass.: Claude Stark Inc., 1974).

11. Ibid., 182.

12. Information provided by Pravrajika Bhaktiprana, telephone conversation, August 6, 1992.

13. *Census of Religious Bodies: 1936*, II, 1662.

14. Gambhirananda, *History of the Ramakrishna Math*, 324–25 and 326; *Prabuddha Bharata* 36 (Dec. 1931), 622–23; ibid., 42 (Dec. 1937), 669; *Message of the East* 27 (Jan.–Feb.–Mar. 1938), 64.

15. *Vedanta Kesari* 25 (May 1938), 38–40, and Harold W. French, *The Swan's Wide Waters: Ramakrishna and Western Culture* (Port Washington, N.Y.: Kennikat Press, 1974), 135–36. See the entire chapter "The Movement in the West in Recent Years," 128–42, which provides an excellent summary up to the early 1970s. Swami Sarveshananda provided details concerning recent developments by telephone on July 13, 1992.

16. *Prabuddha Bharata* 34 (Dec. 1929), 625; ibid., 48 (Mar. 1953), 151–52; *Vedanta Kesari* 26 (Nov. 1939), 275–78. See the biographical sketch in Vergilius Ferm (ed.), *Religion in the Twentieth Century* (New York: Philosophical Library, 1948), 394.

17. Pravrajika Bhaktiprana, telephone conversation, August 6, 1992.

18. *Prabuddha Bharata* 19 (Nov. 1914), 210; ibid., 32 (Apr. 1927), 184–87.

19. *Voice of Freedom* 7 (Dec. 1915), 180; *Prabuddha Bharata* 25 (Jan. 1920), 20; and ibid., 25 (Dec. 1920), 288.

20. Gambhirananda, *History of the Ramakrishna Math*, 262–63, 325.

21. *Vedanta Kesari* 20 (Jun. 1933), 80; ibid., 22 (July 1935), 118–19; Gambhirananda, *History of the Ramakrishna Math*, 357, 401, 431. See also Dorothy Mercer, "The Vedanta in California: The Swamis of the Ramakrishna Order," *Pacific Spectator* 10 (Winter 1956), 38–46.

22. Brahmacharini Bhavani, "Vedanta Centers in the West," 30–31. Recent information on the San Francisco, Berkeley, and Sacramento centers provided by telephone by Swami Sarveshananda on July 13, 1992, and by Pravrajika Bhaktiprana on Aug. 6, 1992.

23. Sara Ann Levinsky, *A Bridge of Dreams: The Story of Paramananda, A Modern Mystic, and His Ideal of All-Conquering Love* (West Stockbridge, Mass.: Lindisfarne Press, 1984), 368.

24. Sister Amiya [Amiya Corbin], "Vedanta in Southern California," *Vedanta and the West* 14 (Sept.–Oct. 1951), 141; see also "Vedanta in Southern California: A Guidebook to the Vedanta Society," originally published as a special issue of *Vedanta and the West* no. 120 (July–Aug. 1956), 7–64.

25. "Vedanta in Southern California: A Guidebook," 43.

26. Information provided by Pravrajika Bhaktiprana, telephone conversation, Aug. 6, 1992.

27. *Prabuddha Bharata* 31 (Jan. 1926), 48; ibid., 37 (July 1932), 362–63.

28. *Prabuddha Bharata* 42 (Jan. 1937), 52; ibid., 43 (Feb. 1938), 104; ibid., 44 (Feb. 1939), 104; *Vedanta Kesari* 45 (Sept. 1948), 240. Recent information provided in a telephone conversation with Swami Sarveshananda on July 21, 1992, and with Pravrajika Bhaktiprana on Aug. 6, 1992.

29. *Prabuddha Bharata* 44 (Oct. 1939), 516–17; ibid., 53 (July 1948), 296; *Vedanta Kesari* 26 (Oct. 1939), 239. In the 1950s Vividishananda also launched a branch work in Hawaii, responding to the invitation of a former student. Though a subsequent report mentions a "Vedanta Society of Hawaii," the infant body seems to have quickly expired for there is no further reference to it. See *Vedanta Kesari* 45 (Nov. 1958), 320. Details on the new center in Vancouver, Canada, provided by Swami Sarveshananda, telephone conversation, on July 21, 1992, and by Pravrajika Bhaktiprana on Aug. 6, 1992.

30. *Prabuddha Bharata* 32 (Oct. 1927), 478–79; ibid., 49 (Feb. 1944), 104; *Vedanta Kesari* 44 (July 1957), 111–12.

31. *Vedanta Kesari* 21 (Aug. 1934), 159; ibid., 22 (Sept. 1935), 200; Gambhirananda, *History of the Ramakrishna Math*, 326.

32. *Vedanta Kesari* 24 (Jan. 1938), 358–60; *Prabuddha Bharata* 43 (Feb. 1938), 101–103.

33. The term is Swami Gambhirananda's; see his *History of the Ramakrishna Math*, 357. Little reference is made to the painful split anywhere in movement histories.

34. Gayatri Devi, *One Life's Pilgrimage: Addresses, Letters, and Articles by the First Indian Woman to Teach Vedanta in the West* (Cohasset, Mass.: Vedanta Center, 1977), 15–16.

35. Ibid., 115–20.

36. Ibid., 116.

37. Ibid., 117, 118.

38. See Srimati Gayatri Devi, "Sister Daya: An Intimate Picture," *Message of the East* 44 (Oct.–Nov.–Dec. 1955), 222–31, and the biographical sketch in Lawrence Veysey, *The Communal Experience: Anarchist and Mystical Counter-Cultures in America* (New York: Harper & Row, 1973), 248–62.

39. See Gayatri Devi's "An Autobiographical Sketch" in *One Life's Pilgrimage*, 2–27.

40. *Message of the East* 47 (Winter 1958), 253–56; ibid., 50 (Summer 1961), 128. Swami Sarveshananda brushed aside my questions about Gayatri's American work in a telephone conversation on July 25, 1992. He was clearly reluctant to discuss the matter.

41. The following discussion is primarily based on the helpful account in "Vedanta in Southern California: A Guidebook to the Vedanta Society," originally published in *Vedanta and the West* no. 120 (July–Aug. 1956), 7–64, and upon interviews, questionnaires, and direct observations assembled during a visit in July 1987.

42. Isherwood, *My Guru and His Disciple* (New York: Farrar, Straus, & Giroux, 1980), 131.

43. "Vedanta in Southern California: A Guidebook," 24.

44. Ibid., 23–24.

45. Ibid., 23.

46. Information provided by Swami Sarveshananda, telephone conversation, July 21, 1992.

7. The Ramakrishna Movement in History

1. Wendell Thomas, *Hinduism Invades America* (New York: Beacon Press, 1930); Raymond Brady Williams, *Religions of Immigrants from India and Pakistan: New Threads in the American Tapestry* (Cambridge: Cambridge University Press, 1988).

2. Emma M. Layman, *Buddhism in America* (Chicago: Nelson-Hall, 1976); Charles S. Prebish, *American Buddhism* (North Scituate, Mass.: Duxbury Press, 1979); and Rick Fields, *How the Swans Came to the Lake: A Narrative History of Buddhism in America* (Boulder, Colo.: Shambhala, 1981).

3. Mrs. Charles Howard, "The Death of Mr. Virchand R. Gandhi," *The Open Court* 16 (Jan. 1902), 51–53; "Virchand at the World Congress of Religions, Chicago, 1893," *Jain Journal* (Calcutta) 3 (Jan. 1969), 103–109.

4. Puran Singh, *The Story of Swami Rama: The Poet Monk of the Punjab* (Madras: Ganesh, 1924). See also "A Short Account of the Life of Rama Tirtha," in Hari Prasad Shastri, *Rama Tirtha: Scientist and Mahatma* (London: Shanti Sadan, 1955), 15–58.

5. John N. Farquhar, *Modern Religious Movements in India* (New York: Macmillan, 1915), 296.

6. Thomas, *Hinduism Invades America*, 177–87, 217–18, and 221–22.

7. "History of Swami Yogananda's Work in America," *Self-Realization* 1 (Nov.–Dec. 1925), 7–11, and Thomas, *Hinduism Invades America*, 134–76. See also Yogananda's own account, *Autobiography of a Yogi* (New York: Philosophical Library, 1946).

8. Yogananda, "Oriental Christianity, Occidental Christianity, and Yogoda," *Self-Realization* 1 (Sept.–Oct. 1926), 5.

9. *Self-Realization* 9 (Mar. 1937), 72.

10. J. Gordon Melton (ed.), *The Encyclopedia of American Religions*, 2 vols. (Wilmington, N. C.: McGrath Publishers, 1978), II, 362–63.

11. The most recent edition is *The Encyclopedia of American Religions* (3rd ed.; Detroit: Gale Research, 1989). See pp. 849–95 and 907–42.

12. See J. Stillson Judah, *Hare Krishna and the Counterculture* (New York: John Wiley, 1974), and Francine J. Daner, *The American Children of Krsna: A Study of the Hare Krsna Movement* (New York: Holt, Rinehart, & Winston, 1976); and E. Burke Rochford, Jr., *Hare Krishna in America* (New Brunswick: Rutgers University Press, 1985).

13. Satsvarupa dasa Goswami, *Srila Prabhupada-lilamrta*. Vol. 2: *Planting the Seed. New York City, 1965–1966* (Los Angeles: Bhaktivedanta Book Trust, 1980), 38. Written by a disciple, the three-volume work presents the most detailed treatment of Bhaktivedanta's effort in the U.S.

14. As Raymond Brady Williams points out in his *Religions of Immigrants from India and Pakistan*, ISKCON has moderated a good deal since the passing of its leader. See pp. 130–37.

15. Judah, *Hare Krishna*, 46–97, and Daner, *American Children of Krsna*, 23–51.

16. Melton, *Encyclopedia of American Religions* (3rd ed.), 868.

17. Williams, *Religions of Immigrants from India and Pakistan*, 131 and 133.

18. John Whitworth and Martin Shiels, "From Across the Black Water: Two Imported Varieties of Hinduism—The Hare Krishnas and the Ramakrishna Vedanta Society," in Eileen Barker (ed.), *New Religious Movements: A Perspective for Understanding Society* (New York: Edwin Mellen Press, 1982), 155–72.

19. Williams, *Religions of Immigrants from India and Pakistan*, 133, 136–37.

20. A scholarly study of Transcendental Meditation and its founder is much needed. Meanwhile, see the sketches in Martin Ebon (ed.), *Maharishi, The Guru: An International Symposium* (New York: New American Library, 1968), 9–11, and Vishal Mangalwadi, *The World of the Gurus* (New Delhi: Vikas Publishing House, 1977), 101–24.

21. See Needleman, *The New Religions* (rev. ed.; New York: Pocket Books, 1972), 128–42, and Robert S. Ellwood, Jr., *Religious and Spiritual Groups in Modern America* (Engle-

wood Cliffs, N.J.: Prentice Hall, 1973), 231–35. Ellwood and Henry B. Partin published a 2nd edition of *Religious and Spiritual Groups* in 1988.

22. J. Gordon Melton, *Encyclopedic Handbook of Cults in America* (New York: Garland, 1986), 191.

23. Cyrus R. Pangborn, "Analysis of a Cliché: Eastern Spirituality and Western Materialism," *Contributions to Asian Studies* 3 (1973), 109–18.

24. See Ann Myren's two recent articles, "American Women Encounter Vedanta," *Prabuddha Bharata* 91 (Jan. and Feb. 1986), 16–23 and 57–64, and "The Challenge of Vedanta to American Women," ibid., 91 (July and Aug. 1986), 302–308 and 344–50.

25. *The General Report of Ramakrishna Math and Ramakrishna Mission: From April 1984 to March 1985* (Belur Math, Howrah: General Secretary, 1986).

Bibliographical Essay

Much of the literature on the Ramakrishna movement has been produced by swamis and devotees, though in recent decades Western scholars and theologians have also begun to explore the order's teachings and influence. Though generally proponents of Hinduism have revealed an indifferent and even hostile attitude toward historical concerns, Ramakrishna leaders have manifested strong interest in preserving their history. Much of this "official" literature may be used by the scholar with considerable confidence despite its obvious bias. Movement histories are rarely critical; nevertheless, they supply the basic facts. Unfortunately, few are footnoted. Many of the standard works have been published by Vedanta presses in the West and can be found in major research libraries. The literary materials consulted for this study consist of six basic types of publications: collected works and reminiscences, official histories and biographies, expositions of Ramakrishna and Vedanta teachings, articles in Vedanta society journals, writings of Western devotees, and outside scholarly evaluations. In addition to these works, the author greatly benefited from interviews and conversations with Ramakrishna movement officials, swamis, and devotees both in India and the United States.

While other nineteenth-century Hindu reform movements such as the Brahmo Samaj and Arya Samaj have attracted attention, Western scholars have so far largely ignored the Ramakrishna movement's critical role in the nineteenth-century revival of Hinduism. David Kopf's *The Brahmo Samaj and the Shaping of the Modern Indian Mind* (Princeton: Princeton University Press, 1979) and Kenneth W. Jones's *Arya Dharm: Hindu Consciousness in 19th-Century Punjab* (Berkeley: University of California Press, 1976) are superb and might serve as models for a scholarly analysis of the Ramakrishna movement. However, several recent essay-length examinations suggest rising Western awareness of the movement's importance. George M. Williams's "The Ramakrishna Movement: A Study in Religious Change," printed in Robert D. Baird (ed.), *Religion in Modern India* (New Delhi: Manohar Publications, 1981), 55–79, offers one of the best brief treatments. Williams characterizes the movement using nine descriptors; according to Williams, the Ramakrishna movement was monistic, monastic, universal, tolerant, nonsectarian, liberal, humanitarian, progressive, and scientific. Adopting a more anthropological approach, Cyrus R. Pangborn argues in "The Ramakrishna Math and Mission: A Case Study of a Revitalization Movement," in Bardwell L. Smith (ed.), *Hinduism: New Essays in the History of Religions* (Leiden: E. J. Brill, 1976), 98–119, that the Hindu reform body may be best understood as a revitalization movement, revealing most of the characteristics (revivalistic, vitalistic, messianic, etc.) originally employed by anthropologist A. F. C. Wallace in his studies of the Handsome Lake movement among the Iroquois. Gerald B. Cooke's description of one Ramakrishna ashrama, *A Neo-Hindu Ashrama in South India*

(Bangalore: Christian Institute for the Study of Religion and Society, 1966), should also be noticed.

Until better studies appear, readers must still rely on Swami Gambhirananda, *History of the Ramakrishna Math and Mission* (Calcutta: Advaita Ashrama, 1957), updated in a 1983 third edition, which provides the "inside" history preferred by officials of the Ramakrishna movement. Like all "official" histories, Gambhirananda's work tends to ignore outside events and influences and to pass over unpleasant occurrences such as internal dissension and schisms. The volume is primarily descriptive and unanalytical, describing the rise of the Ramakrishna movement from obscure beginnings in rural Bengal to its present position as an organization of national and international significance. Though primarily focused on the movement's Indian work, the volume includes brief running summaries of the Order's expansion in the West. Despite glaring limitations, it remains an indispensable reference.

When we turn to the Ramakrishna movement's Western work, the only previous full-length study is Harold W. French, *The Swan's Wide Waters: Ramakrishna and Western Culture* (Port Washington, N.Y.: Kennikat Press, 1974), which presents an admirable analysis written from the perspective of a religious studies scholar. French's summary of the movement's history in the United States might have been fuller; on the other hand, his analysis of the movement's teachings and place in the Hindu tradition (Part II) is excellent. Two earlier treatments should also be noticed. Though marred by a Christian bias, Wendell Thomas's section on the Ramakrishna movement in *Hinduism Invades America* (New York: Beacon Press, 1930), 43–133, provides an interesting assessment *circa* 1930 that should be compared with subsequent evaluations. Carl T. Jackson's bulky dissertation, "The Swami in America: A History of the Ramakrishna Movement in the United States, 1893–1960" (U.C.L.A., 1964), presents the most complete account of the American work to that time. The unpublished manuscript includes a lengthy bibliography and considerable material not to be found elsewhere. Finally, one may consult A Western Disciple [Cornelius Heyblom], *With the Swamis in America* (2nd ed.; Mayavati: Advaita Ashrama, 1946), for an interesting firsthand description of the movement's early days in the United States by a participant.

The primary source for Ramakrishna's life and teachings is "M" [Mahendranath Gupta], *The Gospel of Sri Ramakrishna*, trans. Swami Nikhilananda (New York: Ramakrishna-Vivekananda Center, 1942), the detailed account of Ramakrishna's last four years (1882–1886) of life as recorded by a disciple. Originally published in Bengali, the *Gospel* has appeared in several English translations, including an imperfect 1907 version by Swami Abhedananda. The movement views Swami Nikhilananda's 1942 text as most trustworthy. The *Gospel* is remarkable for the completeness with which it records Ramakrishna's daily life and teaching and has achieved the status of sacred scripture. In the eyes of devotees, Swami Saradananda's *Sri Ramakrishna: The Great Master* (Mylapore: Sri Ramakrishna Math, 1952) ranks second only to the *Gospel* as authoritative on Ramakrishna's life. At the author's death in 1927, the account was still incomplete. Whereas the *Gospel* records the Bengali founder's words almost verbatim, in the biography Saradananda organizes Ramakrishna's rather loosely ordered teachings into a more systematic sequence.

Western writers expressed fascination with Ramakrishna as far back as the end of the nineteenth century, as indicated by F. Max Müller's *Ramakrishna: His Life and Say-*

ings (New York: Charles Scribners, 1899). Though sketchy and unreliable as a factual source, Müller's life continues to be consulted because of the German scholar's eminence and the fact that his work represents one of the earliest Western evaluations. The volume is largely based on materials provided by Vivekananda, whom the famous Vedic scholar met during one of the Swami's London visits. Thirty years later the French writer and idealist Romain Rolland helped spark renewed Western interest in the movement through sympathetic portraits of Ramakrishna and Vivekananda in his *Prophets of the New India* (New York: Albert & Charles Boni, 1930). Like Müller's work, Rolland's volume may now be more significant because of its author's stature than for what it adds to our knowledge. English writer Christopher Isherwood added a new version with his *Ramakrishna and His Disciples* (New York: Simon and Schuster, 1959), published after he moved permanently to the United States in 1939. Authorities in India read and sanctioned the manuscript, which offers an extremely readable account based on intimate knowledge of the movement. Though hardly critical—for many years Isherwood was a disciple of Swami Prabhavananda's at the Vedanta Society of Southern California—nevertheless, the volume offers one of the best brief lives of Ramakrishna available in English.

There is as yet no full-scale scholarly treatment of Ramakrishna's life and teachings despite growing recognition by the academic community of his significance. Modern scholars are beginning to focus upon his remarkable experiences, however, as indicated by several recent article-length analyses. One of the most impressive is Walter G. Neevel, Jr.'s "The Transformation of Sri Ramakrishna," which is included in Bardwell Smith's *Hinduism: New Essays in the History of Religions*, 53–97, a volume previously cited. In a provocative essay Neevel argues that Ramakrishna's commitment to *Advaita* Vedanta has been exaggerated and that his religious views may be better understood by recognizing the strong influence upon him of Vaisnavism and Tantrism. In "The Teachings of Ramakrishna in Relation to the Hindu Tradition and as Interpreted by Vivekananda," *Religion* 11 (April 1981), 171–84, Freda Matchett endorses Neevel's claims concerning the overemphasis on Vedanta, proceeding to argue that Swami Vivekananda did much to encourage the misconception that Ramakrishna was a Vedantist. Claude Alan Stark's *God of All: Sri Ramakrishna's Approach to Religious Plurality* (Cape Cod, Mass.: Claude Stark, Inc., 1974) offers a sympathetic analysis of Ramakrishna's universalistic religious perspective. Two other works should also be mentioned. Richard Schiffman, *Sri Ramakrishna: A Prophet for the New Age* (New York: Paragon House, 1989), provides a brief, uncritical treatment while Narasingha P. Sil, *Ramakrisna Paramahamsa: A Psychological Profile* (Leiden: E. J. Brill, 1991), offers a psychoanalytic interpretation. Sil argues that Ramakrishna's spiritual odyssey arose from a profound emotional and sexual crisis.

One must wonder whether there would be Vedanta centers in the West today without Swami Vivekananda's efforts. *The Complete Works of Swami Vivekananda, Mayavati Memorial Edition* (14th ed.; Calcutta: Advaita Ashrama, 1973) is the indispensable source for the swami's life and teachings. The *Complete Works* has steadily expanded from edition to edition as new material has been uncovered, reaching eight volumes in the fourteenth edition. New editions are published periodically as research turns up additional information. The *Complete Works* reproduce a wide variety of primary source materials, including all of the swami's books, articles, and addresses; notes taken by followers at his classes; newspaper reports of his lectures; interviews and conversations; and a surprising number of his letters. A convenient one-volume selection of the letters has been separately published as *Letters of Swami Vivekananda* (3rd ed.; Calcutta: Advaita Ashrama, 1970). The recollections of such key Western followers as Margaret Noble, Josephine MacLeod, E. T. Sturdy, and Laura Glenn are collected in His Eastern and Western Admirers, *Reminiscences of Swami Vivekananda* (2nd ed.; Calcutta: Advaita Ashrama, 1964). Most of the pieces originally appeared in the movement's periodicals. Several movement biographies have been published, including His Eastern and Western Disciples, *The Life of Swami Vivekananda* (8th ed.; Calcutta: Advaita Ashrama, 1974), which was originally published in 1907. A thick work of over 750 pages, the volume provides a detailed narrative of the swami's life, including lengthy chapters on his years in the West. Swami Nikhilananda's *Vivekananda: A Biography* (1st Indian ed.; Calcutta: Advaita Ashrama, 1964) offers a more compact and more analytical treatment in less than half the pages. Finally, the serious student may wish to look into Ramesh Chandra Majumdar (ed.), *Swami Vivekananda Centenary Memorial Volume* (Calcutta: Swami Vivekananda Centenary, 1963), which brings together essays of wildly varying quality, including such substantial pieces as Swami Tejasananda's "Swami Vivekananda and His Message," 33–161.

Recognized as a nationalist defender of modern India as much as a spokesperson for Hinduism, Vivekananda has attracted the attention of a number of modern Indian historians. Sailendra Nath Dhar's *A Comprehensive Biography of Swami Vivekananda* (Madras: Vivekananda Prakashan Kendra, 1975), published in two volumes, is one of the most ambitious of such works. Largely based on standard printed sources and nearly 1,500 pages in length, Dhar's work provides an extraordinarily detailed narrative that largely avoids analysis. Curiously, Dhar completely omits Vivekananda's thought. Western scholars have ignored Vivekananda even more than Ramakrishna. The exception is George M. Williams, who sheds much new light on the swami's intellectual and religious development in his carefully documented *The Quest for Meaning of Swami Vivekananda: A Study of Religious Change* (Chico, Calif.: New Horizons Press, 1974). Williams's essay, "Swami Vivekananda: Archetypal Hero or Doubting Saint?" 197–226, included in Robert Baird's collection, *Religion in Modern India*, presents a concise summary of his argument.

For Vivekananda's career in America, the key reference is Marie Louise Burke's massive, multivolume work in progress, which reprints in full the voluminous newspaper coverage of the swami's lectures and travel in the United States and Europe. Three volumes have appeared so far: *Swami Vivekananda in America: New Discoveries* (2nd rev. ed; Calcutta: Advaita Ashrama, 1966), which focuses on the swami's movements from 1893 to mid-1895; *Swami Vivekananda in the West: New Discoveries. The World Teacher: Part One* (Calcutta: Advaita Ashrama, 1985), concentrating on the period 1895–1896; and *Swami Vivekananda: His Second Visit to the West. New Discoveries* (Calcutta: Advaita Ashrama, 1973), which surveys the swami's final 1899–1900 visit to the West. Burke, a longtime follower and Vedantist, has done more to dredge up the newspaper reports of Vivekananda's American efforts than any other investigator. The three volumes are primarily chronicles devoid of interpretation, but they are meticulously researched and should remain useful references for scholars for years to come. Inspired by Burke's example, Sankari Prasad Basu and Sunil Bihari Ghosh (eds.), *Vivekananda in Indian Newspapers, 1893–1902* (Calcutta: Bookland Private Ltd., 1969), attempt to provide a similar compendium documenting the Indian reception of the swami between the Parliament of

Religions and his death in 1902. The reader should also consult Satish K. Kapoor, *Cultural Contact and Fusion: Swami Vivekananda in the West (1893–96)* (Jalandhar, India: ABS Publications, 1987), an expanded and revised doctoral dissertation.

As time has passed, all persons who had direct contact with Ramakrishna have been granted special status. Sarada Devi, Ramakrishna's wife, is most venerated and is now ranked by many followers as equal to her husband as a spiritual force. Two key movement biographies are Swami Gambhirananda's *Holy Mother: Shri Sarada Devi* (Madras: Sri Ramakrishna Math, 1955), published in conjunction with the Holy Mother Centenary celebrations in 1954; and Swami Nikhilananda's *Holy Mother: Being the Life of Sri Sarada Devi, Wife of Sri Ramakrishna and Helpmate in His Mission* (New York: Ramakrishna-Vivekananda Center, 1962). Published more recently, *Sri Sarada Devi, The Great Wonder: A Compilation of Revelations, Reminiscences and Studies* (New Delhi: Ramakrishna Mission, 1984) draws together a diverse assortment of reminiscences, testimonies, and essays contributed by disciples, devotees, and scholars. The 1984 volume is especially relevant to this study, including an entire section of testimonials to Sarada Devi by Western women. Swami Brahmananda, who replaced Vivekananda as leader and served as the Ramakrishna Math and Mission's head for two decades, has come to be ranked just below Vivekananda as a movement founder and figure of special veneration. Swami Prabhavananda describes Brahmananda's life and influence in *The Eternal Companion: His Life and Teachings* (Hollywood: Vedanta Society of Southern California, 1944). Swami Gambhirananda (ed.), *The Apostles of Shri Ramakrishna* (Calcutta: Advaita Ashrama, 1967), provides brief biographies of the remainder of Ramakrishna's direct monastic disciples.

Interest in the Indian swamis who launched the Western work has been growing and has primarily focused on Vivekananda, but other early monks who brought the Vedantic message to the West have also begun to attract attention. Swami Aseshananda's *Glimpses of a Great Soul: A Portrait of Swami Saradananda* (Hollywood: Vedanta Press, 1982) focuses on the second Ramakrishna monk to teach in the United States. (He returned home to India after only a few years.) The volume includes a biographical sketch of nearly 100 pages, Saradananda's letters and lectures, reminiscences of his life, and selections from his writings. Swami Abhedananda, the third monk to come west, is the subject of Sister Shivani [Mary LePage], *An Apostle of Monism: An Authentic Account of the Activities of Swami Abhedananda in America* (Calcutta: Ramakrishna Vedanta Math, 1947). A devoted disciple, LePage writes as a partisan, defending the swami at every point, while dismissing his opponents. Abhedananda has been a controversial figure in the history of the Ramakrishna movement. At first a great success in New York, he subsequently broke with his American followers. Following his return to India in 1921, he established an independent center known as the Ramakrishna Vedanta Math, which survives down to the present. The math has kept Abhedananda's numerous books in print, publishing his collected writings in ten volumes as *The Complete Works of Swami Abhedananda, Birth Centenary Edition* (Calcutta: Ramakrishna Vedanta Math, 1967–70). Swami Ritajananda's *Swami Turiyananda: A Direct Disciple of Sri Ramakrishna* (Madras: Sri Ramakrishna Math, 1963) describes the life of still another of Ramakrishna's direct disciples who served in the United States. Turiyananda spent the years 1899–1902 in the New York and San Francisco areas; he was one of the most traditional Ramakrishna monks to labor in America.

Swami Paramananda, who founded Vedanta centers in Boston and Los Angeles, deserves separate treatment, both because of his great success in the United States and because of the voluminous literature followers have devoted to his work. Two key biographies are Sister Devamata [Laura Glenn], *Swami Paramananda and His Work* (La Crescenta, Calif.: Ananda Ashrama, 1926–41), the admiring account of a longtime assistant, published in two volumes; and Sara Ann Levinsky's recent *A Bridge of Dreams: The Story of Parmamananda, A Modern Mystic, and His Ideal of All-Conquering Love* (West Stockbridge, Mass.: Lindisfarne Press, 1984). Levinsky's book is one of the most impressive historical works so far produced by a follower of the movement; the volume draws on unpublished as well as published sources and includes extensive interviews with older members. Though written in admiration of one of the movement's most charismatic swamis, the book approaches its subject in a scholarly manner. Notes would have greatly increased the biography's value. Sister Daya [Georgina Jones Walton], *The Guru and the Disciple* (Cohasset, Mass.: Vedanta Centre, 1976) should also be noted, a volume which presents the abridged memoirs of one of Paramananda's key disciples; the memoir was originally published in its entirety in the Boston Vedanta Society journal, *The Message of the East*. New "inside" biographies devoted to such popular American swamis as Prabhavananda, Ashokananda, Nikhilananda, and Akhilananda seem certain to appear.

A major difficulty in surveying the teachings of the Ramakrishna movement is the sheer quantity of materials one confronts. From the days of Vivekananda, the organization has maintained an extensive publication program, with active presses in both India and the United States. In India, the Advaita Ashrama Press at Mayavati, and subsequently Calcutta, has been particularly important; the Vedanta Press at the Hollywood center has been the most prominent American press.

One must begin, of course, with *The Gospel of Sri Ramakrishna* and Swami Vivekananda's *Jnana-Yoga*, *Bhakti-Yoga*, *Karma-Yoga*, and *Raja-Yoga*—volumes that all Ramakrishna followers study with utmost care. (Vivekananda's works may be most conveniently consulted in *The Complete Works of Swami Vivekananda*, already cited.) As a result of the assistance of a stenographer who became his disciple, most of Swami Vivekananda's early American lectures were preserved. Vivekananda's writings are more systematic and therefore more accessible to Western readers than much of the Ramakrishna movement literature. Swami Nikhilananda (ed.), *Vivekananda: The Yogas and Other Works* (New York: Ramakrishna-Vivekananda Center, 1953), is the most convenient introduction to the Swami's writings.

Though followers of the Ramakrishna movement look especially to the *Gospel* and Vivekananda's works for spiritual guidance, earlier Hindu classics are also considered essential. Ramakrishna swamis have produced English translations of most of the key texts of Hinduism and Vedanta, and most are available in libraries and bookstores. These include Swami Nikhilananda's scholarly edition of *The Upanishads* (New York: Harper, 1949–56), published in two volumes; and a series of readable translations prepared by Swami Prabhavananda and Christopher Isherwood, including *The Song of God: Bhagavad-Gita* (New York: Harper, 1944); *How to Know God: The Yoga Aphorisms of Patanjali* (Hollywood: Vedanta Press, 1953); and *Shankara's Crest-Jewel of Discrimination* (Hollywood: Vedanta Press, 1947). Reprinted in inexpensive paperback editions, the Prabhavananda/Isherwood translations are frequently used as texts in American university classes.

Swamis of the Ramakrishna movement have also published a number of popular surveys of Hinduism, which provide useful introductions to Hindu religious conceptions.

Two of the best are Swami Prabhavananda's *The Spiritual Heritage of India* (Garden City, N.Y.: Doubleday, 1963), published originally in 1960, and Swami Nikhilananda's *Hinduism: Its Meaning for the Liberation of the Spirit* (New York: Harper, 1958). Typically, Ramakrishna writers approach Hinduism from a Vedantic perspective, a tendency that has come under increasing criticism by modern scholars. Westerners who study Hindu religious philosophy must confront an unfamiliar Sanskrit terminology. Such individuals may wish to consult Margaret Stutley and James Stutley, *Harper's Dictionary of Hinduism* (New York: Harper & Row, 1977). Brahmacharini Usha (comp.), *A Ramakrishna-Vedanta Wordbook* (Hollywood: Vedanta Press, 1962), provides compact definitions of key terms from the Ramakrishna movement's perspective.

Swami Satprakashananda's "The Ramakrishna Society," included in Vergilius Ferm (ed.), *Religion in the Twentieth Century* (New York: Philosophical Library, 1948), 395–413, presents one of the best brief statements of the movement's teachings; see also Swami Nirvedananda, "Sri Ramakrishna and Spiritual Renaissance," in Haridas Bhattacharya (ed.), *The Cultural Heritage of India*, Vol. IV: *The Religions* (Calcutta: Ramakrishna Mission Institute of Culture, 1956), 653–728. For more extended expositions, one may turn to the writings of individual swamis. Some representative works include: Swami Abhedananda, *Vedanta Philosophy: How to Be a Yogi* (New York: The Vedanta Society, 1902); Swami Paramananda, *Emerson and Vedanta* (2nd rev. ed.; Boston: The Vedanta Centre, 1918); Swami Pavitrananda, *Modern Man in Search of Religion* (Mayavati: Advaita Ashrama, 1947); Swami Akhilananda, *Hindu Psychology: Its Meaning for the West* (New York: Harper, 1946); Swami Nikhilananda, *Essence of Hinduism* (Boston: Beacon Press, 1948); Swami Prabhavananda, *The Sermon on the Mount According to Vedanta* (Hollywood: Vedanta Press, 1963); and Swami Satprakashananda, *The Goal and the Way: The Vedantic Approach to Life's Problems* (St. Louis: Vedanta Society of St. Louis, n.d.). The very titles of the books point up the desire of Ramakrishna movement swamis to make Hinduism relevant to the modern age. Two anthologies edited by Christopher Isherwood, *Vedanta for the Western World* (Hollywood: Vedanta Press, 1945) and *Vedanta for Modern Man* (New York: Harper, 1945), should also be noted. The articles originally appeared as essays in *Vedanta and the West*, the journal of the Vedanta Society of Southern California. John Yale (ed.), *What Vedanta Means to Me: A Symposium* (Garden City, N.Y.: Doubleday, 1960), a collection of testimonials from individuals connected with the Hollywood Vedanta society, suggests the specific appeals of Ramakrishna teachings for Americans.

Personal reminiscences of life in the Ramakrishna movement by devotees provide one of the best indications of the influence of Vedanta on the lives of Western converts. Sister Nivedita's testimonial concerning her relationship with Vivekananda, *The Master as I Saw Him: Being Pages from the Life of the Swami Vivekananda* (London: Longmans, Green, 1910), is one of the earliest such reports. An English woman originally named Margaret Noble, Nivedita followed Vivekananda to India, where she spent the rest of her life as a leader in the education of Hindu women. Sister Devamata [Laura Glenn], *Days in an Indian Monastery* (2nd ed.; La Crescenta, Calif.: Ananda Ashrama, 1927), recounts the experiences of one of Swami Paramananda's closest American followers during two years at a Ramakrishna monastery in Madras. The life of a Dutch-American named Cornelius Heyblom offers one of the most remarkable examples of Western conversion to Hinduism. Heyblom was drawn into the Ramakrishna movement in the 1890s and was eventually ordained as Swami Atulananda, spending over forty years as a monastic in

India. Taped near the end of his life and published in Swami Vidyatmananda [John Yale] (ed.), *Atman Alone Abides: Conversations with Swami Atulananda* (Madras: Sri Ramakrishna Math, 1978), Heyblom's memories of life in the Ramakrishna movement emphasizes the radical adjustments Western devotees had to make in adapting to Hindu life. John Yale's *A Yankee and the Swamis* (London: George Allen & Unwin, 1961), which grew out of a 1952–1953 journey during which he visited thirty-eight Ramakrishna centers across India, provides a perceptive overview of the Indian movement as seen by a Western follower. Most revealing of all is Christopher Isherwood's *My Guru and His Disciple* (New York: Farrar, Straus, & Giroux, 1980), which describes Isherwood's close relationship with Swami Prabhavananda.

A number of Western devotees who became closely associated with the Ramakrishna movement have subsequently broken away. John Moffitt began as a Protestant, became a follower of Swami Nikhilananda's, and then a fully ordained swami in the Ramakrishna movement; but that was not the end of his spiritual pilgrimage. After twenty-five years as a Vedantist, he shifted back to Christianity to assume the life of a Roman Catholic monastic, a move he attempts to explain in *Journey to Gorakhpur: An Encounter with Christ beyond Christianity* (New York: Holt, Rinehart, & Winston, 1972). Despite his decision to return to the Christian fold, Moffitt apparently retained a high regard for both the Ramakrishna movement and Hinduism. Leopold Fischer, now known as Swami Agehananda Bharati, left the Ramakrishna movement after only two years. Bharati recounts his experiences in *The Ochre Robe* (London: George Allen & Unwin, 1961). An Austrian by birth, he traveled to India after World War II and has subsequently settled in the United States. Since breaking away, he has become a well-known scholar on Indian religion and a professor of anthropology. He has become one of the Ramakrishna movement's most outspoken critics, attacking the order for a puritanical outlook and unquestioning attitude toward the teachings of Ramakrishna and Vivekananda.

Several reports on the work of American Vedanta centers have been published. One of the best is "Vedanta in Southern California: A Guidebook to the Vedanta Society," published as a special issue of *Vedanta and the West* 120 (July-Aug. 1956), 7–64, which describes the life and daily operations of the Vedanta Society of Southern California. Founded in 1930, the society has been one of the movement's most dynamic American centers. Similar accounts are needed for other Vedanta societies. In a quite different work entitled *Seeking Spiritual Meaning: The World of Vedanta* (Beverly Hills, Calif.: Sage Publications, 1977), Joseph Damrell presents a sociological examination of a Vedanta center identified only as "Valley City Church Universal." The study provides a sympathetic portrait of the organization and inner dynamics of one American Vedanta society, based on six years of personal observation and numerous interviews with the resident swami.

In addition to the works listed here and cited in the notes, the following Ramakrishna movement journals were critical in the research for this book and should be consulted by interested scholars:

Brahmavadin (Madras). Vols. 1–18 (1895–1913).
Pacific Vedantist (San Francisco). Vol. 1 (1902).
Prabuddha Bharata (Mayavati, India). Vols. 1- (1896-present).
Star of the East (Melbourne, Australia). Vols. 6–8 (1910–1912). Title changed to
    Vedanta Universal Messenger with Jan.-Feb. 1912 issue.
The Message of the East (Boston). Vols. 1–50 (1912–1961).

Vedanta and the West (Los Angeles). Vols. 1–16 and Nos. 111–206 (1938–1970).
 Entitled *Voice of India* until Jan. 1941.
Vedanta Darpana (New York). Vols. 1–3 (1931–1933).
Vedanta for East and West (London). Vols. 1- (1952-present).
Vedanta Kesari (Mylapore, India). Vols. 1- (1914-present).
Vedanta Monthly Bulletin (New York). Vols. 1–5 (1905–1909). Title changed to
 Vedanta Magazine with Jan. 1909 issue.
Voice of Freedom (San Francisco). Vols. 1–7 (1909–1916).

Finally, several general works may be consulted for religious background. In the case of India, understanding of the so-called Hindu Renaissance is particularly important. Despite its age and Christian bias, John N. Farquhar's *Modern Religious Movements in India* (New York: Macmillan, 1915) remains useful, offering profiles of the Brahmo Samaj, Arya Samaj, and Theosophical movements, in addition to the Ramakrishna movement. Many years of residence in India explain the author's intimate grasp of the religious situation. Robert D. Baird has updated Farquhar in his *Religion in Modern India*, already cited, adding essays on several movements ignored in the 1915 study. D. S. Sarma's *Studies in the Renaissance of Hinduism in the Nineteenth and Twentieth Centuries* (Benares: Benares Hindu University, 1944) considers the Hindu reform movements from an Indian perspective. The essays in Bardwell L. Smith's *Hinduism: New Essays in the History of Religions* (1976), already cited, reveal newer interpretations.

Several background works focusing on the history and role of Asian religions in the United States may be recommended, beginning with Wendell Thomas's *Hinduism Invades America* (1930). It seems astonishing that Thomas's old and flawed volume remains the only general history of Hindu religious groups in the United States. Raymond Brady Williams's *Religions of Immigrants from India and Pakistan: New Threads in the American Tapestry* (Cambridge: Cambridge University Press, 1988) is excellent on developments since the passage of the Immigration and Nationality Act of 1965. Focusing more narrowly, John Y. Fenton's *Transplanting Religious Traditions: Asian Indians in America* (New York: Praeger, 1988) treats immigrant Indian religious patterns in Atlanta, Georgia, between 1979 and 1988. Recent scholars have demonstrated that Americans were already becoming aware of Eastern religious conceptions well before the first appearance of Asian teachers in the 1890s. Two surveys trace the roots of America's first interest in Asian religious ideas as far back as the seventeenth century: Dale Riepe, *The Philosophy of India and Its Impact on American Thought* (Springfield, Ill.: Charles C. Thomas, 1970), which emphasizes philosophers; and Carl T. Jackson, *The Oriental Religions and American Thought: Nineteenth-Century Explorations* (Westport, Conn.: Greenwood Press, 1981), which treats such movements as Unitarianism, Transcendentalism, and Theosophy. Several works on Buddhism in America include background material and comparative data useful for any student of Asian religious thought. Most useful are Charles Prebish, *American Buddhism* (North Scituate, Mass.: Duxbury Press, 1979), and Rick Fields, *How the Swans Came to the Lake: A Narrative History of Buddhism in America* (Boulder, Colo.: Shambhala, 1981). Thomas A. Tweed, *The American Encounter with Buddhism, 1844–1912: Victorian Culture and the Limits of Dissent* (Bloomington: Indiana University Press, 1991), offers a superb scholarly account of the nineteenth-century American encounter with Buddhism.

The growing visibility of Eastern religious groups in the United States since the

1960s has stimulated rising attention to the role of Asian religion and what social scientists call "new religions." Robert S. Ellwood's and Harry B. Partin's *Religious and Spiritual Groups in Modern America* (2nd ed.; Englewood Cliffs, N.J.: Prentice-Hall, 1988) includes a provocative analysis of such key groups as the Self-Realization Fellowship, Transcendental Meditation, and International Society for Krishna Consciousness. Ellwood's *Eastern Spirituality in America: Selected Writings* (New York: Paulist Press, 1987) provides a handy compendium of key texts relating to the history of Hinduism, Buddhism, Taoism, and Theosophy in the United States. The most readable survey is Jacob Needleman's *The New Religions* (Garden City, N.Y.: Doubleday, 1970), which profiles a wide variety of the newer movements, including Zen Buddhism, followers of Meher Baba, Transcendental Meditation, and Tibetan Buddhism. Nathan and Sulochana Glazer (eds.), *Conflicting Images: India and the United States* (Glenn Dale, Maryland: Riverdale, 1990), presents a series of essays focusing on trans-cultural perceptions, including such pieces as Diana Eck's " 'New Age' Hinduism in America," Lloyd I. Randolph's "Gandhi in the Mind of America," and Veena Das's "The Imaging of Indian Women: Missionaries and Journalists."

J. Gordon Melton's *The Encyclopedia of American Religions* (3rd ed.; Detroit: Gale Research, 1989) is an invaluable general reference for Asian religious groups in the United States. Hindu groups and movements are treated on pp. 849–95 and Buddhist bodies are discussed on pp. 907–42. For additional citations, see Carl T. Jackson, "The Influence of Asia upon American Thought: A Bibliographical Essay," *American Studies International* 22 (Apr. 1984), 3–31.

Index

CARL T. JACKSON is Dean of the College of Liberal Arts and Professor of History at the University of Texas, El Paso. His earlier book, *The Oriental Religions and American Thought: Nineteenth-Century Explorations*, won the Ralph Henry Gabriel Prize of the American Studies Association.